Diving Pioneers

An Oral History of Diving in America

by Eric Hanauer

DISCLAIMER
Diving is a potentially hazardous practice and if practiced incorrectly or with incomplete planning and procedures can expose a person to considerable risks including serious injury or death. It requires specialized training, equipment and experience. This book is not intended as a substitute for the above or for the diver to abandon common sense in pursuit of diving activities beyond his abilities. This book is intended as a source of information on various aspects of snorkeling and diving, not as a substitute for proper training and experience. For training in diving, contact a national certification agency. The reader is advised that all the elements of hazard and risk associated with scuba diving cannot be brought out within the scope of this text. The author, publishers and manufacturers presented in this book, are not liable for damage or injury including death which may result from scuba diving activities, with respect to information contained herein.

First Printing 1994
Watersport Publishing, Inc. P.O. Box 83727, San Diego, CA 92138

ISBN: 0-922769-43-5

Library of Congress Catalog Card Number: 94-61985
Hanauer, Eric
 Diving Pioneers • *An Oral History of Diving in America*

Other books by Eric Hanauer
 The Egyptian Red Sea • *A Diver's Guide*

Diving Pioneers

An Oral History of Diving In America

by Eric Hanauer

Cover painting by John Steel

Watersport Publishing, Inc. • San Diego, California

*This book is dedicated
to all the divers of the 1940s and 1950s,
living and dead, whose curiosity,
preseverence, and spirit of adventure
showed us the way underwater.*

ACKNOWLEDGEMENT

Thanks to the following people who helped in the production of this book: Ron Merker, Sam Miller, Ken Loyst, Theresa Slusher, Denise Winslett, Bonnie Cardone, Nick Icorn, Sean Combs, Deborah Day, Mia Tegner, Mark Dorfman, Harry Ruscigno, Brian Miller, Pat Barron, Ron Pavelka, Spencer Slate, Bret Gilliam and all the pioneers whose stories are told here.

TABLE OF CONTENTS

DIVING PIONEERS
HOW IT BEGAN

SCUBA DIVING AS WE KNOW IT BEGAN a half century ago. It was 1943 in occupied France, that a young naval officer, Jacques Cousteau, convinced a friend, engineer Emile Gagnan, to design a regulator which could be used for diving. Gagnan adapted and modified a gas regulator that enabled cars to run on natural gas, and the rest is history. Or so the history books tell us.

Jim Christensen and white sea bass, Catalina Island, 1960.

But the event was little noted at the time, except by Cousteau and his friends. There was a war on, and it took a while for word to get out to a world that was pre-occupied by more important matters. It wasn't until 1949 that the first Aqualungs were imported into the United States, and nearly another decade before diving attained any measure of popularity.

If the truth be told, diving in the United States can trace its origins far before 1943. While Cousteau and Gagnan were tinkering in France, a hardy group of San Diego Bottom Scratchers already had over a decade of underwater experience as free divers. Their founder, Glenn Orr, recorded his first dive in 1929. In the early 30s a group of Europeans, who called themselves gogglers, was exploring the waters of the French Riviera. Their guru was an expatriate American journalist, Guy Gilpatrick. Among his pupils were Hans Hass and Cousteau. Gilpatrick wrote the first book on free diving, **The Compleat Goggler**, which is now de rigeur in the collection of any diving historian.

So we can trace the beginnings of sport diving back over sixty years. That's not very long in the grand scheme of things. But the pioneers who are still alive — and in many instances still finning — are growing old. They won't be around much longer, and when they go a significant part of diving history will go with them.

The past decade or so has been a period of rapid growth in diving. Through favorable media exposure, easier training, improved equipment, and readily accessible travel, scuba has been transformed into a mainstream activity that attracts a wide range of people, including women, children, and older adults. A whole new population of divers has come in that has learned little or nothing about the history and traditions of the sport. Initially the typical new diver is interested in little more than the latest equipment or the current hot dive destination. But eventually a curiosity arises about the origins: where did this activity come from and how did we get here?

> **I wanted to talk to these people who were the movers and shakers when I began, to hear their stories as they lived them. This book is the result, an oral history of diving in America as told by the pioneers in their own words.**

Nobody is better equipped to recall history than the people who made it. A couple of years ago I set out to find them.

By the time I had learned to dive in 1959, the pioneer era was already coming to a close. Formal classes were starting to become established, the single-hose regulator had been introduced, and when a woman went underwater it no longer made headlines. Among the big names in diving those days were Bill Barrada, E.R. Cross, Connie Limbaugh, and Lloyd Bridges. I wanted to talk to these people who were the movers and shakers when I began, to hear their stories as they lived them. This book is the result, an oral history of diving in America as told by the pioneers in their own words.

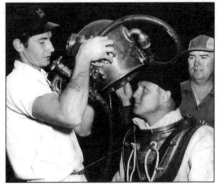

Dick Anderson (L) dresses in E.R. Cross for a commercial dive, 1950's.

Oral history imposes several limitations. First, the people have to be willing and able to talk about the past. Unfortunately, some of them have already passed on. Because I wanted first-hand recollections, this volume covers only living American diving pioneers. (The only exception is Conrad Limbaugh.) That isn't meant as a slight to Europeans and Asians, whose exploits and contributions are as significant as any recalled here. But a totally comprehensive history would require far more space than is available in this small volume. The line had to be drawn somewhere, so we limited the book to Americans who were available for interviews. European pioneers Jacques Cousteau, Hans Hass, Philippe Diole´, Folco Quilici, and Phillippe Talliez all have written memoirs. Although most are out of print, they are still available in some libraries and used book stores.

Many of the pioneers whose stories are presented here made significant contributions to the sport that are still recognized and remembered. Others took part in a specific event, the significance of which perhaps wasn't recognized until later. But all of them provide a first-person window to diving's early days.

It was a man's world, and the few women who participated had to prove themselves every time they went underwater.

When recalling events that took place thirty to sixty years ago, memories sometimes become more vivid than the actual event. Dives become deeper, fish grow larger, and adventures become more dangerous with the passing of the years. Sometimes people have differing viewpoints on the same event. Communication between remote communities of divers was practically nonexistent. So two different people may claim to have invented a new tool or technique, or to be the first ever to do something. It's possible both are right, as neither knew about the existence of the other. No attempt is made here to select one version or viewpoint over another. All are presented as told, except

Gustav Dalla Valle, Zale Parry and Dick Anderson before riding Gustav's wet sub from the mainland to Catalina Island, 1955.

where overwhelming evidence states otherwise.

In the course of these interviews, some people were extremely frank about events of their lives, even unpleasant or tragic ones. The diving community has had its share of scoundrels as well as heroes. But muckraking and personal distress are not the purpose of this book. Our pioneers are people just like everybody else. They had disappointments, tragedies, divorces, and all the other events that make up a lifetime. But except where these events had a direct impact on diving history, they were left out of the narrative. These people were trail blazers who showed us the way underwater. Whenever they preferred to leave skeletons in the closet, I respected their wishes and left them locked up.

Some pioneers were very outgoing in telling their stories, others were modest to a fault. In the latter cases I went to people who knew them to fill in the blanks. This is also why I assume the narrator's role for parts of each story. It allows me to say things that some were too modest to say about themselves, and also leads to smoother transitions in the narrative.

Two unintended biases become evident in checking the roster

of pioneers: most of them lived in California, and there were very few women. Both are reflections of the state of diving in those days. Scuba diving was born in France, but the beaches of California were its incubator. Dimitri Rebikoff's 1956 book, **Free Diving**, purported to list all the dive clubs in the United States. At that time, there were 132 clubs in California. New York was second with 32, Florida third with 24. It took a lot more dedication to dive in the icy waters of the northeast, or the dark, murky quarries of the nation's heartland, or the forbidding caves of Florida. Yet people like Frank Scalli, Dan Wagner, Ralph Erickson, and Tom Mount spread the word in their regions.

Books and magazine articles about diving in the 1950s are dominated by pictures of divers with dead animals. In this age of environmentalism, spearfishing is equated with killing whales or clear-cutting rain forests.

It was a man's world, and the few women who participated had to prove themselves every time they went underwater. Dottie Frazier fought prejudice when she became the first woman instructor. Zale Parry, Norrine Rouse, and Barbara Allen had to be better than the men they dived with. Dr. Eugenie Clark eloquently told her own story in two books published over 30 years ago: **Lady with a Spear and Lady and the Sharks.** She is an obvious but reluctant omission in these pages, because her career is so well known.

Chuck Nickin

The early divers were mostly water people: swimmers, surfers, and lifeguards like the Meistrells, or ex-military divers like Dick Bonin and E.R. Cross. Water experience was important because there were no classes in the beginning. People would buy equipment from surplus stores or fabricate it in their home workshops. If there were instructions they would read them, if not they went diving anyway.

The primary reason for going underwater was catching fish. Books and magazine articles about diving in the 1950s are dominated by pictures of divers with dead animals. In this age of environmentalism, spearfishing is equated with killing whales or clear-cutting rain forests. But beach populations were much smaller then, and the best scientific minds were telling the public that the ocean was a bottomless cornucopia that, by the end of the century, would feed the world. I have de-emphasized the fish-catching exploits of the pioneers, but underwater hunting is part of our legacy, and the exploits of these men and women are larger than life. So when reading about those activities, don't judge the people by the environmental ethic of the 90s, but enjoy the tales of adventure on their own merits. Even the first wave of underwater photographers —Ron Church, Al Giddings, Bob Hollis, and Chuck Nicklin—began as hunters. If you had been diving in the 50s, you probably would have been a hunter too.

This set the stage for the first Aqualung dive in the United States. Rene rented a boat from Bob Vincent and headed out to Point Dume. The divers on board were Cousteau, Bussoz, Vincent, McCall, another Frenchman whose name Glen couldn't remember...and Johnny Weismuller.

Diving today is a big business, with many of the manufacturers part of major conglomerates. In those days gear was made in and sold out of garages. It wasn't until four years after the war that the first Aqualungs were imported into the United States. Rene Bussoz entered this country during the war as a representative of France. After the hostilities ended, he opened Rene's Sporting Goods in Westwood, near the campus of UCLA.

In 1949 his friend, Jacques Cousteau, sent him a consignment of Aqualungs. According to a well-circulated folk tale, there were eleven units in the initial shipment. (About a hundred people claim to have bought one of them.) A few weeks later, the captain is supposed to have called Bussoz, asking if he wanted another shipment. Rene replied to hold off, because the American market was saturated.

It's a good story, but it just wasn't so. I had hoped to identify the actual owners of the original eleven tanks, but Rene is dead, and the only well-known person who worked for him in the early days, Dick Anderson, signed on later. Dick, however, turned me on to Glen McCall, and Glen burst the bubble of the legend.

Now 84 years old, McCall lives in British Columbia. He was an early free diver who was doing repair work for Rene on a contract basis. In 1949 Cousteau brought six Aqualungs to Westwood. The plan was to show Rene and his staff how to use them. He would keep the units as demonstrators to introduce the sport to potential customers.

This set the stage for the first Aqualung dive in the United States. Rene rented a boat from Bob Vincent and headed out to Point Dume. The divers on board were Cousteau, Bussoz, Vincent, McCall, another Frenchman whose name Glen couldn't remember...and Johnny Weismuller. The Olympic champion swimmer and Tarzan of the movies was a friend of Rene's and an invited guest on that first dive. He became an enthusiastic diver, and went out with McCall and Bussoz for quite some time afterward. Eventually he had a 120 cubic foot tank setup made for himself because, according to McCall, he was a big guy and used lots of air. The only thing Glen remembers about the first dive was being a bit scared of the "little sharks" he saw down there.

The first six lungs were in the shop about eight to ten months, and Rene would loan them out to prospective customers. Glen and Bob Vincent eventually bought two of the original six for $35 each, which included the tank and regulator. Subsequent units were sent from France in parts, because they were cheaper to import that way. McCall assembled each one, working nights after his regular job. This made him America's first regulator assembly line. The equipment sold so well that Rene obtained exclusive rights to distibute the Aqualung in this country, and formed a company called U.S. Divers.

Many of these lives are so comprehensive and eventful that a chapter in a book can only skim the highlights. Many are worthy of a book by themselves.

At first they had a hard time obtaining tanks, so they bought Walter Kidde fire extinguisher tanks and hooked up oxygen valves. Glen remembers some of the earliest customers: Parry Bivens, Mel Fisher, and Bob Lorenz. Lorenz opened the nation's first dive shop, Watergill in Venice. Fisher was invited on a trip to the Santa Barbara islands, where McCall taught him to dive. He later opened the second dive store, Mel's Aqua Shop in Redondo Beach. Connie Limbaugh and Andy Rechnitzer of UCLA were also early Aqualung owners. So was Buster Crabbe, another Olympic swimmer and Flash Gordon of the movies.

Bob Hollis with a Rollermarine camera and housing, early 1960's.

As in many of these interviews, fact turned out to be more interesting than legend. It was fascinating to talk to people who were only names and pictures when I began diving. They are still vibrant, interesting, active people who made history then, and in some cases, continue to do it today. In age they range from McCall's 84 to Bob Hollis and Tom Mount in their 50s.

Many of these lives are so comprehensive and eventful that a chapter in a book can only skim the highlights. Many are worthy of a book by themselves. A few are working on their memoirs, and I hope this will be an incentive to finish and get them published. Eugenie Clark, Colonel John D. Craig, and Dimitri Rebikoff wrote theirs during the pioneer era. With so much first-hand material on them already available, I decided to concentrate on those who have yet to write their stories.

In any project like this, some significant names are omitted who may be as worthy as those included. Only two people turned me down for interviews. Some aren't here because of my ignorance of their accomplishments. Others are missing because we weren't able to make connections. It's not that they aren't as important as some of those covered here, but there was a point when everything finally had to be assembled for publication before the book grew to 500 pages.

Lee Somers lecturing for Sea Grant, early 70s.

It is my hope that this book will spark a resurgence in awareness of our beginnings. As long as there is interest, this project will continue. If everybody of significance is covered in volume one, there would be no inducement for volume two.

So on the next stormy day when the surf is kicking up ten feet and visibility is closed down to five, take your vicarious diving fix by turning back the clock and reading these stories of the people who made our sport. And the next time you go down, remember to thank them for showing us the way.

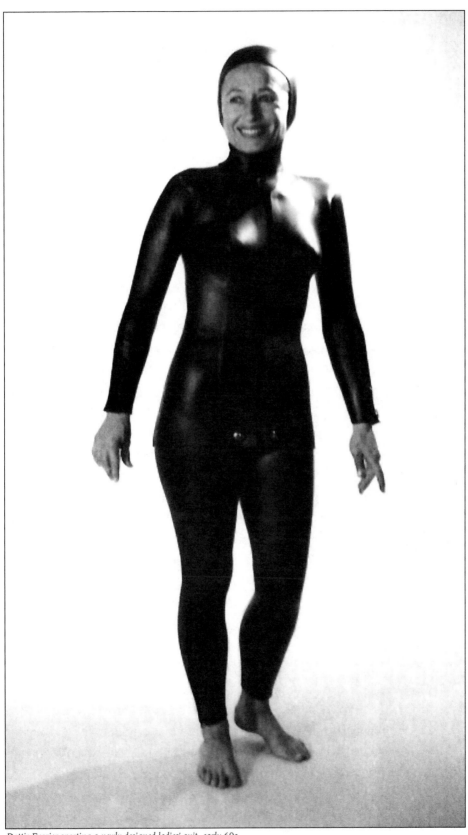

Dottie Frazier sporting a newly designed ladies' suit, early 60s.

Diving History
The Way Things Were

In the early 50s there was an aura about diving, an adventure, that got lost with age. The mystique is gone now; everybody is doing it. It's like driving a damn car.
—Dick Anderson

Diving historians don't have statistics or yearbooks or collectors' cards to feed their interest in underwater nostalgia. (If diving had trading cards, would a 1936 Hans Hass rookie card in goggling gear sell for as much as a 1911 Honus Wagner?) Even the old television series of the 50s aren't running any more, because they were filmed in black and white. (Could **Sea Hunt** inspire as many movie sequels as **Star Trek**?) Dive magazines of the 50s weren't attractive, had no color and few underwater photographs. Even if they had, they would look like a low-budget sci-fi flick of 40 years ago compared with the latest Steven Spielberg epic. If you need an ego boost, just pick up an original edition of Cousteau's **Silent World** and check out the color photographs. The novice division of any dive club competition turns out better stuff than the elite efforts of those days.

Divair was the first regulator designed and manufactured in the USA.

The history of diving isn't visual; it is found in the words of the people who lived it. Many of the people who made that history are still around. What these pioneers lacked in sophisticated equipment and knowledge of the sea, they made up for with a drive for discovery and adventure. They pursued their activity in an ocean not yet diminished by pollution and overfishing. Animals, unused to strange bubble-blowing apparitions, hung around due to curiosity rather than conditioned hunger. Interviews with the pioneers reveal how much hassle it was to go underwater in those days. They did it not for the bottom line, but for the love of the sea and the joy of discovering a new world.

While researching background material for this book, I kept running across a wealth of information about equipment, techniques, and conditions that the early divers had to overcome to pursue their activity. We take for granted such things as full-service dive stores, high-tech equipment, and professional instruction. The pioneers had none of that.

A lot of the early equipment was home-made. One of the first magazine articles on scuba techniques appeared in **Popular Science** Magazine in July, 1953. It described how to build your own "diving lung" out of surplus oxygen tanks and a demand valve. The author, Herb Pfister, began:

"For a brand-new sensation, a feeling of really being out of this world, try the latest thing in water sport—a self-contained diving outfit.

"You can make your lung pay for itself, too. One outboard motor salvaged from the mud, or one boat propeller replaced without pulling the boat up on shore, will net you the price of the parts."

The next three pages explained in step-by-step pictures how to mount two surplus oxygen tanks on a wooden backpack, and how to adapt an oxygen regulator for underwater use. Among the pieces used were automobile heater hoses and various plumbing components. A rubber noisemaker forced over a wooden thread spool served as a flutter valve.

When mounting the diaphragm, he advised, "Seal edge of diaphragm with Permagasket to keep water out of regulator. Apply several built-up layers rather than one thick one. Waterproof diaphragm with several coats of rubber cement. Dust final coat with talcum to prevent it from sticking to cover."

Scott Hydro-Pak full face mask unit, mid 1950s.

Pfister concluded his article with one of the earliest diving instructional lessons in print. Entitled "How to Use your Diving Lung," it is worth reproducing here to demonstrate how things have changed.

"Using a diving lung is as safe as crossing a street. However, you wouldn't send a child across a street without telling him to cross with the traffic light and to watch out for the cars. You, for the first time, are about to cross into a new medium — deep water. Knowing how to act and what to expect will make your trip safe.

• Take several deep breaths before diving. They'll clear your lungs and get you a little ahead on your oxygen needs.

• Dive with someone, or have someone on the surface ready to give aid if needed.

- Take a light rope along on your first few dives. Tied to the boat or pier, it will be a comforting contact with your own world.
- Stay by the rope until you get your weight belt adjusted. If you take too many weights down with you, you'll have to throw off the belt to get back up.

- Establish a rhythm of breathing and maintain it. If the rhythm is upset you may take water in your mask or mouthpiece.
- Swallow any water that enters your mouth. It's easier than trying to blow it out.
- Blow through your nose to get rid of water that enters your mask. The water will leave with the air around the edges of the mask.
- Swim quietly and without undue exertion. This will conserve air and let you breathe normally. Use fins for easy swimming.
- Take your air gradually rather than trying to fill your lungs all at once. You'll find that a long slow breath will bring in all you need; a quick sharp breath may panic you as the air will not seem to come through fast enough. If you get too little or too much air, readjust the valve shown in Photo 16. (Note: This was to be done "...after underwater trials..." using a screwdriver.)

- Important. Never hold your breath while coming up. Air taken into your lungs at the bottom will expand as you rise, forcing your lungs out and possibly injuring them.
- Dive without ear plugs. They trap air inside your ears which reacts to pressure changes to create discomfort. Water pressure can also force plugs deep into your ears.

Sea Dive – The first mask manufactured in the USA, early 1950's

- You'll feel the pressure of the water on your head and ears as you go down. Pause a moment, press your mask tightly against your face and blow through your nose to relieve the pressure. After a few dives, you'll become accustomed to the pressure around you.
- Swim to the surface immediately when you feel your breathing growing difficult. When tank pressure drops to about 300 psi, it becomes slightly more difficult to pull it from the tanks, but easy breathing will get you topside. Beginning with a full charge, the two tanks shown give a useful diving time of about 40-45 minutes.
- Limit your dives to a maximum of 30 feet. If for any reason you must release the outfit, you'll have to swim to the surface; and more than 30 feet is a long way up."

Pfister estimated the cost of a complete outfit at about $40, not including mask and fins. It can be less if you "...shop shrewdly or use only one large tank..." The weight belt was a surplus cartridge belt with lead in the pockets. This was before there were wet suits or BCs.

I wonder how many readers actually built units following these instructions, and how many of them had problems. Can you imagine how this article would read had there been as many hungry lawyers in 1953 as there are today?

Few divers actually built their own equipment to go underwater, because several companies had already adapted Cousteau's patent and were manufacturing scuba gear of their own. In his 1956 book, *Free Diving*, Dimitri Rebikoff describes in detail four US-made units that competed with the Cousteau-Gagnan Aqualung (as it was known then). They were the Divair, Northill Air Lung, Dacor Diving Lung, and the Scott Hydro-Pak.

In many ways 1954 was a more carefree, innocent time. Nobody worried about the ozone layer, and sexually transmitted diseases could be cured with penicillin. The Chicago Cubs had been in the World Series only eight years before.

Perhaps the most unusual of these was the Hydro-Pak. Made by a manufacturer of fire rescue and aircraft equipment, it adapted features from that technology. Its twin tanks were mounted upside-down on the first back pack, a flat aluminum frame. This was done to allow the diver to turn them on and off with ease. (Cousteau's original tanks were also mounted valves down, but by the mid

A CALYPSO *camera, predecessor of the Nikonos.*

50s, valve-up orientation was beginning to dominate.) The Hydro-Pak's full face mask featured the first single-hose regulator and the first purge button. The air intake was mounted on one side of the mask, the exhaust on the other. For surface swimming, a short snorkel tube was supplied, activated by unscrewing its top valve.

The August, 1954 issue of *The Skin Diver* magazine provided a further look into scuba's past. Then in its third year of publication, a copy sold for 25 cents and a year's subscription was $3.00. On the cover was The Creature from the Black Lagoon, and an article inside told about the making of that motion picture. Rico Browning, later a stunt man on the *Sea Hunt* television series, portrayed The Creature. A major share of editorial content was devoted to news from dive clubs around the country.

Even more than the articles, the ads and the photos provided insights on the state of sport diving in those years. In many ways 1954 was a more carefree, innocent time. Nobody worried about the ozone layer, and sexually transmitted diseases could be cured with

penicillin. The Chicago Cubs had been in the World Series only eight years before. (It's now 48 and counting.) However there were some dark shadows as well. The French were being driven out of Indo China by the Viet Minh rebels. People were digging backyard bomb shelters and Joe McCarthy was looking for communists in everybody's past.

Tropical diving meant going down to Florida and hooking up with a dive shop in Miami. Cayman was a sleepy Carribbean island that no one had heard about, and the sunken Japanese fleet in Truk Lagoon had long been forgotten. There was only one tiny foreign travel ad, for a dive operator on the Virgin Islands: La Belle France, "the skin diver's paradise." They offered sales and rental of the top brands of equipment: Aqualung, Cressi, Champion, Hurricane, Pirelli, Squale, and Voit.

US Divers was selling a standard Aqualung (tank, harness, and regulator) direct by mail, for $160. Using a coupon on the back cover, you could pay 1/3 down and make twelve monthly payments, provided you filled in the blanks about monthly take-home pay, bank accounts, and real estate owned. In contrast, one of the new color television sets, with a 12-inch screen, would have set you back $1100.

On any Saturday or Sunday, you could go spearfishing at Catalina Island on board the cruiser *Maray*, leaving Long Beach at 7:30 AM. The fare was $6. A special two-day San Clemente Island trip, including food, was advertised for $15, and chartering the boat for a day, with 20 divers, cost $102.50. Mel's Aqua Shop in Redondo Beach ran an ad featuring a weepy infant in a dry suit. The owner was Mel Fisher, whose subsequent *Atocha* treasure find insured that he wouldn't have to run a dive shop for a living in his old age.

There weren't many underwater photographs in the magazine, and none in full color. Most of the shots were of divers, (almost exclusively males) posing with dead fish. Art Pinder, Underwater Athlete of the Year, stands on a Miami cabin cruiser with his 584-pound jewfish. Ron Church, one of the first great underwater photographers, holds a big grouper at Guaymas, Mexico. A young Ron Merker (owner of Aquatic Center, Newport Beach) displays his gun and a 173-pound

black sea bass shot at Catalina Island. And Bob Givens, later director of USC Marine Lab, poses with his 80-pound bat ray.

In those days divers were shooting anything that swam. Octo-
puses, stingrays, and even turtles were exhibited in these fishmar-
ket photographs. However, environmental concern
was not entirely absent. An editorial urged that limits be placed on commercial lobster fishing, because
too many shorts were being taken. The author, Johnny Logan, charged that 50% of the commercial catch
consisted of shorts, and blamed the courts for letting
violators off with mild fines. Among his recommendations were that lobster traps be designed to let
shorts escape, something that was finally enacted
about 30 years later. Logan also suggested that
abalone should be removed from the sale list because
of "serious depletion and flagrant violations (by) commercials."

A well-equipped diver of the late
1950's looked like this.

Diving activities in those days was centered around clubs, and
most of them were concerned primarily with spearfishing. The names
of these clubs reinforce that impression: Sea Lancers, Davey Jones
Raiders, The Barbs, Depth Devils, Sea Spooks, Hell Divers, Reef
Robbers, and Sea Combers were some of them. Sons of the Beaches and Chickens of the Sea displayed an irreverent sense of humor.
Rebikoff's book lists 132 dive clubs in California alone, by far the
largest contingent of divers in the country. Florida was a distant
third with 24. Instruction was centered around the clubs; veteran
members taught newcomers without benefit of instructor training
or certification.

Scuba diving in the 50s quickly attracted a large number of fol-
lowers. Some observers at the time considered it a fad that would
soon become passe. Others felt this was an exciting scientific tool,
but too complex and dangerous for the general public. Instructional programs, begun in the 50s on a local basis and going national in
the 60s, effectively bridged that gap. Today we take for granted
things like luxury live-aboard boats, equipment fitted to all sizes
and tastes in a rainbow of colors, and classes tailored for all levels
of aquatic ability. Scuba diving has come a long way in the past half
century. I wonder what the next fifty years will bring.

TIME LINE OF SCUBA
A CHRONOLOGY OF THE RECREATIONAL DIVING INDUSTRY

by Mark Dorfman *(reprinted with permission by DEMA)*

We humans have been trying to find a way to swim freely under water ever since our species' expulsion from the Garden of Eden. The earliest evidence of scuba diving is an Assyrian frieze dating from about 900 B.C. It shows armed men using a small breathing device while swimming under water. The word "SCUBA" has somewhat more recent origins. An acronym for "Self Contained Underwater Breathing Apparatus," it started as military jargon coined by the U. S. Navy underwater demolition team (UDT). As used today, the term "scuba" distinguishes self-contained devices from surface-fed "hookah" and "hard hat" types of diving equipment, and from submersible vessels

Early diving systems proved dangerous and difficult to use, and required lengthy training. Modern scuba equipment, first introduced in 1943, comes close to realizing the ancient dream of allowing humans free access to the underwater world. Here are some of the milestones on the path to fulfilling that fantasy.

332 BC:
The Greek philosopher Aristotle's **Problemata** describes a diving bell used by Alexander the Great at the siege of Tyre (a Phoenician town on the Mediterranean coast of what is now Lebanon).

1500s:
Leonardo da Vinci designs the first known scuba. His drawings of a self-contained underwater breathing apparatus appear in his **Codex Atlanticus.** Leonardo's design combines air supply and buoyancy control in a single system, and foreshadows later diving suits. There is no evidence that Leonardo ever built his device. He seems, instead, to have abandoned scuba in favor of refining the diving bell.

1622:
A Spanish treasure fleet on its way home is scattered and largely destroyed by a hurricane near the Florida Keys. The Spaniards will salvage a small part of the treasure with a custom-built diving bell, but most of it stays on the bottom. Storms will also sink treasure transports in 1715 and 1733. Hundreds of people drown in the shipwrecks and the economic losses intensify Spain's national deficit, accelerating its decline as a world power. That's the bad

news. The good news is that for the next 350 years, people will dream about the treasure and fantasize about finding a way...

1680:

Italian physician Giovanni Borelli imagines a closed circuit "rebreather." His drawings show a giant bag using chemical components to regenerate exhaled air. This, he suggests, should allow the air to be breathed again by a submerged diver. Borelli also draws rather bizarre, claw-like feet on his diver. This leads one historian to stretch things a bit and credit Borelli as the inventor of swim fins. Others recognize Borelli as the first to envision the scuba diver as a free-swimming "frogman."

1808:

Friedrich von Drieberg develops his "Triton" apparatus. The system uses an air reservoir worn by the diver but requires that the tank be supplied by surface hoses. The diver obtains air from the backpack reservoir through a valve operated by nodding his head.

1819-1830s:

A German-born inventor and machinist living and working in England, Augustus Siebe, designs a surface-fed helmet for "open dress" diving. (In "open dress" an open-bottomed helmet rests on the diver's shoulders.) He introduces his "closed dress" (with the helmet sealed to the suit) diving outfit in 1836. In 1839, Siebe's hard hat system, along with four other designs, is used to salvage the *Royal George* from the harbor at Spithead, England. Siebe wins endorsement by Her Majesty's Royal Navy and his firm Siebe, Gorman & Co., becomes the leading manufacturer of diving equipment.

1819-1830s:

Charles Anthony Deane and his brother, John Deane develop, manufacture, and market a succession of fire fighters' smoke helmets, diving outfits. and related equipment. The Deanes compete with Siebe for market share, government contracts, and eventually, a place in diving history. They lose the first two battles, but are now winning recognition as the actual inventors of open dress diving equipment.

1825:

An Englishman, William James, develops a system that several historians consider to be the first true scuba. It employs tanks of compressed air and a full diving dress with a helmet. Limits on useful depth and duration keep it from widespread adoption by commercial divers.

1825:

Charles Condert, an American, develops a compressed air reservoir consisting of copper tubing bent into a horseshoe and worn around the diver's body. The system includes a valve to inflate the diver's suit.

1828:

Lemaire d'Augerville patents a "swimming belt" designed to enable divers to swim in mid-water and ascend or descend as needed for their work. We now call such devices "buoyancy compensators." But nineteenth-century salvage divers found little use for the buoyancy device, so d'Augerville netted little compensation.

1836:

Charles Deane publishes the first "how to" diving manual.

1864:

Two Frenchmen, Benoit Rouquayrol and Auguste Denayrouze, develop a diving system that feeds air to a diver carried tank from a pump on the surface, and to the diver through a membrane-controlled "demand" valve. The valve automatically compensates for the pressure of the surrounding water. That makes it possible for the diver to breathe with minimum effort. Their system of surface pump, pressurized air cylinders, and demand regulators goes into commercial production in 1867. The principle behind the Rouquayrol/ Denayrouze system is essentially the same as that of demand valves used in modern scuba.

1869:

Jules Verne popularizes the concept of scuba in **20,000 Leagues Under the Sea.** His central character, Captain Nemo, specifically cites the Rouquayrol/Denayrouze system and theorizes about the inevitable next step—severing the diver's reliance on surface-supplied air.

1869-1883:

New York's Brooklyn Bridge is built, but many of the workmen pay a high price. Emerging after extended hours in high-pressure caissons (dry construction compartments sunk into the riverbed) they become crippled by "caisson disease." Because of the cramped and frozen joints caused by the affliction, reporters dub it "the bends."

1876:

Henry Fleuss, an English merchant seaman, revives the idea of the closed-circuit rebreather. His self-contained system is useful for working in smoke and noxious air and, for short periods, underwater. Fleuss goes to work as an engineer for Siebe, Gorman, and the company puts his design into commercial production.

1880:

Dr. Paul Bert, a French physiologist, completes his pioneering work on breathing under hyperbaric (high pressure) conditions. He recognizes that "caisson disease" is identical to problems experienced by deep sea divers and suggests that it is caused by the release of dissolved nitrogen from the bloodstream. He also shows that oxygen, even the oxygen in compressed air, can become toxic when breathed under pressure. (The oxygen in compressed air becomes toxic only at depths far beyond the 130-foot limit of recreational diving.)

1892:

Frenchman Louis Boutan develops a variant of the closed-circuit system. The Boutan scuba can be used for up to three hours at shallow depths.

1909:

The Draeger company of Lübeck, Germany—a manufacturer of gas valves, fire-fighting equipment, and mine safety devices—plunges into making dive gear. The company creates a self-contained, lined dive system combining a "hard hat" style helmet with a backpack containing compressed oxygen. Over the next few years, Draeger will win numerous patents for diving equipment.

1910:

Dr. John Scott Haldane, a British physiologist, confirms that caisson disease is caused by the release of dissolved nitrogen when surfacing. To enable divers to avoid "the bends," Haldane develops a procedure that calls for gradually staged "decompression." His pioneering research culminates in publication of the first dive tables.

1911:

Sir Robert Davis, a director of Siebe Gorman, refines the Fleuss system and comes up with the Davis False Lung. His reliable, compact, easily stored, and fully self-contained rebreather is adopted (or copied) throughout the world for use as an emergency escape device for submarine crews

1912:

Germany's Westfalia Maschinenfabrik markets a hybrid dive system that blends scuba and surface-fed components with mixed gas technology.

1915:

An early film of **20,000 Leagues Under the Sea** marks the first commercial use of underwater cinematography. The cast and crew uses modified Fleuss/Davis rebreathers and "Oxylite," a compound that generates oxygen through a chemical reaction. (Oxylite explodes if it gets wet, a trait that tends to limit its popularity as a scuba component.) John Williamson shoots the underwater scenes from a chamber, connected to the surface through a flexible metal entry tube.

1917:

Draeger produces a true scuba system that combines tanks containing a mixture of compressed air and oxygen (oxygen enriched air) with rebreathing technology. It is sold for use at depths to 40 meters (130 feet).

1918:

The Ogushi Peerless Respirator passes field tests at 324 feet. The Japanese device combines modified false-lung style closed-circuit rebreather technology with a compressed air reserve. It supplies air to the diver through a manually controlled on/off valve.

1919:

C. J. Cooke develops a mixture of helium and oxygen (heliox) for use as a breathing gas by divers. The mixture enables divers to avoid nitrogen narcosis while diluting oxygen to non-toxic concentrations. It allows commercial divers to extend their useful working depth well beyond previous limits.

1926:

An officer in the French Navy, Yves le Prieur, patents the Fernez/Le Prieur diving system based on compressed air carried in tanks. Le Prieur's device feeds air to a full-face mask worn by the diver. Early models provide a continuous flow of air. Later models use a manual on/off valve to preserve the air supply.

EARLY 1930s:

Guy Gilpatrick, an expatriate American writer living in France, waterproofs a pair of pilot's goggles by lining the edges with glazier's putty. Commercial versions of his window to the underwater world soon follow.

1933:

Jack Prodanovich, Ben Stone, and Glen Orr (later joined by Jack Corbeley, Bill Batzloff and Wally Potts) start a skin diving club in San Diego—the Bottom Scratchers. This pioneering group, the first of its kind, helps define the sport and creates its own folk legends. (In an era preceding the availability of swim fins, would-be members are required to dive to 30 feet. They have to capture three abalone on one dive, grab a five-foot horn shark by its tail, and bring up a "good-sized" lobster) Those who pass the test include underwater filmmaker Lamar Boren and Jim Stewart, diving officer at Scripps Institution of Oceanography.

1935:

Louis de Corlieu patents a broad bladed fin to be worn on the feet by swimmers. The fins make a big splash among free-swimming "goggle" divers. With their help, skin divers and their sport really start going places!

1937:

The American Diving Equipment and Salvage Company (now known as DESCO) develops a self-contained mixed-gas rebreather. It uses a compressed mixture of helium and oxygen in combination with a fully sealed diving suit. Using the new system, DESCO diver Max Nohl sets a new world depth record of 420 feet.

1937:

Georges Comheines creates a scuba system by combining the Rouquayrol/Denayrouze valve with le Prieur's system of compressed air tanks. This breakthrough finally brings to reality the scuba device anticipated by Jules Verne in 1869. Comheines and a group of friends demonstrate the device in a "human aquarium" exhibit at the Paris International Exposition.

1939-1940s:

Owen Churchill helps popularize skin diving, making it a hot sporting craze among cool cats living in coastal areas of the United States.

1942:

The Duke Goes Diving. John Wayne stars as a hard-hatted salvage diver in Cecil B. de Mille's **Reap the Wild Wind**. Co-stars include Rita Hayworth, Paulette Goddard, Raymond Massey, Charles Bickford, Ray Milland, and the giant squid that does in The Duke at the end. Cinematographer Victor Milner is nominated for an Academy Award, but only the squid wins an Oscar (special effects).

1942:

Jacques-Yves Cousteau meets Emile Gagnan, an industrial gas control systems engineer with L'Air Liquide et Cie. They combine their talents and insights. Cousteau, an experienced diver, understands the diver's requirements. Gagnan is an expert on the mechanics of gas valves. Working together, they will soon produce significant advances over Comheines' pre-War scuba system.

1943:

The first Cousteau/Gagnan scuba device fails January testing in the Marne River outside Paris and goes back to Gagnan's drawing board for modifications. Subsequent innovations include a novel device that provides inhalation and exhaust valves at the same level. Several months later, the modified device passes tests in a water tank in Paris.

During the summer, Cousteau and two close friends. Philippe Tailliez and Frederic Dumas, test production prototypes of the Cousteau/Gagnan scuba system in the Mediterranean Sea. The device proves to be safe, reliable, and remarkably easy to use. During July and August, the friends make hundreds of dives, thoroughly testing the system and seeking to determine its limits. (Cousteau's wife, Simone, and sons, Philippe and Jean-Michel, also try out the prototype Aqua-Lung units. That makes the Cousteau family the first to discover that a dive trip makes a great family vacation.) In October, Dumas demonstrates the amazing reliability of the Aqua-Lung with a dive to 210 feet.

That same year, Cousteau and Dumas complete **Au Dix-Huit Metres du Fond ("Sixty Feet Down")**, their first underwater film. To overcome wartime shortages of movie film stock, Jacques and Simone Cousteau splice rolls of still film together. Lacking a darkroom, they work under blankets at night. Cousteau photographs some underwater scenes using a small camera housed in a modified fruit jar.

1946:

Pat Madison and Everett Edmund incorporate M & E Marine in Camden, New Jersey, and create Mar-Vel Underwater Equipment as a division of M & E. Mar-Vel will import and retail diving equipment—primarily commercial hard-hat rigs, but also early skin diving and scuba gear. M & E will also manufacture specialized diving and underwater gear, and become a specialty supplier and contractor with major American corporations, the U. S. Navy, NASA, and other government agencies.

1947:

Jordan Klein starts a small company, Marine Enterprises, Inc., to manufacture spear guns and housings for underwater cameras. His company evolves into a retail store. When he has difficulty finding a good air source, he goes into the business of repairing and

modifying war surplus air compressors. In 1956, Klein will start importing parts from Germany's Bauer organization and packaging his own
compressors under the MAKO name.

1948-1949:

Rene Bussoz imports the Cousteau/Gagnan Aqua-Lung (manufactured by L'Air Liquide through a subsidiary, Le Spirotechnique)
for sale in his Southern California store, Rene's Sporting Goods.
When the Hollywood film community discovers his new gadget,
interest in scuba skyrockets. Bussoz returns to France in 1953. The
store's new management, an executive team from Le Spirotechnique, transforms Rene's Sporting Goods into US Divers which
becomes a leading manufacturer of diving equipment.

1949:

Arnold Post starts selling the Aqualung and related scuba gear
at "Richard's Sporting Goods" (now "Richard's Aqualung Center" and
still operating at the same location) in New York. At the same time,
Charlie Marshall offers the Aqualung for sale at the exclusive New
York outfitter "Abercrombie & Fitch." In Chicago, Vern Pedersen
stocks the Aqualung at his medical gas supply business, "Chicago
Oxygen."

1950:

The International Underwater Spear Fishing Association holds the
first national skin diving competition at Laguna Beach, California.
Organized by Ralph Davis, the competition pulls together many
underwater activities. It is won by the Dolphin Club of Compton,
California.

EARLY 1950s:

Gustav Dalla Valle, the emigre scion of an aristocratic Italian
family, begins importing scuba and skin diving equipment made in
Italy by Eduardo Cressi to the United States. Dalla Valle later sells
the Cressi distribution contract to Dick Kline at Healthways.

EARLY 1950s:

Entrepreneurs in coastal cities all around America launch dive
retail operations. In California, Bob Lorenz opens "Water Gill," presumably the first specialty retail store for scuba divers, in Venice; Mel
Fisher opens "Mel's Aqua Shop" in a Torrance feed store; and Bill
Hardy and Bill Johnston open "San Diego Divers Supply." In Florida, Paul Arnold opens "Aqua-Lung, Inc." and Jordan Klein opens
"Underwater Sports" (originally named "Marineland") in 1951. They
soon face competition from Lou Maxwell ' s "Florida Frogman." Back

on the West Coast. Bob and Bill Meistrell start "Dive 'N' Surf" in Hermosa Beach, California, in 1953. That makes "Dive 'N' Surf" the West Coast's oldest diving specialty retailer in continuous operation. In Boston, James Bliss starts retailing scuba gear at his marine products wholesale distributor in 1954. In 1955, Bernie Freedman starts selling dive gear at "Tommy's Hardware" (now "Tommy's Hardware and Dive Store") of Portland, Maine. And things are just getting started!

1951:

Richard Widmark and Dana Andrews star in **The Frogmen**, a critically acclaimed film about the exploits of the Navy's underwater demolition teams. Industry experts credit this film and other publicity given the exploits of military divers with helping to accelerate the growth of scuba; diving Cinematographer Norbert Brodine earns an Academy Award nomination.

1951:

E. R. Cross invents the "Sport Diver," one of the first American-made single-hose regulators. Cross' version is based on the oxygen system used by pilots. Other early single-hose regulators developed during the 1950s include Rose Aviation's "Little Rose Pro," the "Nemrod Snark" (from Spain). and the Sportsways "Waterlung," designed by diving pioneer Sam Le Cocq in 1958. The "Waterlung" will become the first single-hose regulator to be widely adopted by the diving public. (While some double-hose regulators remain in use. they are no longer manufactured in the United States.)

1951:

Chuck Blakeslee and Jim Auxier create **Skin Diver** magazine. (Many early skin divers refuse to use the new "bubble machines" and look on scuba as "sissy diving.") **Skin Diver** instantly becomes the leading journal of spear fishing and underwater hunting. In later years, the magazine shifts its attention to scuba. **Skin Diver** will continue to play an important role, nurturing  industry growth by promoting underwater photography and travel.

1951:

A European manufacturer, possibly Le Spirotechnique, produces a new tank valve that can be set to reserve part of the air supply. The "reserve" can be used by the diver after the main supply is depleted. The first US Divers catalog, published in 1953, designates the reserve valve with the letter "J," and it becomes known throughout the industry as the "J-valve." Its catalog companion, the "non-reserve" device, is still known as the "K-valve."

1951:

Rachel Carson publishes **The Sea Around Us**. Her scholarly yet poetic book about the oceans wins several prestigious awards and tops bestseller lists for almost seven months. Today, more than 40 years later, **The Sea Around Us** continues to win new friends for the marine environment

1951:

John Steinbeck publishes **The Log from the Sea of Cortez**. His book chronicles a 1940 research and collecting expedition undertaken by Steinbeck and Ed Ricketts. It introduces a wide audience to the Sea of Cortez, then more commonly called the Gulf of California. It also attracts many adventurous scuba divers to La Paz and nearby islands. (The original, full report of the journey appeared in 1941 as Steinbeck and Ricketts, **The Sea of Cortez: A Leisurely Journal of Travel and Research**.)

1951:

Hans Hass publishes **Diving to Adventure.** With its descriptions of diving with sharks, whales, manta rays, and other animals, the bestseller enhances diving's image as grand adventure. It also makes Hass a role model for the diving public.

1952:

Jacques-Yves Cousteau, Frederic Dumas, and James Dugan publish **Silent World**, a book about the early days of Aqualung diving. It too becomes a bestseller.

1953:

Dr. Eugenie Clark publishes **Lady With a Spear**. It becomes a Book-of-the-Month Club selection and will be translated into eight languages plus Braille. The popular book gives women divers a role model of their own.

1953:

Robert Wagner, Gilbert Roland, Terry Moore, Peter Graves and an antagonistic rubber octopus star in **Beneath the 12 Mile Reef**, a film about diving for sponges off the Florida coast. The critics say it's a sinker. But crowds flood the theaters and the underwater cinematography of Edward Cronjager receives an Academy Award nomination.

1953:

The July issue of *Popular Science* publishes directions for modifying surplus Air Force oxygen systems for use as scuba regulators. (There is no indication of who was supposed to pay for the product liability insurance. It was, indeed, a simpler, albeit more hazardous era!)

1953:

E. R. Cross publishes **Underwater Safety**, the first modern diving manual in the U.S. Later distributed by Healthways, well over 100,000 copies of this 86-page book will eventually be sold. Cross also publishes **Underwater Photography and Television**. Since there are only a few hundred underwater cameras in the country at the time, this one proves to be a book whose time has not yet come.

1954:

Al Tillman, director of sports for the Los Angeles County Department of Parks and Recreation, and L. A. County lifeguard Bev Morgan develop the first formal skin and scuba diver training programs. In 1955, the L. A. County program will begin certifying diving instructors.

1954:

The first full textbook of recreational diving, **The Science of Skin and Scuba Diving** is published by the Council for National Cooperation in Aquatics. An expanded edition appears in 1959. The third edition appears, under the title **The New Science of Skin and Scuba Diving**, in 1962. By 1974, when the fourth edition is published, more than a million copies have been sold.

1954:

Kirk Douglas, James Mason, Paul Lukas, and Peter Lorre star in Walt Disney's popular remake of **20,000 Leagues Under the Sea**. It wins Academy Awards for art direction and special effects.

1954:

Television's first underwater documentary series, **Kingdom of the Sea**, makes its debut. The program includes live broadcasts of a "diver education" segment starring diver Zale Parry. The same year, Parry makes a record setting dive to 209 feet near Catalina Island. National publicity accompanies her exploit, and diving will never again be perceived as "for men only."

Zale Parry after 209 feet record dive near Catalina Island, 1954.

1955:

Jane Russell, Richard Egan, and Gilbert Roland star in a Howard Hughes film, **Underwater**! Promotional posters feature scantily clad

Hollywood newcomer Jayne Mansfield. The film premieres at a Florida spring. Some of the guests wear scuba gear to watch divers search for sunken treasure. Or maybe they just watch Jane and Jayne.

1955:

Sam Davison, Jr., introduces the "Dial-A-Breath," a double-hose, double-diaphragm regulator, complete with a built-in low-pressure reserve and variable breathing resistance. It helps touch off a competitive frenzy as other manufacturers seek special features to distinguish their own lines of equipment. Davison goes on to build his own equipment manufacturing company, Dacor.

LATE 1950s:

Dive retailing shifts into high gear. Jim Cahill and Bob Gurette open "New England Divers" in Beverley, Massachusetts. Mike Kevorkian opens "Tarpon Skin Diving Center" in Miami. In Vermont, Harold Simpers transforms his auto dealership into "Victory Auto and Dive." In Connecticut, Navy diver Bob Barth starts "Aqua Sports" and Lenny Green offers diving gear at his "Surplus Trading Post." In Rhode Island, John McAniff adds dive equipment to the photography equipment sold at the "Bellvue Camera" chain. Out on New York's Long Island, Archie Orenstein opens "Central Skin Divers." In Schenectady. New York, Howard Goldstock opens "Goldstock Sporting Goods. ' Joe Dorsey opens the "Divers Den" in Baltimore and Smokey Roberts opens "Smokey's Divers Den" in Pennsylvania. In the Midwest, Vern Pederson changes the name of his business from "Chicago Oxygen" to "Vern's Scuba Center"; "Ed Thorne's Hardware" in Rockford, Illinois, adds a line of scuba gear; Jack Blocker opens "Jack the Frogman" in Minneapolis; and Ralph West opens "Sport Diver" in Milwaukee. In the Northwest. the man to see is Gary Keffler at Seattle 's "Underwater Sports. " Down South, Bill Tant opens "Southern Skin Diver Supply" in Alabama and Roland Riviere opens "Roland's" in New Orleans. Texas checks in with Jack Rich's "Village Sporting Goods" and "Copeland's," owned by Jim Copeland. The Sooner State makes its entry a little later when Phil Bayouth opens "Phil's" in Oklahoma City. Even the arid Southwest discovers diving when Boris Innocenti opens "Aqua Sports" in Phoenix. And many other pioneering retailers also take the plunge.

1956:

Dr. Hugh Bradner at the University of California is researching thermodynamic principles as applied to the protective properties of Arctic long johns. Instead of perfecting polar underwear, he invents a new type of outerwear for divers. The fabric: a neoprene foam manufactured by Rubatex as automobile insulation. The concept: replace a physical barrier (the supposedly watertight diving suit) with a more user-friendly thermal barrier. That means that the wearer gets wet but stays warm, anyway. The product becomes known, logically enough, as the wetsuit. Early production models are 1/8" thick, made by EDCO, and marketed by the Beaver company of La Jolla, California.

1956:

Jacques Cousteau and co-director Louis Malle win the Golden Palm at the Cannes Film Festival for **Le Monde Du Silence ("Silent World")**. The documentary introduces worldwide audiences to Cousteau's research ship and floating film studio, Calypso.

Commander Lionel Philip K. Crabb of the British Navy disappears while diving in Portsmouth harbor, near a visiting state-of-the-art Soviet cruiser, Ordzhonikidze. The British admiralty cries "foul," claims that Crabb was innocently testing new scuba gear, and demands an explanation from the Soviets. The USSR strenuously denies knowing anything at all about whatever could possibly have happened to the British frogman. Media coverage stresses Crabb's extraordinary career as a military diver and creates widespread interest in scuba diving. The event remains diving's greatest unsolved mystery.

1956:

Ted Nixon introduces a distinctive red and white "diver down" flag to warn boaters to stay clear or slow down to avoid injuring nearby divers. (There is no record of who becomes the first boater to respond by cruising over at high speed "to see what those guys are up to.")

1957:

Zale Parry and Al Tillman organize the first international underwater film festival in Los Angeles. The popular event gives diving a new artistic and cultural dimension. Similar popular events soon follow in Mexico, Canada, New York, Miami, Chicago, the Virgin Islands, and other locations.

1957:

Bob Soto opens "Bob Soto's Diving. Ltd," the first successful full-service, full-time dive operation on Grand Cayman Island.

1958:

A small hotel, Sunset House, opens for business on Grand Cayman. Its beach front location makes it an immediate success. It becomes especially popular with scuba divers. Over the next decade, Sunset House (now "Sunset Divers") will become a popular dive resort.

1958:

Sherwood Manufacturing purchases the patent for the piston regulator. (The price asked and received by the inventor is that he be taken to lunch once a year.) Sherwood engineers modify the regulator for use in scuba equipment, as a replacement for the diaphragm regulator originally created by Rouquayrol and Denayrouze in 1864. Sherwood will manufacture piston-valved regulators in various configurations for sale by U. S. Divers, Voit, Healthways, Swimaster, Scubapro, Dacor, Nemrod-Seamless Rubber, and others for many years. Various versions of the device are still widely used throughout the industry.

1958:

Executives from several diving equipment manufacturers exhibiting at the National Sporting Goods Association (NSGA)—Voit, US Divers, Healthways, Dacor, and Swimaster—decide to form the "Organization of Underwater Manufacturers." They hope it will become a vehicle for the gathering and exchange of valuable commercial information, and will help professionalize recreational diving. The group continues to meet at NSGA shows for a few years, but it fails to become much more than a social club.

1958:

Ivan Tors ' **Underwater Warrior** (1958) starring Ross Martin and Dan Dailey spotlights the career of Doug Fane and his U. S. Navy UDT divers. One critic calls it "a semidocumentary drama, unlikely to win any recruits," but enlistment of UDT volunteers soars, anyway.

1958-1961:

Sea Hunt, produced by Ivan Tors and photographed by Lamar Boren, becomes one of America's most popular television series. The exploits of Mike Nelson (played by Lloyd Bridges) make the character a role model for a generation of wanna-be and someday-will-be scuba divers.

1959:

Hollywood's love affair with the underwater world bottoms out with Jerry Lewis on scuba gear, some wayward Weeki Wachee mermaids, and a wimpy, wacky octopus in **Don't give Up the Ship**.

1959:

The YMCA 's National Aquatic Council offers the first nationwide diver training and certification program.

1959:

The Boston-based Northeast Council of Dive Clubs hosts the First National Convention of Skin Divers. The group forms an umbrella organization representing many diving clubs. councils, and constituencies—the Underwater Society of America. Organizers include John McAniff, who serves as director of competitive skin diving. The Society will become an industry advocate and an active forum for skin diving activities, including a variety of national and international competitions.

1960:

Diving pioneer Connie Limbaugh drowns while diving in a cave in France. Limbaugh, the first diving officer at Scripps Institution of Oceanography, is among the most admired divers in the world and a leading marine scientist. His death saddens everyone in the industry—and makes divers everywhere feel vulnerable.

Conrad Limbaugh

1960:

Neal Hess and Al Tillman organize the National Association of Underwater Instructors (NAUI) in cooperation with the Underwater Society of America. Its first instructor certifying course, held in Houston, draws participants from all over the United States.

1960:

Dick Birch opens the four-room Small Hope Bay on Andros Cay in The Bahamas—the earliest known dedicated dive resort. Small Hope Bay offers a remote location sheltered by the Andros Barrier Reef, less than 200 miles from Miami. Now with 20 rooms, it is still in business.

1960s:

Mel Fisher, Burt Webber, Kip Wagner, Fay Field, and others find scattered treasure from wrecks of Spain's 1715 fleet and create new technology for the hunt. By the end of the decade, they recover much of the salvageable treasure from the 1715 and 1733 fleets. But new finds will continue to be uncovered in the 1990s, and, perhaps, beyond.

1961:

Maurice Fenzy patents a device invented by the underwater research group of the French navy. The device includes an inflatable bag with a small attached cylinder of compressed air. It rapidly becomes the first commercially successful buoyancy compensator. Within a few years, divers throughout Europe. and a few well-traveled Americans, are wearing "Fenzys."

1961:

Ed Replogle invents a "sonic alarm" that automatically warns its user (and everyone else in the vicinity) of low air pressure. The device manufactured by Sherwood and sold by Healthways, signals that safety remains a major concern in the recreational diving industry.

1962:

Two highly publicized experiments give the world a glimpse of underwater experimentation and research. E. A. Link becomes the "Man in the Sea" with an experimental 24 hour dive (on heliox) to 200 feet. And Jacques Cousteau conducts "Conshelf One," with a habitat housing six men breathing oxygen enriched air (nitrox) at 35 feet for seven days.

1963:

Equipment importer and distributor Gustav Dalla Valle and his partner, former Navy diver and dive equipment retailer Dick Bonin, start their own diving equipment manufacturing company, Scubapro.

1963:

Art Stanfield and Charlie Jehle (Voit), Dick Bonin (Scubapro), Sam Davison, Sr. (Dacor), John Culley (U. S. Divers), and Randy Stone (Healthways) revive the idea of a national trade association. They form the Diving Equipment Manufacturers Association

Scubapro co-founder Dick Bonin (R) with Engineers Jim Dexter and Mark Lamont.

(DEMA) "to promote, foster, and advance the common business interests of the members as manufacturers of diving equipment."

1963:

Flipper, a movie featuring Chuck Connors and Luke Halpin, but starring a tail walking, playfully squeaking bottlenosed dolphin, wins modest box office success. The film, its sequels, and the popular television series that follows will change popular attitudes toward marine mammals—and toward the oceans.

1964:

Richard Adcock launches *Marisla*, possibly the first dedicated live-aboard dive boat, in La Paz, Mexico. Adcock has been teaching diving and guiding dive tours of the Sea of Cortez since 1956.

1964:

The U. S. Navy launches *Sealab* for a different kind of live-aboard diving experience. In the first experiment, four divers stay underwater for 11 days at an average depth of 193 feet.

1965:

Al Tillman develops the UNEXSO Diving Resort at Freeport in The Bahamas. Created with the dawn of the jet age, it soon becomes a major attraction for teaching diving and a magnet for traveling divers. Programmed to protect the environment, the resort promotes hunting with cameras instead of spear guns. UNEXSO becomes the prototype of a complete dedicated dive travel destination.

1965:

U. S. Navy *Sealab* II team leader Scott Carpenter, living and working in the habitat at a depth of 205 feet, speaks with astronaut Gordon Cooper in a *Gemini* spacecraft orbiting 200 miles above the surface. No longer will humanity be able to view space, sea, and land as separate entities. Instead, we are learning to view Spaceship Earth as a single system. This is the real dawning of the Age of Aquarius.

1965:

Thunderball, starring Sean Connery, glamorizes and updates the image of scuba with waves of diving extras and starlets galore. Agent 007 saves the world but gives diving retailers fits as customers demand to buy scuba gear "just like James Bond's." The special visual effects win an Academy Award.

1966:

The Professional Association of Diving Instructors (PADI) is formed by John Cronin and Ralph Erickson.

Ralph Erickson (R) with a newly certified instructor at a Sweden ITC.

1967:

The Undersea Medical Society (now the Undersea and Hyperbaric Medical Society, UHMS) is founded in Bethesda, Maryland. UHMS and its members will significantly advance knowledge of the medical aspects of diving.

1969:

Travel agent Dewey Bergman starts See and Sea Travel based in San Francisco. The new agency offers tour packages designed for scuba divers traveling to such off-the beaten-path destinations as Bonaire, Grand Cayman, and Cozumel.

1970:

John McAniff and the University of Rhode Island create the National Underwater Accident Data Center (NUADC). The statistics and accident information gathered, analyzed, and reported by McAniff will advance industry awareness of many aspects of diving safety. Originally funded by the U. S. Department of Health, NUADC will later attract support from the National Oceanic and Atmospheric Administration (NOAA), DEMA, PADI, and other groups within the dive industry.

1970:

The macho image of underwater exploration has its chest hairs tweaked when marine biologist Dr. Sylvia Earle leads a highly publicized mission in the *Tektite* habitat. Earle's all-female team of aquanauts successfully completes a two-week saturation stay at 42 feet, providing researchers with much valuable data.

1970s:

Mel Fisher and his group find scattered traces of *Nuestra Senora de Atocha*, a treasure ship lost in 1622. Treasure fever fires the imagination of the nation. Burt Webber' s group later finds the remains of *Nuestra Senora de la Conception*, another rich treasure ship, and the world has a relapse of treasure fever. As research, technology, and search skills improve, more finds will follow.

1971:

Peter Hughes opens the first full-service dive business on Roatan at "Anthony's Key Resort," then a 17-room resort hotel catering to the sailing crowd. Hughes' remarkable and rapid success demonstrates to beach resort operators throughout the Caribbean that "underwater treasure" can take many forms.

1971:

Scubapro introduces the Stabilization Jacket. A combination backpack and jacket style buoyancy control device (BCD). The "stab jacket" and its imitators increase diver acceptance of BCDs. Jacket-style BCDs become the industry standard for most uses. ("Horsecollar" BCDs will continue to be popular with cave divers and others who use multi-tank dive rigs.)

1972:

The U. S. Congress passes the Marine Protection, Research, and Sanctuaries Act. The Act seeks to extend the kind of protection afforded by national park status to estuaries and coastal waters. It recognizes that marine sanctuaries are "part of our collective riches as a nation" and charges NOAA with managing the program. The first National Marine Sanctuary, designated in 1975, protects the remains of the Civil War ironclad *Monitor*. Today, the system embraces thirteen sites including the three newest: Monterey Bay, California; Stellwagen Banks off the New England coast, and the Hawaiian Islands Humpback Whale National Marine Sanctuary.

1972:

"Captain Don" Stewart of Bonaire starts setting concrete "sea tethers" (now known as mooring buoys) at popular dive sites. The buoys successfully prevent damage to fragile reefs caused by falling and dragging boat anchors. In 1979, to further protect the reefs for and from divers, Bonaire designates its surrounding waters as a marine park. Tom van't Hof, head of the Caribbean Marine Biological Institute (Curaçao), formalizes the mooring buoy program. The reef protection idea gradually (actually far too gradually) takes hold at other popular dive destinations.

1972:

Carl Roessler joins See & Sea Travel and expands the organization's live-aboard dive boat program. The live aboard idea popularizes dive travel to the Cayman Islands (aboard Paul Humann's pioneering *Cayman Diver*), the Great Barrier Reef and Coral Sea (aboard Wally Muller's *Coralita*) and other distant seas.

1974:

Baja Expeditions expands dive travel opportunities in the Sea of Cortez aboard *Poseidon*, then the *Baja Explorador* and the *Don Jose*. Dive guides working for Baja Expeditions include neophyte underwater photographers Marty Snyderman and Howard Hall.

1975:

Hollywood rediscovers the underwater world in a fearsome way with the box office blockbuster, **Jaws**. Stephen Spielberg's bodacious beast makes a bunch of bucks for novelist Peter Benchley but takes a big bite out of the diving business. Shark-o-phobia chases people out of the water in droves, ending 15 consecutive years of industry growth. Aftershocks echo in 1977 with **The Deep**, and in 1978 and 1983 with **Jaws 2** and **Jaws 3**.

1977:

The first DEMA trade show convenes in Miami. The show establishes itself as "neutral ground" where the entire industry can meet. The trade show becomes remarkably successful, and within a few years, DEMA makes itself a potent force for professionalism and unity within the recreational diving industry.

1981:

DEMA designs and tests its GEM program of streamlined diver training in cooperation with NAUI, PADI, and a group of diving retailers. The program suggests a kinder, gentler philosophy of dive instruction—along with courses that require less pool and classroom time. The certification programs that follow in GEM's wake make diving more accessible to busy professionals entire families, and other new participants.

1982:

The Institute of Diving opens the "International Diving Museum" (now the "Museum of Man in the Sea") in Panama City, Florida. The museum's collection will become one of the most comprehensive in the world. It includes the U. S. Navy's *Sealab* I and the *Deep Dive System Mark* I. The museum also houses diving equipment from England, France, Germany, and Japan, as well as a research library of rare books, video tapes, photographs, and films.

1983:

DEMA produces **I'd Rather Be Diving,** a film that promotes recreational diving and is widely used by retailers as a sales aid. In the best Hollywood tradition, it will be followed by three sequels: **Treasure Diving** (1984) spoofs adventure films; **The Seven Wonders of the Diving World** (1985) promotes dive travel; and **Scuba Diving in America** (1986) promotes local diving at domestic sites throughout the United States.

1983:

Co-inventors Craig Barshinger and Karl Huggins, and ORCA Industries founder Jim Fulton, introduce The Edge, the first commercially successful American electronic dive computer, at the DEMA trade show. The device automatically tracks dives and continuously calculates remaining "no decompression" time and depth limits. It helps spark a new era in dive instrumentation.

1984:

Dive travel via live-aboard boats surges with the arrival of a new group of charter boats custom-designed for scuba divers. They include the *Cayman Aggressor* serving the Cayman Islands; the *Tri-Star* in the Philippines; and the *Fantasea* in the Red Sea. Larger, more stable, and more luxurious than their predecessors, they will attract and satisfy diving's increasingly upscale market. The new market, in turn, will attract new players to dive travel.

1984, 1985:

American popular culture shows a revived affection for the underwater world. Two movies—**Splash** and **Cocoon**—portray the ocean as a revitalizing, nurturing environment and feature lovingly photographed underwater scenes. Rising sales throughout the recreational diving industry reflect the appeal of the new image.

1985:

Mel Fisher's team finds the main body of the 1622 wreck A*tocha*, along with its fabled $400 million in gold, silver, emeralds, and priceless historic artifacts. The event marks the ultimate fulfillment of the treasure hunter's fantasy. Publicity given Fisher's find (not to mention the lawsuits that follow) helps fuel America's reviving fascination with recreational diving.

LATE 1980s:

The recreational diving industry continues to evolve, with a growing emphasis on underwater photography and video. Domestic and international dive travel attract a rapidly growing following. With increasing popularity comes a new emphasis on the style, color, fashion. and visual excitement of diving equipment. Books about the ocean, especially lush "coffee table" presentations of underwater photography, become bestsellers. These years also witness continuous improvements in the comfort, durability, and efficiency of equipment, and in diver education, training, safety, and environmental awareness.

1991:

Recreational divers form Ocean Futures, an environmental organization "Dedicated to the Sea Around Us." The new group recognizes that the dive industry has a responsibility to the oceans and marine life throughout the world. The 1992 DEMA trade show in Houston features an "Environmental Pavilion" with displays and information provided by many of America's leading marine environmental organizations. As part of the show's "Industry Convocation," NOAA Administrator Dr. John A. Knauss and Chief Scientist Dr. Sylvia Earle designate the Flower Gardens reef system as a National Marine Sanctuary.

1993:

Dive travel continues to grow rapidly, and takes another giant step with the addition of numerous new boats to the charter fleet. They include luxurious live-aboards serving Borneo, Papua/New Guinea, the Solomon Islands, Fiji, the Sea of Cortez, the Coral Sea, and many other new destinations around Planet Ocean.

1993-2001 AND BEYOND:

We can only fantasize about accomplishments yet to come. Revolutionary new technologies such as rebreathers for recreational divers are already in prototype. Remarkable new live-aboard dive boats and luxurious resorts are under construction at this moment. Whatever form your diving dreams may take, you can be sure that diving educators, inventors, scientists, explorers, and other visionaries are already working to fulfill those fantasies.

DEMA Hall Of Fame, 1993. From left to right: Jean Michel Cousteau, Stan Waterman, Zale Parry, Bob Meistrell, Eugenie Clark, Glen Egstrom, Jim Stewart, Dick Bonin and Scott Carpenter.

SECTION 1

FREE DIVERS

THE SAN DIEGO BOTTOM SCRATCHERS

(All photos by Lamar Boren except the 1939 photo.)

The world's first diving club, the San Diego Bottom Scratchers, was organized in 1933. That was about three years before Jacques Cousteau and Hans Hass began goggling in the Mediterranean, and a decade before the invention of the Aqualung. An exclusive organization that numbered only 19 members, the Bottom Scratchers roster included some significant contributors to sport and scientific diving: Conrad Limbaugh and Jim Stewart, Professor Carl Hubbs and Lamar Boren. But to spearfishing enthusiasts, the biggest names are Jack Prodanovich and Wally Potts.

NOW IN THEIR 70s, these Bottom Scratchers are living legends of spearfishing. A self-taught tinkerer and inventor, Jack is credited with the invention of the first American diving goggles, the first practical mask, the first mini camera housing, the powerhead, and the first American speargun. Potts was his diving buddy, also an inventor, and one of the big guns in spearfishing through the 50s. He is the historian of the Bottom Scratchers, maintaining biographies, photos, and artifacts that keep the tradition alive. Today both are noted for the innovative, custom spearguns they still make to order.

The major thrust of the Bottom Scratchers was spearfishing, an activity frowned upon by much of today's diving public. But environmentalism is a luxury of hindsight from the perspective of the 90s. Chasing edible fish and invertebrates is what first brought man underwater. There were few divers then and lots of fish, and everybody thought it would last forever. For the first two-thirds of this century, the most distinguished ocean scientists were telling us that the wealth of the sea was inexhaustible. So when the killing of fish is discussed, let's try to keep it in the context of those times. We divers wouldn't be where we are today if people like the Bottom Scratchers hadn't shown us the way.

The name of the club comes from their initiation ceremony. A prospective member had to capture three abalones on a single breath, catch a 10-pound lobster, and grab a horn shark bare-handed. Of course, all this had to be accomplished while breath-holding, and without swim fins. The abalone and lobster requirements were not as difficult as they would be today, because both animals were plentiful in the heyday of the Bottom Scratchers.

Horn sharks have a small horn in front of both dorsal fins. A new member had to remove a horn from the shark he caught, and hang it from the zipper on the coin pocket of his swim trunks. As they swam along the bottom, those horns left scratch marks in the sand. This is how the club got its name.

The first diving mask and diving goggles, developed by Jack Prodanovich in the mid-1930's.

The late Glenn Orr is credited with being America's first skin diver. According to a **Sports Illustrated** article ("The Old Men of the Sea" by Coles Phinizy, August 1965), Orr was a part-time commercial diver who also dabbled in rum running during Prohibition. After the crash of 1929, while others were lining up in soup kitchens, Orr and his friends kept their families fed from the bounty of the sea. Two of those early buddies, and co-founders of the club, were Ben Stone and Jack Prodanovich.

At first they hunted abalones and lobsters, which were slow enough to be grabbed by hand. Later they fabricated hand spears from straightened fish hooks and wooden poles, which were used to stick jack smelt. Masks, fins, protective suits, and rubber-powered spearguns were far in the future. Potts: "In those days you were fully equipped if you had a glass to look through and a pair of trunks to wear."

Orr found some goggles that were designed for salt-water swimming. These allowed limited sight underwater, but the lenses were in different planes, resulting in double vision. Prodanovich had to close one eye when "punching" a fish with the spear. In addition, Orr's was the only set of goggles. The other club members took turns using them.

Jack was head custodian at Point Loma High School. Like Wally, he arranged to work the night shift so he could dive all day. An inveterate tinkerer, Prodanovich sought a way to improve on Orr's goggles. First he took the hoses from an automobile radiator. The round, mirrored glass in women's compacts was the correct diameter, so he scraped off the backing, attached two of them to hose fragments, and the first American diving goggles were made. These were bet-

Bottom Scratchers Diving Club in 1939 at La Jolla caves area, before swim fins, rubber shirts, etc. From left to right; Glenn Orr, Jack Corbeley, Ben Stone, Bill Batzloff and Jack Prodanovich.

ter than the Japanese version, but Jack wore glasses and needed something to accommodate them. So he designed the first diving mask, inspired from a stereoscope viewer he saw in the high school science classroom. Its body was made of copper, with a glass faceplate attached. Rubber from ignition wire formed the seal. To fit people with different sized noses, the nose was left outside the mask. Prodanovich: "The Japanese dive goggles had bulbs on each eyepiece. We couldn't figure out what they were for. Then I remembered when I dive down to 10 or 15 feet, I'd get this squeeze. By gosh, I figured the water pressure would squeeze the bulbs, then I could dive 25 feet with no strain. Amazing." Potts: "Most of his ideas, he gets from something he sees,...which can be used for something else,...which becomes an invention."

This solved the problem of mask squeeze, but ear squeeze was another matter. They realized that pressure hurt the ears, but nobody knew what to do about it. Even today, many doctors do not fully comprehend the mechanics of pressure injury, and continue to advocate ear plugs. Pain in the ears was considered a normal part of diving, and the early pioneers just endured it. The Bottom Scratchers used custom-molded earplugs which hung on strings from their mask straps. All the surviving members have paid the price of pioneering and wear hearing aids today. Potts blames part of it on the noisy environment at the aircraft plant where he worked. Prodanovich adds, "I've got two brothers and a sister, they've got hearing aids and they never dove a day in their life. My mother is 102 and she can hear as well as I do."

By the late 1940s there were an estimated 8,000 skin divers in Southern California, according to an article featuring the Bottom Scratchers in the May, 1949 issue of **National Geographic**. Because it was a male-only organization, their wives and girl friends formed the first women's dive club, the Sea Nymphs.

The early history of diving illustrates the principle of convergent evolution. In other parts of the country and the world, people were working on the same problems and coming up with similar solutions. But there was no communication among them. So masks were also developed in Europe, in Japan, and in Florida. Each was an original, based solely on the experience and ingenuity of its inventors.

Then as now, divers sought a way to convey visually what they saw underwater. Although he wasn't a serious photographer, Prodanovich in 1934 fabricated a waterproof housing for Kodak's Baby Brownie camera. A year later Potts, a sheet metal worker at Solar Aircraft, came up with his own version. Although the fuzzy black and white images don't measure up to today's photographs, they remain the only underwater record of the early exploits of the Bottom Scratchers.

In 1943 another diver joined the club who would have a major impact on underwater photography: Lamar Boren. During World War II he was working for the electric utility company, and owned a photo studio on the side. Wally: "He was a fair diver too. A rugged old guy, he rarely used a shirt (wet suit), even after they came into being. So any time the water cleared, Jack and I were out there punching fish,...Lamar would shoot pictures of us. Now that we are over the hill, we can look back and say, 'I did that one time.'

"We got a lot of pictures before Lamar's time, but they were box camera types. Lamar started out in still photography." Potts helped him make a housing for his Speed Graphic, which allowed one picture before reloading. He moved on to movies when club member Bill Batzloff fabricated a housing for his 16mm Bolex. Boren's first film depicted the Bottom Scratchers diving for abalones and lobsters, and was shot entirely while breath holding.

By this time the photo business was so successful that he quit his job with the utility company and shot pictures full time. He founded an aerial photo service, working both as pilot and photographer. In 1950 he was recruited to shoot the sub-surface scenes for the Jane Russell film, "**Underwater,**" using his own movie camera, because no other was available. That was the start of a 30-year career as Hollywood's leading underwater film maker. His credits include the "**Sea Hunt**" television show (which he helped originate), the "**Flipper**" TV series, four James Bond films, "**Old Man and the Sea**",

"Day of the Dolphin", **"Around the World Under the Sea"**, **"Brewster McCloud"**, and numerous TV shows. Recipient of many awards including a NOGI and lifetime membership in the Explorers Club, Boren died in 1986 at age 69.

Wally Potts and his world-record black sea bass, 401.5 pounds. This photo appeared in the 5th issue of **Sports Illustrated**, 1954.

When shooting the pilot film for the **"Sea Hunt"** series, Boren recruited Potts and Ben Stone to play the villains. In the final scene they ride a boat into the sunset, dressed in swim suits and handcuffs. The original heroes were a pair of unknown actors; the title of the pilot was **"Sea Divers."** Lloyd Bridges wasn't involved at the time. He was signed to play Mike Nelson after the project was sold to TV.

Conrad Limbaugh joined up in 1953. At this time, Connie was the first diving officer at Scripps Institution of Oceanography. He also had a long background in free diving, dating back to the pre-war years. Limbaugh was part of the Bottom Scratchers' Scripps connection, begun two years earlier by Jim Stewart and culminating with Dr. Carl Hubbs. Hubbs was invited to join for his contributions to oceanography rather than his limited diving background. He used observations from club members in his research, and in turn advised them on conservation.

The relationship dates back to 1945, when Jack and Wally began using their newly developed powerheads. For the first time they were able to get big fish. Wally shot the first one over 100 pounds, a broomtail grouper off Boomer Beach, using Jack's powerhead mounted on a 12 foot pole. "The following day I speared another one, a gulf grouper with a smooth tail. We figured the one with the ragged tail was the same fish, had got in a fight or something. That's where Carl Hubbs came in." Hubbs informed them that this was a limited population, perhaps stranded there by a warm water episode. They immediately declared the fishes off limits. Unfortunately other spearfishermen didn't honor the ban.

Other Scripps scientists enlisted the Bottom Scratchers for research projects as well. Potts recalls, "We always told people we held our breath three minutes, but we never took a watch down and timed ourselves. Early on, Scripps did some studies on this. They put us on an exerciser bike in a pool, put (instruments) all over us. Glenn Orr did four minutes underwater with that stuff, riding a bicycle. And he was a smoker. Of course he's dead now; probably held his breath too long (laughs)."

Between them, Potts and Prodanovich are credited with the invention of the American speargun. Through their efforts it evolved from a 10-foot hand spear with a frog gig on the end to a sophisticated rubber-powered gun with a slip-tip or powerhead, and a line pack or reel. Jack states, "Wally and I feel the modern speargun is derived from all of our experience. Everything on the market was influenced by our early guns. I've been making essentially the same gun for 20 years, only change it to improve it." Others were making guns as well, in Europe and in other areas of the United States. But blue-water spearfishermen gravitated to Jack's and Wally's designs.

> They put us on an exerciser bike in a pool, put (instruments) all over us. Glenn Orr did four minutes underwater with that stuff, riding a bicycle. And he was a smoker. Of course he's dead now; probably held his breath too long.

Prodanovich first experimented with springs, pieces of inner tube, even 1/2-inch diameter bungee cord used on the landing gear of biplanes. But the rubber of the day just wasn't resilient enough. He eventually hit on the idea of a powerhead on the end of a hand spear, using a .38 caliber cartridge. But before he got it to work, he lost his right eye testing it in a swimming pool. "I had a malfunction in the retrieving line. Normally, at 10 feet it's got enough momentum to counteract the recoil. The retrieving line got hung up, it slowed the shaft down to where it just set itself off. I had a plywood target, the shaft became the projectile and came back and went through my mask. I was wearing glasses inside my mask; it went through...and into my eye. So (my eye) bought the ranch."

When better quality surgical tubing became available after the war, Prodanovich set out to improve upon the European speargun. He eventually sold the design to Swimaster, who produced the first commercial American version. Later Scubapro bought Potts' design for its guns. The custom units that Jack and Wally produce today are practically works of art, made from mahogany, maple, ash, walnut or metal tubing. Actually they make the mechanism, and the buyer installs it in the gun. To an avid spearfisherman, buying a gun made by these two would be like buying a baseball bat made by Ty Cobb or Honus Wagner.

Spearfishing competitions began in the late 40s, but the Bottom Scratchers didn't participate for very long. At the time, winners were based on the aggregate poundage of fish. The easiest way to win was to shoot as many small reef fish as possible. Potts recalls, "A guy came in with 200 little shiner perch. I bet they weren't 4 inches long. They put them on the scale and weighed the whole mess.

And he became the big shot. Our stance was the fish had to be at least a foot long, and had to be an edible fish, not a stingray or something. We wanted only one fish of a species. That didn't go either. We said, 'That's enough for us,' and we

Wally Potts and Jack Prodanovich with three white sea bass shot off the La Jolla shores, 1951.

never did that any more... We realized the competitions weren't the right way to go. You don't have a contest to see who could shoot the most deer."

The biggest fish Wally ever shot was a world-record black sea bass: 401 1/2 pounds. In 1954 Lamar Boren was asked by the editor of Time-Life's new magazine, **Sports Illustrated**, for some spectacular underwater photos. He contacted Wally and Jack, hired an 18-foot boat and set off for the Coronados Islands, just across the border in Mexico. Wally: "We all got up on the right side of the bed that day. This big old guy (the fish) was sitting there, probably asleep. He didn't even know he was hit. Immediately he takes off, as far as he's concerned he's free. He slowed down until he had used up slack line. When he felt resistance...he again took off with a full head of steam. Jack takes the line from the surfboard and is working the fish. I hit it with the powerhead, but not exactly where we're supposed to, and it was just like an old drunk, alive but didn't know it. That was lucky, because in pictures a dead fish looks like a dead fish. The background was dark (so) Lamar says take it to Moonlight Cove where the sand background is better for photography. We dragged it down there where we could take pictures, about a two minute ride...I'd aim that old fish at Jack, he'd aim it back at me, and all the while Lamar was shooting." The resulting photo appeared in fifth issue of **Sports Illustrated**, the first underwater shot in that publication's history.

It is difficult for divers of today's environmentally conscious society to identify with killing fish. In the 30s, with a relatively small coastal population and a wealth of marine life, attitudes were different. Even then, part of the Bottom Scratchers' membership oath was to do everything possible to prevent waste of sea life. With the perspective of nearly 60 years of diving, Potts and Prodanovich are in a unique position to comment on the situation.

Prodanovich: "If you had been with us, you'd have done the same thing...Everything that exists, once they find it, whether it's a trout stream in Timbuktu or a spot in the ocean, it's just common practice for people to work on it. Now we're taking stuff faster than it's growing....People just depleted it..I remember the day that, if you were a good swimmer...I could put my mask on you and make you a hard core diver on one dive. Get you in 6 feet of water, ... grab hold of a ledge...peek in and might be twenty abalone, might be three lobsters in there. You've never seen anything like that, you go ape. Take an abalone iron, I tell you how to pop him off there real quick, and I've made a diver out of you for sure. Today I could take a young kid out there to LaJolla, and I'd probably have to dive umpteen hundred times before I found an abalone. Now this guy will figure 'If he can't find anything, how does he expect me to?'...The reason diving took hold then was that there was something there for the people, and they became really fired up over it."

Potts: "At Scripps early on, they were teaching that the ocean was going to feed the world. You don't hear that no more. The commercials (fishermen) just wiped out stuff, they are making a desert out of the ocean. We fought them gill nets for years. In 1951 there was a good run of white sea bass, and the second day they had the nets out and that was the end of diving there. We tried to tell Fish and Game and they didn't want to hear this; they had their fingers in their ears."

The advent of scuba wasn't welcomed by the Bottom Scratchers. They all tried it, Jim Stewart and Connie Limbaugh made their living from it. Yet they all preferred free diving. Prodanovich: "We knew what was going to happen. We told our members to go out to 15 feet and leave the intertidal stuff to the waders. Scuba divers started going in 10 feet of water with tanks, they were going to strip it. We tried to get a laws passed that to use scuba for hunting you should be in over 20 feet."

Potts: "I wasn't thrilled about the Aqualung at all...Connie Limbaugh came in with the original tanks, and opened the field to a lot of people that would not normally be divers. Jack and I knew that

> We realized the competitions weren't the right way to go. You don't have a contest to see who could shoot the most deer.

would have a bad effect on available sport fish. We attended a Fish and Game committee meeting; we wanted scuba restricted to fairly deep water...I've seen tank divers crawl into holes we could never reach, fins flopping around in open air. They could stay down there forever and get the last ab..."

I wasn't thrilled about the Aqua lung at all... Connie Limbaugh came in with the original tanks, and opened the field to a lot of people that would not normally be divers.

In his 1965 article on the Bottom Scratchers, Coles Phinizy quotes Lamar Boren describing a fully equipped scuba diver hunting for abalone: "...a floating hock shop. All dressed up for very slim pickings. When I see him I cannot help thinking that the really sad part of it is he's come along about 20 years too late."

Scuba opened the ocean to the occasional visitor, and was resented by the water people that had been there before. These men were swimmers, surfers, and paddle-boarders before they took up diving. Photos of the time reveal athletic bodies built by years of physical activity. Prodanovich: "Being a custodian in a three-story building, you walk up and down steps all day long. Swimming and surfing is part of it too." In 1941 he won the paddle board race in the La Jolla Rough Water Swim: Scripps Pier to La Jolla cove.

Jack doesn't see or hear well any more, but is still sharp and active at 79. "When you get older it gets tougher, but I bear with it...My wife and I ride bicycles every morning. I swim whenever possible, and work out in a friend's pool." At the time of our interview he had just returned from a diving trip to the Socorro Islands. "I still like to get out and see if I can nail one, but ...you gotta have a lot of beans and I found out on that trip I'm old enough that I don't have enough beans."

Potts has recovered from coronary bypass surgery, and is no longer an active diver. But he continues to make custom guns and line packs in his garage workshop. Recently Jack and Wally were featured in a PBS television documentary, **"Blue Water Hunters."** It included rare footage shot by Lamar Boren in the 40s and 50s. To make it look old, the producers showed it in black and white, but Wally revealed that it was originally shot in color.

Potts has this advice for today's divers: "First of all, snorkel in shallow waters to become comfortable with the underwater environment. Be able to recognize rip current spots and learn how to conduct yourself in surf...Become proficient as a breath-hold diver before considering using scuba...You will see more on the first dive than on any other dive you ever make. "

THE BOTTOM SCRATCHERS ROSTER

(The year of induction follows the name)

The Bottom Sctratchers Founders 1933

Glenn Orr

Jack Prodanovich

Ben Stone

Bottom Sctratchers

Jack Corbeley, 1933

Bill Batzloff, 1938

Wally Potts, 1939

Lamar Boren, 1943

Tucker Miller, 1943

Rob Rood, 1943

Don Clark, 1950

Jim Stewart, 1951

Conrad Limbaugh, 1953

Beau Smith, 1954

Carl Hubbs, 1955

Earl Murray, 1955

Emil Haabecker, 1960

Bill Johnston, 1964

Harold Riley, 1969

Jack Taylor, 1969

FREE DIVERS
WALTER DAVIS

Walter Davis was one of the first to dive the wrecks of Truk Lagoon, using primitive gear and lots of free-diving skill. Davis was born in New Orleans, Louisana and later went to Texas where he went to Southern Methodist University and has lived since 1950, he was instrumental in starting scuba instruction there as well.

THE SHIPWRECKS OF TRUK LAGOON had been down only three years when Walter Davis arrived on the islands. It was 1947. He was a pilot on duty with the postwar Navy, assigned to fly C 54 transports from Honolulu to Guam, with stops in such places as Enewitok, Truk, Midway, Tahiti, and Samoa. Needless to say, spending all that time in the tropics during peacetime would grab the interest of anybody with a spirit of adventure. Davis, a Texan who had joined the Navy right out of high school, took advantage of the opportunity and learned free diving from the native Hawaiians.

"I watched them going to 60, 70 feet spearing fish, using Hawaiian slings. I made friends with one or two of them, so they tolerated me." Using a primitive combination plastic and rubber mask, plastic fins, and no snorkel, a 25 foot dive was a deep effort. But over the next six months, he kept improving. "We just speared what we wanted to eat, then cooked them like the Hawaiians, wrapped in banana leaves. I never got as good as them until later."

Walter's flying route was the milk run: Honolulu, Johnston Island, Kwajelain to Guam . "One night in Guam we were talking about spearfishing... Somebody asked 'What are you wasting your time for, why don't you get an oxygen regulator out of an airplane? Take it to the machine shop and they'll rig it up for you.'

"They hadn't actually done this, just had heard about it. Next day we found some beat up oxygen regulators scrounging around old airplanes." According to the men in the oxygen shop, rigging the outfits for diving would be no problem. They found some tanks, purged them, and filled them with air. Walter and his buddies slipped them a few dollars.

"Only two or three of us were involved, nobody else wanted anything to do with it. We weren't really interested in diving with the tank, but more in using it to extend our depth and bottom time." Walter had learned the consequences of free diving too deep the

hard way. Exceeding his usual 75 feet one day, he came up spitting blood. Later somebody told him about lung squeeze, and that got his attention. "I didn't dare go to the dispensary (and) didn't do another dive like that for a long time."

Walter Davis in the Navy, 1947.

The pilots took their equipment back to Hawaii and started practicing with it. Tanks and regulators were towed out on an inner tube. A hose hung down to 25 feet, the maximum depth to which the regulators would supply air. Davis would free dive to the end of the hose and hyperventilate off it a few minutes before heading further down.

"When the tank got to 2/3 down, 20 or 15 feet was the maximum depth at which we could breathe. But we could go deeper and hold our breath longer (than before), one or two minutes after hyperventilating, on a good day maybe two and a half minutes."

What about air embolism? "We didn't have any clue about anything. When we came up we could feel our lungs starting to expand. I got to thinking I'd better let out some air, so we just did it. We didn't know anything about tables or decompression sickness (either)."

Truk was a regular stop on their route, usually with a day or two layover. They knew about the big "Turkey Shoot" in 1944 that had sent over 40 Japanese ships to the bottom of the lagoon. Walter decided it would be fun to take a look at the wrecks. "The crash boat crew took us out there; they thought we were crazy...I looked down and wondered whether I could go that deep...I went down about 20 feet, started hyperventilating and looked at the ship, with no idea of its name or the depth. It had a lot of guns, no growth, the paint was still on it. You could see the numbers...some of the glass was still intact. On the first dive, I got to the top of a mast and that was it. I asked if there was anything shallower. One of us got behind the boat and they kind of dragged us around. We stopped at another wreck."

This one looked closer, but it was a long haul just to get to the deck. Frustrated, the pilots went back to the officer's club that night and discussed the situation. One of the locally based sailors told them they were looking in the wrong place. He knew where there were some shallower wrecks, and on the next day, took them out there. "We dove on that one. It looked kind of like a transport... also had a couple of guns on it. You could go down and swim by a porthole and see a skeleton, you could look in the bridge and see more skeletons. We did a few dives on it and decided that was too eerie." Asked whether he took any souvenirs, Davis replied that it was just too spooky. Besides, the Navy didn't allow anybody to touch anything, and at that time nobody questioned orders.

> We didn't have any clue about anything. When we came up we could feel our lungs starting to expand. I got to thinking I'd better let out some air, so we just did it.

Not even the Trukese were diving on the wrecks at that time. Davis recalls that very few locals were living on that particular island. He isn't sure of the name, but it was probably Eten, which served as the primary Japanese airbase on Truk. "There wasn't a living thing on that island after the ships were sunk. Everything was blown up; they called it the Japanese haircut....It was just desolate, everyone who flew into Truk couldn't wait to get out."

Walter continued using his booster setup for free diving, and eventually heard about others using the same technique. Some took the tanks underwater, but the regulators were unable to supply air below 25 feet. He also experimented with rebreathers, but decided against it after hearing about accidents when using them below 30 feet.

Through the grapevine, Davis learned that better masks, fins, and snorkels were available in Yokuska, Japan, home base of the Ama divers. On his next leave, he flew there. "We took a case of cigarettes, because they brought a fantastic price in Japan. We thought we was hot stuff... figured we could handle our own against Japanese women. We bribed our way on the boat with cigarettes, they wouldn't take money.

"I heard that the water was chilly, (so) we had sweatpants and shirts. The women dove nude. They had big broad shoulders, huge chests, practically no breasts. They were muscular all over; it wasn't sexy or anything.

"They were diving about 55 feet. The first one went off, I went right behind her. She was doing her thing and pretty soon I needed air. So I went up, hyperventilated about 30 seconds, back down again, and pretty soon I was low again and she was still working away. I went back up to the surface again, was hyperventilating, and finally she comes up. I says 'Geez, I'm not that good at all.' The next one I timed, and she was down there three and a half minutes. I froze my tail off.

Davis rides a manta ray in Baja, 1980's.

"There were two men in the boat. (The women) came up with a basket full of oysters... they swam up with that damn basket full. I got some respect in a real big hurry. Then I found out the story. They had been doing this for 300 years, basically bred until they had these tremendous lungs and real staying power."

Walter Davis' Navy experiences were the beginning of a lifelong involvement with scuba diving. He bought his first equipment in 1953, then essentially taught himself to dive, because there were no courses offered in Dallas at the time. Tanks were filled at a local welding shop. Eventually he began teaching at the Irving YMCA, and had the very first instructor class at Southwest Council of Scuba Diving Clubs. When they ran their first course in 1955, Walter became certified as instructor number 29. He still owns the stainless steel card, his first official certification.

Davis became a builder and an insurance agent, but diving and travel continued to be an important part of his life. In 1956, he made an early Baja California diving expedition on a Jeep, carrying his own tanks and compressor. Eventually he began taking people on trips, then opened one of Texas' first dive travel agencies, Voyages. Today he owns The Scuba Shop in Dallas, and continues to travel around the diving world. When asked his favorite destination, Walter wouldn't limit himself to just one. He listed the Red Sea, Galapagos, the northern Great Barrier Reef, Sea of Cortez, Costa Rica, and Tubitaha.

Outside of Texas, few people know about this diving pioneer. But for Walter Davis, those first dives in Hawaii and Truk started something that is still going strong.

SECTION 2

FROM HARDHAT
TO SCUBA

From Hardhat To Scuba
E.R. Cross

"E. R. Cross is diving's renaissance man. Sometime, somewhere in his astounding 60-year diving career, he's done it all. He will be 80 years old in December (1993) but you'd never know it. His mind is sharp as a tack, and a whirlwind of ideas and projects."—Bonnie Cardone, executive editor, **Skin Diver** Magazine.

TODAY'S DIVERS KNOW ELLIS ROYAL CROSS primarily as the author of "Technifacts" in **Skin Diver.** At 29 years and counting, it is the longest running column in diving history. But Cross is responsible for some significant milestones in military, commercial, and recreational diving, beginning in 1934 as a Navy salvage diver. He worked on the Bikini atomic bomb tests, ran a commercial diving school, helped train many of the early leaders of scuba instruction, and wrote the first books on diver training, underwater photography, and television. He is also a renowned malacologist (mollusc specialist).

Cross will talk about diving's past, but prefers discussing today and tomorrow. And he isn't shy about expressing his opinion on controversial subjects:

"I think specialty courses are the future of recreational diving. It will sort of fracture and come back together in layers of qualification. There might even be different qualifications of wreck divers: external wreck diver, wreck photographer, penetration wreck diver. Each of these require different training. It will be a beautiful thing for diver training agencies; they will have nine thousand things they can qualify divers for. I like it, provided they don't do it just for money, provided they make people properly trained. Unfortunately diving has become very commercial and everybody wants to make money at it, irrespective of whether they do a good job, or irrespective of whether the equipment is good."

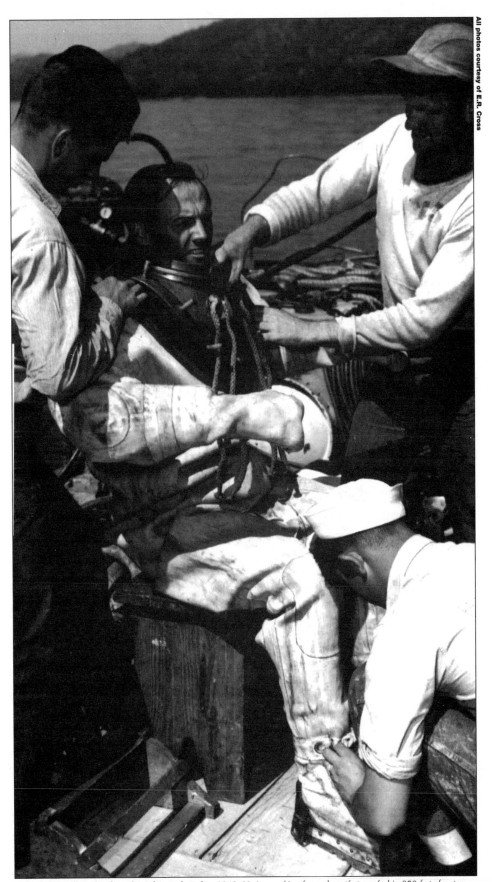

Cross is being dressed in for a dive job in Lake Tahoe, 1948. He is searching for a plane that crashed in 250 feet of water.

Raised in Southern Oregon, Cross (as he is called by his friends), grew up in Washington, Montana, Idaho and Oregon before he moved to California, and enlisted in the Navy out of high school, because there were no jobs in the depression era. "I joined the Navy in 1933 because I was hungry...I worked on a farm for $1 a day, (then)...took a pay cut. Roosevelt gave us...$18 a month (at the time). But you could have a good liberty on $2, dinner was 50¢."

Assigned to the destroyer tender USS *Dobbin*, Cross' cleaning station as a swabbie was the deck area where the divers' hand pump was located. While polishing brass, he made acquaintances with the divers and tenders. Eventually they took him to the diving locker, dressed him in the old Mark V helmets, and finally let him go down. In May 1934, he passed his exams as a second class diver in San Diego Bay. "A neat place to dive. 6 feet of mud to land on, you couldn't get hurt." Cross did most of his work on the tending crew, while the divers did torpedo and aircraft recovery.

In 1936 he was assigned to the Orient for three years, but his duty station did not rate having divers. This cost Cross his qualification. But he discovered a new way to go underwater at Zamboanga in the Philippines, watching the native pearl divers doing their work. "Those were my first recreational dives. I really began taking breath hold diving seriously...The pearl divers taught me the techniques, including hyperventilation. They helped me carve a pair of wooden goggles, using some thin kind of clear shell (for the lens). Air volume in them was almost nil, basically they touched your eyeballs. Sometimes they gave me double vision.

"There were some horrendous currents. That's when I first learned to study the environment and water conditions. When I first started, I couldn't find a pearl shell. Once I found what to look for, the rest were easy. (But) I don't remember many impressions from then; 1937 was a couple of days ago."

On December 7, 1941, Cross was having breakfast in Panama with a pretty blonde girl when news of the Pearl Harbor attack was announced on the radio. A warrant officer by this time, he was skipper of a patrol craft. But that didn't last long, because the Navy needed experienced divers. They asked Cross to volunteer, and sent him to diving officer school in Washington. By October 1942, he was doing salvage on the liner *Normandy* that burned and sank in New York harbor.

"I taught helmet divers how to do mechanical things off floats...from 8 till 4, from then till midnight I took the salvage course and became a qualified salvage diving officer." During the war his assignments ranged from Norfolk to Bermuda. It wasn't combat duty, but he became commissioned as a lieutenant and developed more training programs for salvage crews. This experience was pivotal to his later career. The significant military experience was yet to come.

BIKINI

Cross intended to return to civilian life after the war, but the Navy had other plans. They were setting up the first atomic bomb tests at Bikini Atoll, and needed divers: 300 of them plus 50 diving officers. The channel at Bikini had to be blasted with explosives to deepen it. Then buoys had to be installed, and the target vessels moored to them. One of the most demanding tasks was to moor four submarines at various depths, to determine the effects of the explosion on submerged vessels. "They weren't junk, they were good subs, but we just had too many."

> **Test Baker required a lot more salvage because it sunk a lot of ships. The vessel that the bomb was suspended under disintegrated; there was nothing left. A 38,000 ton battleship moored fairly close went up in the water column... and landed upside down.**

The first blast was an aerial drop. "I watched the blast from six miles away. On an air blast you've got your back to it. Instantly you turn around. Across that whole lagoon, which was several miles, everything was on fire. We had to salvage ships, keep them from sinking, and put out fires. We went right back in...to get any test animals. There were over 1,000 of them on the ship. We had monitors for radioactivity, but no protective clothing. We did know that a person would have a tolerance of about ten minutes, so you would go on for ten minutes, and you didn't board any more for that day. But the next day you could have ten more minutes of exposure. We saved animals, put out fires, and recovered instruments from ships that sank. If we could do it quickly we raised ships, because in another month we had Test Baker, which was an underwater blast.

"Test Baker required a lot more salvage because it sunk a lot of ships. The vessel that the bomb was suspended under disintegrated; there was nothing left. A 38,000 ton battleship moored fairly close went up in the water column...and landed upside down. A lot of other ships sank. We tried to keep the Saratoga afloat, but it was too late. We beached some of the other ships that were sinking.

"We did some underwater photography, and had the first underwater television ever made. It was big and cumbersome, but it worked. The admirals could sit in the wardroom with their coffee, and the diver was down below with the camera.

"We weren't trained, that was the first time we had ever seen the damn things. They just told us to take pictures. (Eventually) they turned all this over to me and I became the ex officio underwater photography expert."

Cross at work on Chevron's submarine pipeline in Hawaii, 1974.

THE SPARLING SCHOOL

About three months after Bikini, Cross finally left the Navy after 14 years. During the war he had met Joe Sparling, who started the world's first commercial diving school in Los Angeles, and had promised him a job. He became manager of the school. Sparling's primary work was on tank farms and pipelines for oil companies. When he received a lucrative offer in Edmonton, Canada, he left and sold the school to Cross for almost nothing, provided he would teach the students already enrolled so their tuition wouldn't have to be refunded.

By mid 1947, Cross had rewritten the curriculum in military style and the school was approved for veteran training. "I opened the Sparling School of Deep Sea Diving. I kept the name (because) **Newsweek, Life**, and a whole bunch of other people had written it up...It was an instant success, the right time at the right place. My first class was his six students, my second class was 20, and the next thing you know, I had students lined up for five years ahead. "

Recreational scuba gear hadn't made it to the United States yet, so Cross did his fun diving off the California coast with commercial and military gear. "In that era until 1950 I probably made as many recreational dives with Mark V helmet gear as with self contained equipment. For years I used Desco oxygen rebreathers; I loved the damn things. With that tiny bottle of oxygen I could stay underwater four hours. Oxygen toxicity is a function of depth and time and individual tolerance. It's treacherous. I limited my diving to 30 feet; if I was going to be there all day it was less. But I would make deeper excursions to get or see what I wanted. Because the beautiful part about oxygen toxicity is if you feel it coming, you pop up to a shallower depth and it goes away. Narrow vision is usually the first symptom. But the trouble is with a diver's mask you have narrow vision (anyway). So you have to learn that your peripheral vision isn't seeing the mask any longer. It takes training, experience, constant realization of what you are doing to keep from getting killed."

The Sparling School had one of the first compressors in the area, so sport divers came in to get their tanks filled. Cross also had a recompression chamber and films on diving, so the school became a hangout for the fledgling sport diving fraternity. Every month there were special programs. "Boy Scout and Girl Scout groups were the guests of honor. If you don't get the youngsters diving, there won't be any after us old buggers are dead. I knew they would be my customers eventually."

Cross in a rebreather unit, 1940's.

Cross' first sport diving class was a technical affair intended to improve the skills of already active divers. This was long before anybody thought about certification. Part of the class was a chamber dive to 110 feet, where students had to do math problems under pressure to illustrate the effects of narcosis.

"It cost about $25, a lot of money in those days. (I'd treat an easy case of bends for $50.) ...I remember the first class because there were two pretty girls: Twila Bratcher, her sister Billie...They were probably the first organized class of recreational divers in existence...Twila was an interesting lady. She probably started diving in 1946 (and later) had one of the first Aqualungs." Like Cross, Ms. Bratcher later became a renowned shell collector.

If you don't get the youngsters diving, there won't be any after us old buggers are dead

Some of the curriculum and training programs that Cross wrote during that period were applicable to sport diving. The first one aimed primarily at recreational divers was a 1951 manual called **Underwater Safety**. "Nobody in the industry would touch it. I published it on my own, printed 10,000, and sold them in about four months. Dick Kline, who owned Healthways, took over the publication and sold well over 100,000 copies.".

Included in the book was an outline of ten pool lessons, along with written tests. Even after the early training organizations began, that outline was used to train thousands of divers nationwide, including this writer. It was also the first civilian book to use the Navy's acronym for self-contained underwater breathing apparatus; at that time it was spelled out as S.C.U.B.A.

The 60-foot schooner **Four Winds**.

In 1952 Cross wrote the first underwater photography book, but it wasn't so successful. "The publisher wanted to do 2500, I told him I know they will sell 5000. He would if I would pay for the other 2500, and I did. It sold 2600; I ate mine. There was probably only 50 underwater cameras in the whole country."

The Sparling School became a mecca for the early pioneers of sport diving. "They came for films, chambers, opportunities to talk technical diving. Also I had the biggest and best coffeepot in town. **Skin Diver** Magazine was born around that coffeepot. I had a little in-house magazine there called **Faceplate**. It was eight pages mimeographed; I printed 300 copies for my students and people that were interested. By the fourth issue I needed a thousand and didn't have time; I was running a diving school. Chuck Blakeslee and Jim Auxier used to hang around my coffeepot. One day they wanted to talk to me about starting a magazine for divers. I had just run the last issue, I wasn't going to do any more. They decided to go for it...It almost didn't fly; I think they had 12 pages and seven ads in the first issue, I took a couple of them." After some early struggles, the magazine finally caught on.

Among the regulars at Sparling was Connie Limbaugh, who is credited with developing the first organized course of basic scuba instruction at Scripps Institution of Oceanography. "I don't think Connie ever took any courses from me, but he did gather my curriculum. We discussed science a lot, and how diving could be used in science."

Cross was asked by Al Tillman and Bev Morgan to serve on a panel for Los Angeles County to help outline a training program. Others included Fred Schwankowski (Red Cross), Rusty Williams (Lifeguards), and an ex-Navy doctor trained in diving physiology. The result was the nation's first instructor training program. Qualification was by experience; most candidates were lifeguards and surfers.

"My next association was on an advisory committee for CNCA (Council for National Cooperation in Aquatics). We went to Yale two different years. The first year was to outline a program that all the recreational people could use, the next year we each wrote chapters for *Science of Skin and Scuba Diving*. I wrote two chapters.

"The Los Angeles County program was really the thing that got California diving going, but they would not let people from outside the state come in and take those courses. Everybody else wanted that training too. That's how NAUI was born. I never had my own C card until the 1970s in Hawaii when I was teaching some classes there. They asked me what certification I had, and gave me a mossback C-card. That's for some old bastard who's been in the water so long that moss has grown on his back."

I never had my own C-card until the1970s in Hawaii when I was teaching some classes there. They asked me what certification I had, and gave me a mossback C-card. That's for some old bastard who's been in the water so long that moss has grown on his back.

While running the school, Cross did freelance commercial diving, mostly underwater surveys around dams. Some of those experiences seem impossible, even with today's equipment. He has written stories about that era, including one project in a flooded uranium mine that almost killed him.

THE *FOUR WINDS*

"I closed the Sparling School (in 1955) for two reasons: one, I trained 2300 commercial divers in 7 or 8 years, and there weren't 2500 jobs, I felt a little guilty about it. The other thing, a couple of my really good students got killed because they violated the rules. You know, mankind can survive without stress only in his natural environment, surrounded by things that protect us. The minute you leave that, you have a potential threat to your life. Diving is an unnatural place. If you don't take some steps to protect yourself you are going to get killed. I learned this in commercial diving, because I took jobs that others refused. The only way you are going to get out of something like that is to know your avenues of escape. Don't ever make a dive that you don't know you can get out of if the worst happens."

Cross offered the school to Harbor Junior College free of charge, but they refused. So he cut up the diving tank, sold everything he owned, and bought a 60-foot schooner he named the **Four Winds**. His plan was to sail around the world where hazardous commercial diving was going on, and teach people how to make it safer. Accompanied by his wife and four crew members, Cross began in Baja California. They spent four months working with the Baja abalone divers, who had one of the highest bends rates in the world. Eventually, the Mexican Navy hired him to expand the program for all divers in all the ports in the country. He sent everybody home except his wife, traveled around Mexico teaching, and wrote four instructional manuals which were translated into Spanish as quickly as they were written.

The recreational diver today is overequipped and underskilled and undertrained. You don't get watermanship in a class. You get that by being almost drowned a few times; you learn to survive in the water.

"They wanted me to stay, but I had my sights set on the Tuomotus, northeast of Tahiti. I visited three of the pearl diving atolls, and read all I could find on deaths over the years. They were all breath-hold divers, the disease was called taravana. I thought part of the problem was an anoxia thing, and there is a reverse gradient that takes place on a rapid ascent from a breath-hold dive. I also thought they were getting bent. They are great divers, staying two minutes at 130-140 feet, they don't rest long on the surface. So the nitrogen saturation is greater than their desaturation; a breath hold diver can definitely get bent."

The **Four Winds** voyages continued for three years. But Cross was going broke and finally headed back for California. First there was a 30 year detour in Hawaii. "One of my crewmen broke his leg. It was a hard beat back to California from the Marquesas. I went to Honolulu to put the kid in a public health hospital. I was there for about three months, piddling around on odd jobs to keep beans on the table." Cross applied for work at Chevron, which was planning to build a refinery in Hawaii. But at 42, he was considered too old. He left a resume, and they hired him as a contractor to check out a tanker mooring that was behind schedule. He photographed it underwater, making a full report on what was wrong, with recommendations.

"A week later they told me Bechtel was going to hire me as marine superintendent. So I worked for them two years, that's what it took to do the job. A tremendous problem of hard coral, nothing to hold a anchor in place. My theory was to blast trenches into the coral, so the tanker could moor. I shot 700 tons of explosives making those trenches."

In 1959 Chevron contracted Cross as their chief diver, a job he held for 28 years. When he wasn't working, he became involved in collecting seashells, discovered some new species, had others named after him, and edited the **Hawaiian Shell News**. He also became involved with NAUI, teaching sport diving classes.

TECHNIFACTS

Now retired in the Seattle area, Cross continues to write the "Technifacts" column for **Skin Diver**. At 29 years and counting, it is the longest running column in the history of the activity. How does he stay current? "A lot of the questions are correspondence. I make phone calls, find out the answers. I have a huge library, have been collecting diving things over 50 years. The column keeps itself going. One thing I do is present things that need further discussion and investigation.

Stan Waterman presents Cross with the DEMA Reaching Out Award commemorating his induction into Diving's Hall of Fame in 1992.

I wrote a column about diving during pregnancy, just to start dialog. High altitude decompression was another. I got bent diving one of the dams, some of them are at high altitudes. I developed the Cross Conversion Tables, and nobody has ever been bent on them. Now they use a more simplified table.

"I've missed a couple of months here and there, during a period of problems with Chevron's pipeline system when I got only about five a year."

Cross offers a few pertinent thoughts on the state of recreational diving today, and as usual he pulls no punches. "The recreational diver today is overequipped and underskilled and undertrained. You don't get watermanship in a class. You get that by being almost drowned a few times; you learn to survive in the water. They don't teach that, you have to learn it by experience.

> The most beautiful thing about recreational diving is that it's a self regulated sport, and we've got to keep it that way.

"I'm amazed that you can even dive with all that equipment. My concept of proper diving equipment is as little as you need to accomplish a specific task. If you are going to do two or three things on a specific dive (penetrate a wreck, take pictures), you take the equipment you need to do one job, then go back up and get another one, and go back down and do it. Too much equipment is environmentally damaging to start with, and it's liable to be dangerous In movies I see people going down with two cameras and stuff...That's not enjoyment, that's slave labor.

"The most beautiful thing about recreational diving is that it's a self regulated sport, and we've got to keep it that way. That's one reason I'm against (technical) diving getting involved with recreational diving. They've had some problems with nitrox and mixed gases. They've had some people killed. They may have been killed with air too, you never know. If enough of that happens, the government will step in and try to make it safe for us, and then they'll probably kill everybody. I know nitrox is good, I've used it all my life. I'm against it as a recreational thing, it's a specialty thing."

The hardest thing about writing this article was deciding what to leave out. Cross has been too busy to write an autobiography, but when he or somebody else finally does it, they are going to have a huge, fascinating book. This man has led that kind of a life.

This photo was taken in 1953 during work in Utah while recovering 530 rounds of fused, live 105mm shells.

DICK ANDERSON

Inventor, engineer, writer, humorist, filmmaker, treasure hunter, adventurer. All these words describe Dick Anderson, as brilliant and controversial a figure as has ever been on the diving scene. Never afraid to speak his mind, Dick gave a free-wheeling, four hour inteview, revealing inside stories on some of the sport's legendary events and figures. Whether you agree with him or not, it's all intriguing, and his iconoclastic voice deserves to be heard.

1950. RENE BUSSOZ HAD JUST SPUN OFF US Divers from his Westwood sporting goods store, and was advertising for a common laborer. 18 year old Dick Anderson, an enthusiastic free diver and high school dropout, came in to apply. As he walked in the back door of the plant, there was Sterling Hayden looking at an Aqualung.

In hiring Anderson, Bussoz got more than he bargained for. Dick had a strong mechanical aptitude, developed in a depression era Oregon foster home where, if one wanted a toy he made it, if something was broken he fixed it. He had run away from home at 15, working in Oregon as a carpenter, on dairy farms, in the woods, and as a longshoreman in Alaska. When he returned home, his mother asked, "When are you getting a job?" Ever since seeing John Wayne battle a giant squid in **Wake of the Red Witch**, Dick had been fascinated with the underwater world. In 1946 he bought his first mask for $1.98, and began spearfishing off the Los Angeles coastline.

US Divers was a tiny company, just getting its feet wet. Anderson's first mentor there was Rene's former gardener, Glen McCall, who came in as an outside contracter a few times a month to work on regulators (see Chapter 1). McCall, an early skin diver, knew all the Bottom Scratchers and was a friend of pioneers Herb Sampson and Doc Mathieson. He took Anderson under his wing and showed him what he knew about Aqualungs. Soon Dick was teaching repair to expedition leaders and UDT teams. The Navy adopted Aqualungs

Anderson as a commercial diver in the 50's.

early on, but all publicity pictures were taken with rebreathers because it didn't look good for them to be using a foreign product. "It was the first time I ever got into some work that really clicked, and got to show some creativity. Before long I knew as much about the workings of the Aqualung as anybody in the United States"

In the early 50s there was an aura about diving, an adventure, that got lost with age. The mystique is gone now; everybody is doing it. It's like driving a damn car.

When Rene appointed him to teach special customers how to use the equipment, Anderson became (according to Rene) the only authorized Aqualung diving instructor in the country. "I would load the guy in my '35 Ford and drive him to Rene's pool near Sunset Boulevard. These were mostly expedition leaders and people who were going to put a diving department in their sporting goods stores. They would get one pool lesson. I'd show them how to mount the unit, put them in the water, have them breathe, clear the mask, take the mouthpiece out and put it back. The only celebrity I remember was William Randolph Hearst Jr., who gave me a tip of $15."

The fascination began to wear off the job for Anderson when his many requests for pay raises were denied. "Rene Bussoz was...a cheapskate beyond all belief. Here is an example. When Glen first showed me how to disassemble the Aqualung, the high-pressure-block-nut was clamped in a vise and unscrewed by pounding on a protrusion on the body with a brass drift pin. It was crude and brutal treatment, and left scars. I designed a jig to hold the regulator so it could be removed with a wrench. I made a cardboard mock-up and showed it to Rene. He told me that if I wanted one I could take my sample to (a welding shop), during my lunch hour, and have one made. It cost me ten bucks, which was a day's pay...Rene would not pay me the ten dollars. (After I left) he began manufacturing my jig and supplying it to his dealers. It became a standard Aqualung repair fixture."

When Sam LeCocq was hired, Bussoz asked Dick to teach him everything he knew. "I was a begrudging tutor to Sam; we were never quite pals. Rene saw something in him that I didn't. In retrospect, perhaps he was a threat to my position (and) was a lot smarter than I gave him credit for." Denied a raise one last time, Dick quit and took off for Miami in 1952.

"Before I left, Rene told me that I should open a dive shop. I said, 'Rene, there's already two of them.' That shows how much foresight I had."

He worked in Florida about a year as an instructor and equipment technician for Diving Corporation of America. Then Walt Disney began filming **20,000 Leagues Under the Sea** in Nassau. They needed an Aqualung technician, and Dick was the only one on the east coast, so his employer subcontracted him. This was the beginning of an off and on association with Hollywood which continues to this day.

When the filmwork was finished, Dick went back to DCA. Every weekend he would drive to the Keys. "It was like skin diving paradise. In the early 50s there was an aura about diving, an adventure, that got lost with age. The mystique is gone now; everybody is doing it. It's like driving a damn car."

> **The reason I dropped out of Boy Scouts after a week was that they wanted me to wear a uniform. I can't take regimentation.**

Some of the divers on the Disney project had attended the Sparling School of Deep Sea Diving in Wilmington, California. Commercial diving seemed like a promising career, so Dick returned to California and worked out a deal with owner E.R. Cross. He repaired the school's Aqualungs in return for reduced tuition. "I developed a real friendship with Cross (and) respected him greatly. (It was) the last class he had there." On the day of graduation Dick Kline, president of Healthways, offered Dick a job in his new scuba division. They had licensed a regulator called the Divair, invented by Bill Arpin in Miami, the only one ever to get around the Cousteau-Gagnan Aqualung patent.

During this time, Los Angeles County inaugurated its pioneering underwater instructors program. Anderson was certified in 2 UICC, receiving card number 27, but never did any formal instruction.

In 1955 Cross bought a boat, the **Four Winds**, and invited Anderson to sail around the world as part of the crew. Dick quit his Healthways job and spent the next two years helping get the boat ready. "I began to get cabin fever and a got bit bugged with Mrs. Cross. She wanted everybody to wear a uniform: white dungarees and a Hawaiian shirt. The reason I dropped out of Boy Scouts after a week was that they wanted me to wear a uniform. I can't take regimentation.

"So I left and joined the divers' union in San Pedro. I was the only one in the union who admitted to being a scuba diver. But my biggest thrill, and biggest scare, came about in helmet diving.

"In 1955 I was working off Gaviota (on an oil exploration site). The sea was too rough to transfer my gear so another diver, who was saturated, offered to let me use his. It was lightweight Japanese gear that I'd never used before. Around 1:00 AM I got dressed in. The phones weren't working; the tender was swatting them. I was diving in a moon pool, hanging on to a greased descent cable, screwing around with my control valve, and wasn't getting a lot of air. My tender was still working on the phones, so a roughneck was handling my hose. He starts throwing hose over, I start to descend involuntary. I yelled, 'Hold it,' but nobody heard me. I'm sliding down this cable at a tremendous rate, can't stop myself, and can't inflate enough to get buoyancy.

I hardhat dived for 10 years after that, but I knew that if anything was going to kill me it would be helmet diving. I finally made the decision not to dive in anything I can't swim away from.

"The next thing I remember is my head banging inside the helmet, regaining consciousness with convulsions at 240 feet. No idea how long I was out, I'm getting a slight trickle of air in the helmet. Walking around looking for the big sling I was supposed to hook up, I pass out again just from the exertion. Coming to a second time, I'm dimly aware I'm in trouble. I could hear my sister's voice saying 'Dickie, wake up.' My first thought was at least I'm alive and in a hospital. I come out of it and I'm lying on a platform on the bottom of the ocean. I feel my legs start to float up. With legs up and helmet down, if you hit the head button it just lets water in, doesn't let air out. There's nothing you can do. It's like blowing up a balloon and letting go of the s.o.b. Just out of reflex I grabbed the edge of the bird cage (platform) and held on. I felt my suit getting bigger and bigger. Pretty soon I had 2 to 300 pounds of buoyancy. 240 feet above me was the bottom of this barge, which was like half a football field of steel waiting there for me to hit. As my hands ripped loose, I thought, 'Oh shit, I'm dead,' and off I went.

"I regained consciousness again, this time at 150 feet. I was aware of the phones saying, 'Hey Anderson can you hear me?' I say, 'Yeah, pull me up.' When I blew off the bottom, by the greatest good fortune, by providence alone, my leg had come up between that sling and when it hit the big shackle it had turned me right side up and my suit had vented. My other good fortune: something on me hung up on this cable mechanism at 150 feet and held me there when I was out cold.

"They said I was down for 25 minutes. The problem had been a kink in my air hose between my belt and helmet. I was lucky to be alive.

"I hardhat dived for 10 years after that, but I knew that if anything was going to kill me it would be helmet diving. I finally made the decision not to dive in anything I can't swim away from. I still go back to it every once in a while, (usually) for a movie, just for the money."

During his first stint at Healthways, Dick met Gustav Dalla Valle. Their working relationship was tumultuous, but would have a significant effect on the shape of scuba diving. "(He was) brilliant...

unscrupulous...a tremendous sense of humor, the most charismatic s.o.b. you will ever meet in your life. He used me for an education about technical things."

In 1955 Gustav was supplying the Cressi line for Healthways. He imported a two-man submarine, produced by the company

1955, Healthways two-man wet sub with Dick Anderson in a front-entry dry suit, holding first Cressi Rondine fins molded in the the U.S. others: Dick Kline and Gustav DallaValle

that made the Italian pig boats of WW II. "It was dangerous...it had a gasoline engine; every time you turned the ignition on you expected an explosion." A 75 foot snorkel tube fed air to the engine, while the pilot and passenger breathed off scuba tanks. As a promotion for Healthways, Gustav arranged an underwater crossing to Catalina Island with himself, Anderson, and Zale Parry alternating on board. "Zale and I did it for the glory and excitement, but very little money."

In 1958 Sam LeCocq introduced the first successful single hose regulator, the Sportsways Waterlung. "The sales manager for Healthways, Randy Stone, talked me into going back to work for them. He felt positive that the so-called 'single hose' regulator would one day command the market.

"I got hold of the models that were selling, the Calypso and the Waterlung. US Divers was marketing the Calypso in the most negative way you can imagine, as if they were trying not to sell it. (It was) tremendously over complex, but with excellent breathing characteristics. The Waterlung was as simple as a mud fence. To me simple was good, complicated was bad. I came up with a regulator called the Scubair. If anything, it was inspired more by the simplicity of the Waterlung than the breathing excellence of the Calypso. The Scubair took a significant share of the market but had the same breathing limitation as the Waterlung, the tilt-valve second stage.

"Around 1960, Healthways started an R&D department with Gustav at the head; I was an engineer. Dalla Valle was the god, sometimes brilliant, sometimes ridiculous. I could no longer ignore the fact that the venturi assisted Calypso breathed just as easily at 250 feet as at the surface. A tilt valve in the second stage just couldn't cut it. I've got to hand it to Gustav, he and I tested every breathing apparatus to 250 feet. I got tremendous pressure from Healthways

About 1951 Dick Anderson tests V.R. Monroe's one-man diving sled at the Santa Monica pier.

to get around the Calypso venturi patent. I tried all kinds of things, but the Healthways patent attorney (turned each one down) as an infringement.

"One day I decided to try aiming the demand valve orifice at the mouthpiece tube, so some of the air deflected into the tube creating the breath-assisting venturi. The rest circulated around inside the case to balance the venturi effect. I set up a bench test and it did exactly what I hoped....The next day I dropped to 250 feet at Catalina with Gustav. ...My prototype (was) not quite so smooth breathing as the Calypso, but on a scale of 100 mine was about a 97, the tilt valve was 2 or 3. I was the happiest s.o.b. in the whole world.

"The good news was that I had a regulator that beat the unbreakable Calypso patent. The fitting that allows the pressure gauge to swivel (also) came right out of my nimble noggin but no patent was applied for because Gustav did not want Healthways to own them. The bad news was that in those days Dalla Valle was discouraging me from patenting anything ....His main goal in life was to out-Cousteau Cousteau. He wanted his own diving company...a big boat, expeditions, the whole deal. "

Anderson is sometimes credited with developing the o-ring piston first stage, although that is not his claim. Actually the concept is from a medical oxygen regulator, made by Sherwood before that company got into the scuba business. They had tried to peddle the idea to every other sport diving manufacturer, but were turned down because of Emile Gagnan's opinion that an o-ring piston wouldn't stand up in salt water and sand. Anderson had been trying to develop an o-ring regulator for Healthways' Scubapro division, using air pressure instead of a spring to maintain secondary pressure. As soon as he saw the Sherwood version, he knew it would work. "I put it in a bucket of seawater and sand and cycled it thousands of times. I gave it more exposure in a week than a diver would in 100 years. So Healthways introduced this new first stage on the Scuba Star, the first o-ring piston first stage on a diving regulator. I enlarged that a bit for the Scubair II."

This was in 1963, the year of the tragic Hannes Keller dive (see Jim Stewart story Pp. 124-5). "Al Tillman got me in there as a safety diver. Some people were invited to participate as observers (but) Dalla Valle was not." Gustav ordered Dick not to go, which pushed the wrong button and precipitated a heated argument. Over his boss' vehement objections, he went.

> It's easier to be trusting and get screwed once in a while than to walk around with the burden of mistrust on your shoulders.

Anderson was teamed with a young Englishman named Chris Whittaker as a safety diver, meeting Keller's diving bell at 260 feet on its emergency ascent. The bell was leaking because something was stuck in the bottom hatch. "I had taken Whittaker's knife and shoved what I thought was a fin tip, it could have been a belt or anything...The hatch clicked shut, but it was still leaking. But it wouldn't leak while I held it down. So I motioned for Chris to surface and have them raise the bell while I held the hatch shut. He got the message and took off toward the surface, but I didn't feel the bell rising. I stayed there till my decomp meter was creeping into the red zone. The hatch wasn't leaking any more so I decided to get the hell out of there. I swam to the surface and the second I got there they asked, 'Where's Whittaker?' It had been five to eight minutes (and) I didn't pass him on the way up. He had just lost consciousness and drifted away into nothing. The unfortunate thing was that he was a safety man on this event because they thought his services would never be needed. He had made about 50 dives or something like that, but most were shallow...But his best friend was Peter Small, the journalist who was inside the bell with Keller. He wanted Chris to be part of this adventure. Whittaker was a brave young man and the only thing he did wrong was to die trying to help his friend...."

About two weeks later, Anderson and Dalla Valle were on Jim Christensen's boat at Catalina to test some equipment. Still angry at Dick for disobeying him, Gustav was making sarcastic remarks about the Keller incident. "I felt really bad about that kid's death...I still do." Anderson blew up, let out a violent string of invective, and threatened to rearrange Gustav's profile. Cooler heads prevailed, but nobody had ever talked to Dalla Valle like that. This episode had a profound effect on their future relationship. "I thought I was going to ride to glory hanging on to Gustav's shirt tail. Cussing him out for five minutes cost me hundreds of thousands of dollars."

Healthways was on the road to bankruptcy, and Anderson

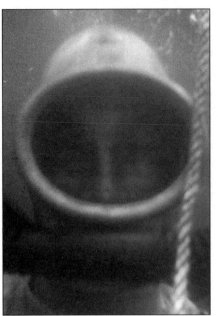

1951-52, Dick Anderson's first underwater photo self-portrait, Point Dume above Malibu. The camera was a Brownie Hawkeye, housed in a plastic bag with a lens, called "The Terry Blimp."

bailed out before the crash. (See Dick Bonin story, pp. 194-203) In the ensuing settlement, Dalla Valle got the Scubapro name, some product tooling, and equipment manufacturing rights. With Dick Bonin as president, he started his new diving company. An all-new regulator was needed, so he swallowed his pride, and had Anderson design the first Scubapro regulator for a promised royalty of 35 cents per unit.

"After that my association with Dalla Valle became more remote. Some time later he invited me to a party celebrating the sale of the one thousandth Scubapro regulator. Gustav hands me a check for $350. He says, 'Finis, finito, end of contract. That's it, no more.' I said that wasn't the deal. He says, 'That's the deal now.'

Anderson has collected royalties on everything from chairs to diving regulators, but confesses to having the business acumen of a gerbil. He has made some good deals and some bad deals. He explains, "It's easier to be trusting and get screwed once in a while than to walk around with the burden of mistrust on your shoulders."

I thought I was going to ride to glory hanging on to Gustav's shirt tail. Cussing him out for five minutes cost me hundreds of thousands of dollars.

Gustav never again called personally, but several times he contracted Dick for counsulting jobs, using Jim Christensen as spokesman. Jim asked Dick to think about something to glamorize the second stage of the regulator. Anderson came up with the adjustable second stage concept. "The regulator didn't really need it, but it seemed like something new and important. I designed an external adjustment for the venturi, which they didn't use....they made it much more complex.

"A year or two later Christensen called me about the Mark V regulator. They were having problems with a sudden air stoppage....My former assistant at Healthways was now the chief engineer at

Scubapro, another guy who was a lot smarter than I gave him credit for. He opens up the regulator, lo and behold, here is my top secret balanced piston first stage. I though there was just one in existence, my prototype. I asked, 'Who the hell invented this?' The guy's ears got red and he said 'I guess I did.' I told him if he'd made it more like my prototype, he wouldn't be having problems right now. There was another engineer who was making the rounds of companies, and pretty soon everybody had a balanced piston first stage. I made the first one and never got anything out of it. That's not to say someone else couldn't have done it spontaneously, there's a natural progression in development work."

Another of Anderson's talents is writing. When he and Zale and Gustav made the channel crossing in the submarine, a newspaper reporter asked

1955-56, Dick Anderson and his pal Jack Reynolds holding the remains of the auxiliary ship's wheel from the Star of Scotland, 70 feet below.

Dick to jot down some notes and impressions. A few days later, Anderson's entire manuscript was published in the **Herald Examiner** under the reporter's byline. "I said, 'Hell, I could have written that, in fact I did.' So I started writing things for **Skin Diver**...Funny things...Buffoonus aquarius, bad manners in diving...not having the slightest idea of what writing was about. Later I got some kind of feeling for literary flow. Coles Phinizy of **Sports Illustrated** said one time that Anderson writes as though he were on a first name basis with every reader. The readers love this, editors are uncomfortable with it."

"Right now I consider myself to be a very readable writer. I don't do much any more since I changed from being a diver working two or three days a week to being a studio prop maker working five and six days a week (which I like as a matter of fact).

"I've got a book coming out, **Diving and Dredging for Gold**. Jim Joiner (Best Publishing) is publishing it. It's about how to do it, where to do it, and an anthology of my gold diving articles."

Dick got into film making in the mid 60s on a dare. When asked by host Al Tillman how he liked the Santa Monica International Underwater Film Festival, the outspoken Anderson told him it was a case of egos entertaining themselves and ignoring the paying audience. Tillman replied, "If you're so goddamn smart, why don't you make a film yourself?" While preparing for the **Four Winds** cruise, Dick and E. R. Cross had taken a cinematography course at Brooks Institute. "I took my kid Rick, almost 2 years old, into the Beverly Hilton pool and filmed him diving with four different types of dive gear. It was entertaining. It wasn't some s.o.b. up there talking about how he defied death...filming sea fans with fish swimming over them. The audience almost tore the house down. Al Tillman says, 'I got the point. What will you have next year?' The next year, 1965, I did a film on diving in the Yuba River for gold, and that s.o.b. tore the house down too." His best remembered film, **Gold from the Winfield Scott**, received the film of the year award. "It was not a comedy film, but an educational film that was very entertaining."

Although Anderson still dives for fun, a little work, and for occasional movie jobs, he doesn't miss the commercial aspect. It provided a good living and material for lots of exciting stories. "But I wanted to get out of commercial diving while I was still alive.

"That was when I started looking around...I wasn't ready to retire, I'm reasonably well fixed and live a comfortable life. But I like to build and create." After serving as divemaster on **Jaws, the Revenge**, Dick became a studio prop maker and has been doing that ever since. "I get a big kick out of making something good, seeing it on film, having your contemporaries say, 'Wow, that's good.' I get a special thrill out of making something that hasn't existed before. It's like writing. Mark Twain said, 'Anyone can write a book; all the words are in the dictionary' But it's nothing until you put them there and somebody reads it."

"For a few years I was an arrogant son of a bitch. I knew I was opinionated...for example I should have invented a submersible gauge, but I thought anybody who didn't know how much air was in his tank shouldn't be diving. Instead I waited until about 1960 to make the swivel for it. The second thing which I completely ignored through the 50s was a buoyancy device. If a guy couldn't swim he shouldn't be diving. Stupid. The ultimate of macho arrogance.

"I've got a fun side and a serious side. Very very few people know both sides. Randy Stone once referred to me as 'the man nobody knows.' It's easy to make the argument that I'm just a nut. That always has kind of bugged me. I'd like to be remembered as something more than somebody who showed nutty films, perhaps as a reasonably competent commercial diver. Very few people remember that I did some really serious engineering."

SECTION 3

SCIENCE UNDERWATER

Science Underwater
Wheeler North

A PhD in marine biology from Scripps Institution of Oceanography, Wheeler North developed many of the techniques now standard in scientific diving, including the study and transplanting of kelp. Many of today's leaders in the diving field owe their start to this distinguished underwater scientist.

North's influence extends into sport diving as well. He was one of this nation's first scuba instructors, a dive store owner, and editor of one of the early diving magazines. But he will be best remembered for his contributions to California's kelp forests. Studying them since the early 50's, North developed methods to control urchins, and to transplant healthy giant kelp plants to resurrect depleted beds. He developed the world's first deep-water kelp farm, and is presently working on a plan to utilize this marine alga to counter the greenhouse effect. The healthy kelp forests off Palos Verdes and Orange County are his lasting monument.

THERE ARE ABOUT A THOUSAND DIVERS who claim to have bought one of the original Aqualungs from Rene's Sporting Goods in Westwood. The original six will probably never be accurately identified. But one of the earliest Aqualung divers was a Caltech undergraduate named Wheeler North.

There were no formal courses in those days, so Wheeler just read the cursory instructions packed with the unit, remembered not to hold his breath, and went diving. The water was cold, and wet suits were still about six years in the future. Finding a place to get a tank refilled was a major operation. Another Caltech student, Howard Teas, owned a Cornelius compressor which he used to fill his own war surplus tank, so he was a source of air for a while. But when Teas blew up his tank, along with a side of a laboratory, and caught a piece of shrapnel in his butt, he lost his enthusiasm for diving.

After graduation from Caltech, North attended Scripps Institution of Oceanography, where he earned his PhD. In those days, marine biologists were essentially landlubbers, doing their work intertidally or in labs. But that was beginning to change. Connie Limbaugh, Scripps' first diving officer, was teaching a research diving course — the first formal course of instruction in this country — and North was one of his early students.

Wheeler North, early 60's.

Then as today, Wheeler was a notorious packrat; he never threw anything away. Eventually, his collection of dive gear, motors, specimens, and bottles of chemicals outgrew his house, located on a cliff facing La Jolla cove. So North excavated caves in the soft sandstone cliff to store his treasures, securing them with wooden doors and padlocks.

1958, North taking underwater pictures with an early movie housing.

As the caves filled up, he had to keep excavating new ones. One day while he was digging, the cliff face gave way. North tumbled about 30 feet to the beach below. Lying helpless and unable to move, he realized that his back was probably broken, and that the tide was coming in. The only chance for rescue depended upon his dog, a boxer named Benny. Wheeler hastily scrawled a note, stuck it in Benny's collar, and sent the dog for help. Just as in the movies, the rescuers arrived in the nick of time. But North still has a mangled vertebra in his spine, and has little feeling in his legs. He walks with a limp, and is unable to use a dive ladder. But underwater it is hard to tell the difference. He essentially pulls himself along the bottom, at a pace most younger divers can't attempt to maintain.

Routine diving days begin at 4 AM. An underwater workaholic, Wheeler typically dives twelve hours in a ragged wet suit with worn-out knees. He doesn't believe in surface intervals, often not even bothering to take off his fins between dives. There are no lunch breaks unless his colleagues force the issue. As concessions to age, he now dives a with computer and spends an occasional safety stop on the anchor line, reading a magazine.

After a post doc at Cambridge University in 1954 and 55, North returned to Scripps and received a major grant for kelp research. "I was the only diving PhD around, so they hired me," he recalls.

Qualified help was hard to obtain, so he hired a high school student as a part-time assistant for the summer, at $16 per month. The lucky youngster was Chuck Mitchell, today the president of MBC, a marine consulting company and a leader in the scientific diving community. Mitchell, an enthusiastic storyteller, was the source of many anecdotes used here. North, a modest individual, isn't comfortable talking about himself.

For Mitchell, this was the beginning of experiences that would turn his life around. Imagine being 15 years old and one of the nation's first scientific divers. North took him to Baja California to survey the kelp forests of the Vizcaino Peninsula, the southernmost on the continent. Eventually, their travels brought them to the tip of the 1,000 mile peninsula, a sleepy fishing town called Cabo San Lucas. In many of these places, they were the first ever to dive.

His first research boat was a 20 foot runabout, nicknamed the Great Green Urinal. According to Chuck Mitchell, it encompassed every mistake in boat building over the last 200 years.

North's team made a pioneering study of an oil spill on the marine environment. In the late 50s a diesel tanker, the *Tampico*, ran aground some 60 miles south of Ensenada. The spill killed virtually everything in the bay, including urchins. But within six months, the bottom was covered by a rich growth of juvenile *Macrocystis*. For the next dozen years, North continued to monitor the area and developed a linear database on its recovery.

It hardly looked like a major scientific expedition. They drove down on dirt roads, in a van filled with scuba tanks, and camped on the beach for a week at a time. North recalls one particularly close call during that project. "The start of our transect was marked by an inner tube, but the rope was a bit short. I was coming up the rope and turned around, when a wave came by. The trough wrapped the loop around my regulator wing nut, and I was trapped underwater. Meanwhile, Chuck had gotten back into the boat. I was completely out of air, and it hadn't dawned on me to ditch my equipment. Just when it seemed it was all over, another trough went by, the line undid itself, and I was free."

This story illustrates North's basic concern with getting the job done. He considers everything a tool for science, and maintenance often interferes. Consequently, he drives everything till it drops. His first research boat was a 20 foot runabout, nicknamed the Great Green Urinal. According to Chuck Mitchell, it encompassed every mistake in boat building over the last 200 years.

North's regulator eventually turned green because it was stored in a moldy burlap and never rinsed. Once, when doing research at Diablo Canyon, he was refused permission to dive in that gear. "Buy some new stuff and send us the bill," he was told.

But Mitchell is quick to point out, "Wheeler is the kindest, gentlest person I've ever met. He's not a dynamic leader, but points people in the right direction, then leaves them on their own. He has remarkable powers of observation and recall."

In the 1950s, the division between sport and technical diving wasn't so sharply delin-

Jim Stewart and Wheeler North launching a boat off Scripps Pier, 1958.

eated as today. There were few experienced divers, and the public was anxious to learn from them. North, along with some other Scripps divers, was pressed into service. "We started a diving instruction program under San Diego Parks and Rec department. I was chief instructor; classes were held in the Mission Bay swimming pool. Jim Stewart was one of the instructors, a grad student named Ray Ghelardi was another. Our program was based on Connie Limbaugh's...When the students finished the pool lessons, they were on their own, because the city didn't want the liability for ocean instruction. The course cost $15...they gave us a very small compensation, that mainly paid for gas to Mission Bay." The city terminated the project when dive stores began to open in the area.

One of the first was Diving Locker, owned by North, Stewart, and several other partners. "Connie Limbaugh had formed a consulting company. The scientific diving consultants were me, Jim Stewart, and Earl Murray...we made money doing surveys for the sewage outfall, and decided to invest it in a dive store.

"We hired Chuck Nicklin to run it. He had been operating a grocery store, loved diving, and knew retailing. The day before the Diving Locker opened (in 1959), a shark came in and took a skin diver at La Jolla Cove. Poor old Chuck sold one face mask the first week, and that was to his best friend." Eventually, business improved to the point that Nicklin bought out everybody and became sole owner.

North also did a term as editor of a diving magazine. In the early 60s, he became involved as a lecturer in the Los Angeles County instructional program, and got to know Zale Parry. She had been approached by Al Hubbard, an underwater film aficionado, to publish an **Arizona Highways** type of magazine for divers. Parry recruited Wheeler as editor, and **Fathom** was born. It was a beautiful magazine, with more color photography than any up to that time. But after two issues and lots of red ink, Hubbard backed out. North was actually relieved, because of the time it took away from his scientific work.

That work involved *Macrocystis pyrifera*, the plant that forms California's magnificent kelp forests. Early research had examined the effect of harvesting. Limbaugh found no harm in a 5 year study, but that had been funded by Kelco, the harvesting and processing company. Fishermen didn't accept the results, and lobbied Fish and Game to fund an independent study. This was where North came in. "We studied what happens when you remove the top of a plant, what lives in the canopy, etc,...and came up with the same answer.

> We were flying by the seat of our pants where methodology was concerned. We had to build our own transect lines, quadrats, and tags that would last underwater. Underwater bearings and triangulation were unknown; we developed that ourselves.

"We were flying by the seat of our pants where methodology was concerned. We had to build our own transect lines, quadrats, and tags that would last underwater. Underwater bearings and triangulation were unknown; we developed that ourselves. Our fish biologist, Jay Quast, developed new techniques for estimating numbers of fishes. He would swim in midwater, count everything he saw, and adapted methods used in estimating the numbers in flocks of birds."

The kelp forests at Point Loma and Palos Verdes were declining. Huge numbers of urchins were foraging through and destroying the kelp. Biologist David Leighton developed a method of controlling urchins by dumping quicklime on them. After he cleared out 100 square meters off South Pt. Loma, the kelp came back. This experiment established that it was urchins, not sewage, that led to decline of kelp. However quicklime was indiscriminating, destroying other invertebrates as well as urchins. A better solution, proposed by Charlie Martin of Kelco, was to kill urchins one by one with a hammer. Obviously this would be quite labor intensive, and dependent to a great extent on volunteer help. North recalls, "I obtained a grant from Kelco to pursue that, and spent the next 10 years hammering urchins."

One problem of urchin removal was documentation of results. Wheeler decided the best way to do it was aerial photographs, so he took flying lessons and bought a Piper Cherokee Trainer. Shooting through the windows wasn't satisfactory, so he cut a 6-inch hole into the floor, big enough to fit a 50mm lens. This allowed the direct overhead photos he needed. His technique was to fly the plane in a slow bank, shoot the picture, then take over the controls again. Owing to FAA regulations, the plane is North's only piece of equipment that is well maintained, to the extent that Mitchell recently purchased it.

1961, Wheeler North fastens a kelp transplant to the bottom. The specimen of giant kelp (Macrocystis) was about 60 feet long and was taken from a bed 400 miles from the site of transplanting.

In 1963 Cal Tech made Wheeler an offer he couldn't resist: to join their environmental engineering group. This meant moving to Pasadena, but it was a hard money position, which alleviated some of pressures of the scientific grantsmanship game. Caltech operated Kerckhoff Marine Lab in Corona del Mar, and that became the base of Wheeler's operations.

"Los Angeles conservation organizations asked me to bring back the Palos Verdes kelp bed in 1965. By the time we got there, there were only two plants left, and they soon succumbed to urchins. We would kill the urchins, but would get *Laminaria* and *Pterygophora*, (smaller species of kelp) but not *Macrocystis*. We had to develop transplant techniques to get spores for reproduction." At first they were unaware of the scope of the project. Fifty plants were brought in from other locations, but within a week herbivorous fishes (halfmoon and opaleye) cleaned them out. "We just kept feeding them plants," North recalls. A critical mass of about 2,000 plants was needed before they began to see juveniles that would survive to be young plants. To obtain healthy plants, they had to go to San Clemente, and tow them 44 miles to Palos Verdes. This couldn't be accomplished in one day; they were left overnight, then towed the remaining distance. "We bought scrap chain for 50 cents a pound and used it to anchor plants. All told, we had about 3 tons of scrap chain at the bottom of Abalone Cove." But they also had a kelp forest.

Nearby White's Point was an urchin desert. "We couldn't hammer them all by ourselves, so we went to LA Parks & Rec Department. They put on a volunteer program, called PURP (Palos Verdes Underwater Restoration Project). On the first day 250 divers bopped about 800,000 urchins according to their counts... It took only 500 plants to get White's Point started...(we) got it stabilized and growing in 10 years."

One of North's best known projects was a deep-sea kelp farm of the 1970s. This was a direct outgrowth of the gas crisis, when everybody was looking for alternate energy sources. Howard Wilcox, a retired nuclear physicist with funding connections, recruited Wheeler to run a

project on growing plants in the open ocean to produce methane. A major participant was the Navy, so the first attempt was made off their San Clemente Island base. A 500 by 600 foot grid of ropes and buoys was anchored at a depth of 40 feet, in water 300 feet deep. Because of powerful currents, it turned out to be a poor choice. When UDT divers tied kelp plants to the grid, they had to hang tightly to the buoy ropes like a spider on a web, otherwise they were on their way to Baja. The plants lasted less than a month, owing to rough water, strong currents, and no nutrients.

1975, *Wheeler North at White Point examing the sea urchins.*

North built a smaller grid (20x50) offshore of Corona del Mar, originating in 150 feet of water with the plants at 40 feet. With nutrient-rich water pumped up from below, the plants lived there for over a year. Grazers were no problem out there, but North observed some animals on the plants that were normally never seen offshore, like *Melibe* nudibranchs.

Wilcox had a more grandiose idea: a hexagonal shaped structure that looked like upside down umbrella, with spokes radiating from a hub, and kelp plants on the spokes. The handle of the umbrella was the buoy. "I explained to Howard why this wouldn't work, but he didn't buy my arguments. It was a problem of scale. At 100 feet across, the nutrients pumped up from below would be swept away by currents. But if it's 100 miles across, you create your own environment and the currents will be stopped."

General Electric, who entered the program after the Navy dropped out, decided to hang a curtain around the farm to keep nutrients there. Within a week, it was torn up and swept away by ordinary currents. There were also serious problems with the module. Its movements were completely out of phase with those of the plants, so they were torn up by the forces and the sharp edges. Essentially the module ate the kelp, and within a month all the plants were destroyed.

A year later the Gas Research Institute became interested in measuring the productivity of the kelp bed, and the whole focus changed. North set up a hemi-dome experiment located at Fisherman's Cove, site of USC Marine Lab at Catalina. It consisted of a semi-circular bag, 50 feet in diameter, that held in nutrients. Unfortunately it was installed in spring 1982, just in time for the El Niño. The warm waters destroyed kelp beds throughout Southern California, including this one. "When that experiment failed, the oil glut came along, and they said 'Thank you, but there is no longer an energy problem.' "

What did North learn from this? "You can grow kelp on an ocean platform if you can handle the engineering problems. You've got to keep it from being torn apart. Economic studies show that methane from kelp costs about $12 per million BTU; getting it out of the ground costs about $4 per million BTU. If the cost of natural gas climbs, maybe it will come about. But we are getting into the greenhouse effect, and that changes the economics. If there is going be a per ton tax on carbon emissions, it's a whole new ballgame. It's better to stay away from structured farms. Barnacles, sea urchins, and other hard-bodied creatures attracted to them will shred the plants."

His latest idea: an unstructured kelp farm, starting out as a kelp paddie. He would culture baby plants, move them to a quiet bay, and let the fronds intertwine. Eventually it will be towed out to sea, still in juvenile stage, a few hundred feet across. Put it in the California current, harvest it when it's off Baja, and burn it. The question is: can you create a kelp paddie that will maintain its integrity if a big storm hits it? He has written a proposal based on this idea.

The purpose is to counter the greenhouse effect. Increase in atmospheric CO_2, caused primarily by burning fossil fuels, threatens to raise global temperatures to disruptive levels. Plants take up carbon dioxide and give off oxygen. To stabilize atmospheric CO_2, you would need a kelp farm over 1200 miles on each side. Using the California Current as a conveyer belt, kelp paddies perhaps 10 miles square could keep coming down the track.

Using plant biomass to take up CO_2 has been proposed before. But what happens to the biomass? If you burn it, it goes back into the atmosphere; if you let it rot, bacteria release CO_2. But in the deep ocean, CO_2 is trapped in lattices called hydrates, which will effectively keep it out of the atmosphere.

So North proposes to capture CO_2 with kelp, digest kelp with bacteria to produce methane, burn methane to produce CO_2 in a concentrated form, pump that into ocean depths to form hydrate, which would settle to the bottom where there is already lots of hydrate. Some interest has been shown in this proposal. The electric power industry is responsible for about 30% of the CO_2 from burning fossil fuels. Ten years from now there may be a tax on carbon emissions, resulting in a major economic impact on these industries.

The most difficult part will be growing the kelp.

Daniel Burnham once said, "Make no small plans. They lack the fire to stir men's souls." As he nears retirement, Wheeler North still makes big plans, and dreams big dreams. When asked how he would like to remembered, he replied, "What I'll be remembered for is restoring kelp beds, but if this CO_2 caper comes off, maybe I'll be remembered for that too."

Science Underwater
Andy Rechnitzer

Nine years before Apollo landed on the moon, the bathyscaph Trieste reached the deepest hole in the ocean: seven miles down. The scientist in charge of that expedition was Dr. Andreas Rechnitzer, a key figure in the Golden Age of Submersibles.

Rechnitzer's career spans the entire era of scuba diving in America. He and Conrad Limbaugh collaborated on the first scientific and recreational scuba courses, introducing methods in both fields that are in standard use to this day. As an administrator and consultant, he was responsible for many of the advances in our understanding of the deep ocean. Biologist, engineer, consultant, sport diver, underwater photographer, marine archaeologist: All these titles are part of Dr. Rechnitzer's resume. His diving experiences range from Mayan cenotes and Spanish shipwrecks to under Antarctic ice.

WHEN UCLA GRADUATE STUDENT CONRAD LIMBAUGH walked into Rene Bussoz' Westwood sporting goods store and saw his first Aqualung, he knew he had to have one. Connie told his major professor, Dr. Boyd Walker, that this new gadget had a place as a tool for marine scientists of the future. Although Walker wasn't a diver, he was persuaded to purchase one of the first Aqualungs ever sold in the United States.

Walker's graduate assistant at UCLA was a Navy veteran of Danish descent, Andreas Rechnitzer. A native of Escondido, California, and an avid free diver and spearfisherman, Rechnitzer had served in Hawaii at the end of World War II. Like Limbaugh, he was attending school on the GI Bill with the ultimate goal of a PhD in marine biology at Scripps Institution of Oceanography. At that time Scripps was a branch of UCLA, and all graduate students had to spend a year at the mother institution making up coursework.

When the first Aqualung arrived, the two graduate students set out to master its use. There were no courses and no instruction books, so like all early divers they learned through trial and error. Since there was only one unit, one of them would scuba dive while the other followed with a snorkel. "On my first trip I wore big holes in my shoulders," Andy recalls, "because I was still trying to use my arms to swim. We had no protective gear, those early straps were rough and tough.

Rechnitzer's diving equipment in 1951 was typical of divers of that time. The wet suit was still four years in the future.

"We dived out of the back end of Connie's car. We had bathing suits, Aqualungs , faceplate, and fins, that's all." By the time Rechnitzer and Limbaugh arrived at Scripps in the summer of 1950, they had obtained a second unit. There was no compressor in San Diego, so for refills they had to cascade air from a storage system of six 160 cubic foot tanks. When those ran out, the tanks were shipped to Los Angeles for refilling, causing a temporary hiatus in diving activity.

Andy poses with a model of **Trieste.**

Trieste's *hull was filled with gasoline for flatation. The seven-foot pressure sphere below could accommodate two persons.*

This was the beginning of the Scripps scuba diving program. It served not only as the model for research diving in this country, but also led directly to the first sport diving courses, which eventually evolved into diving instruction as we know it today. Procedures such as the buddy system, buddy breathing, and ditch and recovery were introduced and developed there by Limbaugh and Rechnitzer.

In the early days many things were jerry rigged, resulting in close calls when equipment sometimes came apart. Andy's first emergency ascent, from 65 feet, became necessary when his intake hose came off the mouthpiece and inhalations produced nothing but water.

There were no standard tanks, and one particular set of new ones was about 15 pounds negative. Limbaugh discovered this when he sank directly to the bottom and couldn't ascend. This was long before buoyancy compensators were introduced, but he did have some plastic collecting bags. Filling them with air from the regulator brought the divers back to the surface, but weight belts had to be dropped to make it back to the beach.

"Limbaugh and (Jim) Stewart and I wanted others to enjoy what we were enjoying, and show them what it could do for their scientific work," explained Andy. "So it wasn't long before we started a training program. Interest was slow to build, and those first courses were almost private lessons. We didn't really teach the first divers, we just demonstrated and told them, 'This is how you do it.' But they were divers or snorkelers to start with. It wasn't until 1952 that we finally organized it into a written syllabus. By that time there were no more than four or five (scientific) divers."

Psychologically, in anything that has a side of danger, you assume the other guy has the answer. You just do better when there are two. So that's how the buddy thing got started.

The first official Scripps diving course came out of necessity. A student at another branch of the university was lost underwater, and the administration temporarily canceled all diving. It was determined that there was a need for more formalized training. "We figured, 'What problems might someone have down there? If someone kicks my faceplate off, what do I do?' So you've got to breathe without a faceplate on. What else? We've got to swim, so there has to be some endurance swimming. Then we had to figure out how to make entries."

Ditching equipment and recovering it from the bottom were done for psychological preparation. Harassment was also part of the program, consisting of kicking off the faceplate and turning off air by pinching the hoses.

Rechnitzer said to Limbaugh one day, "I feel comfortable when we are diving together, we ought to have a buddy system." Connie agreed it was a good idea, then asked, "What do we do as buddies?" One thing was sharing air. They swallowed a lot of salt water while developing the technique, because the early regulators lacked non-return valves, causing the hoses to fill with water. Andy recalls, "Psychologically, in anything that has a side of danger, you assume the other guy has the answer. You just do better when there are two. So that's how the buddy thing got started."

Today, diving operations for universities and scientific organizations are governed by a diving control board. This originated when Limbaugh refused to certify a student on the grounds that he was not psychologically balanced enough to be a diver. "He proved our point when he threatened to kill Limbaugh. He really meant it. We said, 'We've got to take that burden off you and set up a committee, so he will have to pick on five or six people.'

"At that time no one was overseeing us except Carl Hubbs. We got him to go diving when he was 55. He used to be a great swimmer, but that's the only dive he ever made. Mrs. Hubbs once got furious with me. 'When are Connie and you going to get to work? You are out diving all the time.' But old Wesley Coe, a Scripps professor, said, 'Son, you go on out there. You will learn more in an hour (underwater) than you will learn in ten hours with books.' "

Early on, these pioneers recognized the need for self-regulation of diving. In an article written for the second issue of **Skin Diver** Magazine (1951), Rechnitzer wrote that "...we should license ourselves and keep the bureaucrats out of our business. This is one of my proudest things. We are an outstanding organization, despite the internecine fighting among the training agencies. We have good training, cross certification, and it derived from what Limbaugh and I put together years ago."

The Scripps program crossed over into the sport diving world when Al Tillman, Ramsey Parks, and Bev Morgan were sent there to take one of the early diving courses. They originated the first formal diving instruction and certification program offered to the public: the Los Angeles County program, which was essentially the Scripps course. This became the basis of all the instructional programs which are taught today. The major differences are a greatly lessened emphasis on swimming and free diving, and no harassment.

New research techniques also had to be developed at Scripps. Fish identifications were especially difficult, because they had been learned from preserved, colorless specimens in bottles. It was like bird watching without a guidebook. One time Rechnitzer, Stewart, and some others were at Guadelupe Island off the Pacific coast of Baja, collecting fishes. "I sallied down to 100 feet and this very orange fish went by. I said, 'I don't know you.' So I got my frog spear and went back down, but couldn't find it. But then a scythemark butterflyfish, swam by and I said, 'I don't know you either,' and speared it. That was the first one." *Chaetodon falcifer*, since then discovered in deep waters of Scripps Canyon, is now the logo for Scripps Aquarium.

Connie Limbaugh, acknowledged as the founder of dive instruction in the United States, died tragically young. He was lost in a 1960 diving accident in a cave in France. At the time he was the diving officer at Scripps, still working on his PhD. Rechnitzer had earned his degree by then, and was working for the Naval Ocean Systems Center.

Although his formal training was in biology, Rechnitzer is best known today for his work with submersibles. It was under his leadership that two men made the world's ultimate dive: 35,800 feet in the bathyscaph *Trieste*, to the bottom of the Marianas Trench. How deep is that? If Mount Everest were dropped into that hole, its summit would be more than a mile below the surface. That dive was made in 1960, and like the brief period of manned lunar exploration, no one has been back since then.

Rechnitzer and Jacques Piccard look cordial in this 1959 photograph, but today Andy feels he was aced out of the deepest dive.

Rechnitzer became interested in the deep ocean while a graduate student at Scripps. Carl Hubbs and John Isaacs were experimenting with a deep water trawl, and Andy would spend nights identifying the creatures brought up. When he joined NOSC after graduation, there was an invitation from the Office of Naval Research for scientists to apply for dives on the bathyscaph *Trieste*. The vessel had been built in Italy by Auguste Piccard, the famed Swiss balloonist, following the principles of the sealed gondola used on his historic stratosphere flights of the 1930s. The *Trieste* was essentially an underwater balloon with a huge, gasoline-filled float and a two-man pressure sphere to carry the crew. Iron shot would sink it to the bottom; then be released to allow the vessel to rise back to the surface. There was no significant horizontal propulsion; it could only go up or down like a seagoing elevator. Piccard and his son, Jacques, had made the early dives in *Trieste*, but the project ran out of money. So Jacques sought the US Navy's sponsorship for a test dive series in the Mediterranean.

It was at this point that Rechnitzer entered the scene. By 1958 he was in charge of the Navy's deep submergence program. "I thought I would really love to have one of those to go down and look at all the deep sea animals," Andy recalls. "I wrote up a white paper that the Navy should buy it for the US oceanographic community and they should deliver it to me in San Diego. Lo and behold, they did it."

National pride was at stake, because the French Navy was building a submersible intended to make the world's deepest dive. The immediate challenge was to get there first: the Challenger Deep in the Marianas Trench, seven miles beneath the surface. Oceanographers call it the Hadal Zone, because the environment at that depth is as inhospitable as Hades. In contrast to a fiery hell, the Hadal Zone is cloaked in perpetual darkness, with near freezing water temperatures. Ambient pressure on *Trieste's* 7-foot sphere would be 16,000 pounds per square inch.

"First we needed a new sphere built that could go full depth. The original was only good for 20,000 feet. We got one for $60,000 from the Krupp Works in Germany, that was nominally good to 43,000 feet.. Of course there was no way to test it; you have to do that in the environment. So we went to the Marianas Trench to get that deep dive out of the way, simply because it would always be bugging us that we should go there."

It was called Project Nekton, and Rechnitzer was the chief scientist. Included in the program were measurements of gravity, sound velocity, and temperature, and a spectrum of manual and audio

Rechnitzer (left) with astronaut Scott Carpenter at the Santa Monica Film Festival.

observations. (It was actually colder at 20,000 feet than at 35,800 owing to adiabatic cooling of rising deep water. The lowest temperature was about 37 degrees at 20,000 feet.)

"We disassembled the craft and took it to Guam to began a series of dives. On the first one, Piccard and myself set a new world record of 18,150 feet. When we surfaced there were two horrendous explosions, or at least we thought they were explosions. We thought we were going right back to the bottom again. But we stayed on the surface and emptied the entrance tube, which took 15 minutes or so. Piccard went up and looked, didn't see anything wrong. So I slipped out through that 15 inch hole, slammed that 400 pound door, and secured to daylight. ...Back in port the next day, we found several gallons of water inside the sphere...

"The sphere had been made in three parts and epoxy bonded over 4 1/2 inches. Those bonds had parted by shearing and that's where the noise had come from. There was no way to put it back together there, and flying it back to Germany would have cost $40,000. So we made 15 more dives with it in that condition. It leaked all the time, but as long as it only went drip-drip and not drip-drip-drip...let's go diving. The deepest dive was made with it in

photo courtesy of Andy Rechnitzer

three parts, and we made one to 24,000 feet before that. The slippage of the joints is still present, you can see it in the Washington Navy Yard museum."

That shear cost Rechnitzer the opportunity to go on the deepest dive. He had been selected to make it along with Navy lieutenant Don Walsh. But Piccard had a clause in his contract that specified he would be aboard on dives that might involve unusual circumstances. He convinced the Navy brass that a dive seven miles down met that criterion. (In our interview, Rechnitzer didn't mention this part of the story. The information comes from **Diving for Science: a History of Deep Submersibles** by Edward Shenton. Andy later confirmed that version.)

On January 23, 1960 Piccard and Walsh rode Trieste into history. It took five hours to reach the bottom, where they gasped in amazement as they saw a flounder-like fish, a shrimp, and a jellyfish through the viewing port. It had been postulated that nothing could live at that depth.

For his role in the expedition, Rechnitzer received the Navy Department's Distinguished Civilian Service Award from President Eisenhower. Big and ungainly as she was, Trieste launched what is now called the Golden Age of Submersibles. Within the next ten years, over 50 manned submersibles were built. The vessels that followed were smaller, more maneuverable, and far more sophisticated. Yet Trieste, outfitted with a new pressure sphere and christened Trieste II, lasted another ten years. In 1963 she found the wreckage of the nuclear submarine Thresher. But neither its new hull, nor that of any subsequent submersible, was qualified for the ultimate depth. So the mud of the Challenger Deep has remained undisturbed by man since 1960.

"You can hardly pick up a book on oceanography that doesn't have the Trieste in it," says Rechnitzer. "The bathyscaph era lasted for 26 years, which I thought was pretty great because when we started no one was really interested. Now the Navy spends about $100 million a year for their submersible activities, including the remotely operated ones..."

But immediately after Trieste's deep dive, the Navy lost interest in submersibles. Admiral Hyman Rickover stated that anything deeper than 2500 feet was a waste of money. Frustrated by this lack of progress, Rechnitzer resigned from NOSC.

He became director of North American Aviation's new marine sciences department, heading up the program for their submersible,

Beaver Mk IV. Among his staff in 1962 was Bob Ballard, then a college student. Ballard later became a key figure on the *Alvin* team, culminated by his discovery of the *Titanic*. "It was just by a fluke that I didn't build *Alvin*," said Rechnitzer. "I didn't take a president or a vice president from North American back to Woods Hole but General Mills did. They told me later, 'We wanted you to build it but we didn't think your company was behind you." According to another source, it was General Mills' low bid that won the day (**Water Baby, The Story of Alvin** by Victoria A. Kaharl).

> **Most engineers, I have found, are not inventors or creative people. That was a big shock to me at North American, where we had thousands. To find one who was really creative was rare.**

"I don't claim to be an engineer but a lot of people think I am. I've received several engineering awards...but it's mostly for fostering and catalyzing things in engineering. The *Beaver Mark* IV was really my baby, a complete seafloor oil and gas production system, created to operate at 2,000 feet.

"If the truth be known, I can't handle all the math and all the formulas but I have common sense and creativity. Most engineers, I have found, are not inventors or creative people. That was a big shock to me at North American, where we had thousands. To find one who was really creative was rare."

By 1970 the submersible era was beginning to fade, and North American Rockwell phased out its ocean systems program. Rechnitzer went to work for the Navy again. He initially served as a Science and Technology Advisor to the Chief of Naval Operations, then later headed up the International and Interagency Affairs Branch for the Oceanographer of the Navy. Today, he is president of Viking Oceanographics in El Cajon.

Throughout his career, Rechnitzer has remained active in the sport diving community. While at Scripps he formed Scientific Diving Consultants in partnershop with Limbaugh, Jim Stewart, and Wheeler North. They put the profits from the company into San Diego's second dive shop, The Diving Locker, and hired Chuck Nicklin to run it. Andy was an active participant in the annual Santa Monica Film Festival, winning several awards for his motion pictures. In 1968 he received the coveted NOGI award from the Underwater Society of America.

Today Rechnitzer's primary diving interest is marine archaeology. This began in the early 50s, recovering ancient Indian bowls and artifacts from the La Jolla submarine canyon. "I've had artifacts in my hand that had some real history on them...amphoras from Julius

Caesar's army from the Mediterranean off France, treasure from Spanish wrecks off Yucatan, nails from the HMS *Bounty*, and others from Paul Revere's foundry.

"I really cut my teeth on underwater maritime history in 1964. After a...meeting in Mexico City, we went to Akumal. It was like something out of Edgar Rice Burroughs: a pristine beach, palm trees, thatched huts, and the only way to get there was by boat from Cozumel." They dove the Spanish wreck *El Mantanceros*, which went down in 1746. She was carrying "dime store stuff," used as trade items. But Andy was bitten by the bug, and vowed to return on a regular basis.

Subsequent trips brought him to Scorpion Reef, 70 miles off the coast of Yucatan. He and his friends found a number of 16th to 19th century wrecks, recovering breech-loading cannons and anchors dating to circa 1525. One of the

*Andy examines the propulsion unit of the one-man submersible, **Deep Rover**.*

most memorable wreck sites was the *Tweed*, a Royal Mail Steam Packet that went down in 1847. Its huge reciprocating steam engine had 6 foot diameter cylinders. Gold and silver coins, pistol butts, and false teeth were some of the artifacts found there.

A memorable incident of the time was recalled: "Six of us, including Chuck Nicklin and (astronaut/aquanaut) Scott Carpenter were diving off Cozumel, and got caught in the wonderful current. We came up 45 minutes later, looked around, and the boat was so far away you couldn't see the people in it. We were headed for New Orleans the hard way, no BC's, nothing but bathing suits. I'm carrying a brand new 70mm camera custom made for North American Aviation. Not about to drop it, I dropped my weight belt. I wished I had a flare. 'Hey,' somebody said, 'you've got a strobe.' I flashed it several times, the boat got bigger and bigger, and picked us up. That would have been one of the most embarrassing things, all those big-time divers and they got caught unprepared."

Perhaps the premiere historic shipwreck find in America was the Civil War ironclad *Monitor*, and Rechnitzer was involved in its confirmation. It began in 1974 when Harold Edgerton (inventor of the strobe) received a U.S. presidential award. He thanked the president, then mentioned what he would really like to do is to check out the site John Newton had found, to determine if it really was the *Monitor*. The chief executive put in a word with the Secretary of the Navy, who found the necessary money. At the time, Rechnitzer was

I've gone through the fish sticking stage and the photography stage and finally got into underwater archaeology. That is unique in of all the occupations you can get into underwater; your appetite for it is never fulfilled.

working for the Oceanographer of the Navy, and was invited aboard the *Alcoa Seaprobe* for the expedition. They were using an early sidescan sonar and a remote television camera, which could see about a tabletop at a time in the 50-foot visibility. "We went around snapping pictures and finally came across the turret. It was sitting underneath the gunwale. Fortuitously it had broken off as the ship sank in 210 feet of water. It turned over and went down stern first, and that sheared off that big heavy turret with the cannon still in it. That was the key that we had found the *Monitor*.

"I've gone through the fish sticking stage and the photography stage and finally got into underwater archaeology. That is unique in of all the occupations you can get into underwater; your appetite for it is never fulfilled."

In 1990 Rechnitzer was one of the first Americans to dive Russia's Lake Baikal, the largest body of fresh water in the world. He stayed there a month and recalls, "That was something else...You had these shoals like an emerald reef, covered with a forest of sponges standing up to two feet high. There are 60,000 seals in the lake. The crustaceans and other critters living there are all derivatives of marine forms. 20 million years ago it was attached to an ocean."

Andy is supposedly retired now, but is still working on engineering projects. He claims the current one could solve the California water problem. "We can salvage 80% of all the sewage water that is now being pumped into the Pacific Ocean. Reclaimed water, purified, clarified if you want it, all the way back to potable water, and all at a reasonable price. The technique is all electric and environmentally benign. Twenty units will take care of San Diego County. We can provide the water reclaimed for the same price as they are importing it now. We can desalinate seawater, and for every three acres of seawater you can still have an acre of fresh water at the end of each year if you recycle it through this system. The challenge is to bring it on line. You can't scale this technology down. We are going to sell the first unit to Caltech within a month. That's what I do in retirement."

The joy of discovery still radiates from Andy Rechnitzer. He concluded, "Young people may think that everything has been discovered or written about, but that's not true...So much to be learned and discovered, lots of wide open fields. It's pathetic that people work eight hours then go home and watch TV. There is so much to do."

Andy rests while exploring a cave in Capri, Italy in 1956. He is holding a motorcycle battery that powers his underwater light.

SCIENCE UNDERWATER
CONNIE LIMBAUGH'S
LAST DIVE

A report by Dr. Wheeler North

At the time of his death in a cave diving accident, 35 year old Conrad Limbaugh was considered one of the world's leading divers. Self taught as a UCLA undergraduate, Connie went on to Scripps Institution of Oceanography as a doctoral student and became its first diving safety officer. His research diving course at Scripps was the first civilian course of instruction in the United States, and the model for all those that came afterward.

It wasn't easy. Among the swimming pool requirements were: swim 1000 feet under 10 minutes, swim underwater 150 feet surfacing not more than 4 times, swim 75 feet underwater with no breaths, surface dive to 10 feet and recover a swimmer, carry a swimmer 75 feet at the surface, pick up a struggling swimmer, demonstrate back pressure arm lift artificial respiration. In the ocean, candidates had to swim 1000 feet without fins in less than 12 minutes (around the end of the pier), surface dive to 18 feet, and do a ditch and recovery at the end of the pier in 30 feet of water.

The first scientific diving manual was written by Limbaugh, and is the basis of those still used by universities and consulting companies around the world. He was a consumate observ-**He was probably** er and note taker, leaving detailed field notes about marine crea-
a hippie before tures he studied, dating back to 1948. These were some of the first
there were ever written by a diving scientist. Many of them were done in Scripps
hippies... Canyon, where he also made the first accurate charts. Research trips
took him to Clipperton Island, Mexico, the Virgin Islands, and the Bahamas.

Limbaugh taught the founders of the Los Angeles County program, as well as running their first instructors' course in coordination with Al Tillman and Bev Morgan. With Jim Stewart, Wheeler North, and Andy Rechnitzer he formed the first scientific diving consulting company, and later opened one of the nation's first dive shops with the same partners.

Pioneer Sam Miller calls him the leading figure in American diving through the 1950s. He recalls his first meeting with Connie, expecting a tall, blonde, tanned adonis. Instead, here was a chunky, balding fellow wearing glasses.

Chuck Mitchell recalls, "He was probably a hippie before there were hippies...He never wore shoes...went barefooted or had just flaps on...pants usually kind of baggy, walking on his cuffs. One of the nicest guys you ever want to meet, he was very methodical, and did things very slowly. A remarkable individual. I used to marvel at how we would dive an hour someplace rather unexciting, usually the sand dollar beds at the end of Scripps Pier...He would come back, sit down at the typewriter, and it would be almost like he had a videotape running the whole time. He would fill 15 or 20 typewritten pages with notes of incredible detail. Nothing was taken for granted, everything was recorded. That's how Howard Feder at University of Alaska was able to write some of the papers that came out later under Connie's name .

Connie Limbaugh 1957.

"Connie was a good family person, always had his kids around. They were dressed just like him, barefooted... Always asking lots of questions and he was always patiently answering them. If you saw him today on the beach you would probably think he was some surfer. His death really took everybody by surprise. We were in disbelief, it couldn't happen, there was no way."

No history of scuba diving in America can be written without paying tribute to Connie Limbaugh. The accounts of many of the pioneers in this volume — Mitchell, Andy Rechnitzer, Jim Stewart, the Meistrells, Chuck Nicklin, Wheeler North and the Bottom Scratchers — include recollections of his full, brief life. However the exact details of his fatal accident have become obscured by time. The official report by his colleague, Dr. Wheeler North, is reprinted here in edited form, courtesy of the Archives of Scripps Institution of Oceanography.

On 20 March 1960, Conrad Limbaugh, one of the most experienced, cool-headed, and safety-conscious divers in the world, lost his life while diving in a submarine cave at the tiny harbor of Port Miou, near the Mediterranean resort town of Cassis, France, about 10 miles east of Marseilles. A thorough investigation of the accident was made because of the concern of the entire diving community of the world in developing an accurate account of how such a serious mishap could overtake a man as careful and canny as Limbaugh, and because of the necessity of ensuring that no misconceptions be left as a source of ill feeling between American and French divers. In retrospect, the accident does not appear to have resulted from negligence on anyone's part, but rather was precipitated by an understandable conclusion, which, under normal circumstance, would have been considered a triviality; the gravity of the error was doubtless not recognized until too late.

The American aspects of the investigation were conducted by Drs. Menard, Sargent, and North, assisted by US. Navy Lieutenants Sobiesky and Thomson. ...The first American investigators did not reach the scene of the accident until 3 days after it occurred. All available witnesses were questioned and Menard and North reconnoitered the submarine cave for a distance of about 200 ft. from the entrance, under close supervision by French divers. ...

Mr. Limbaugh had been sent to Europe as one of the American representatives to a meeting of the International Underwater Confederation at Barcelona, Spain. After the close of the conference, he visited France to familiarize himself with and to photograph the Mediterranean coast, and the French developments in underwater research and techniques. ...The day before his death he returned all his borrowed diving equipment...(he had brought only his face mask from America) and stated that he did not contemplate any more diving while in France.

Some time after returning his equipment Limbaugh apparently changed his mind about further dives and he made arrangement with M. Clouzot to borrow equipment and undertake another dive on March 20th. ....he left his valuables including his wallet and Rolleiflex camera with Mme. Clouzot and drove with Clouzot to Port Miou where they met Messrs. Girault and Poudevigne who were to participate in the dive....

Girault has taken his 15 year old daughter in as far as the well. Poudevigne regarded it as such a simple task and had heard so much of Limbaugh's capabilities that he did not consider it necessary to have contact maintained between the two by means of a short rope.

Girault and Poudevigne did not speak English while Limbaugh knew very little French, but Clouzot acted as interpreter...Limbaugh, Clouzot and Poudevigne set out in the latter's small boat (approximately 16 feet in length) along with a young boy, Michel, ...who had begged to come along on the chance of getting in a short dive. Limbaugh was to use a triple tank Aqualung with a conventional reserve, plus Aqualung weight belt, and flashlight borrowed from Girault, while his rubber shirt with attached hood, and fins and mask were borrowed from Clouzot. ...They decided that the most interesting place to dive was a limestone cave, located near the entrance to the Port, a few hundred yards from the boatslips. About a thousand feet of the interior of the cave had been fairly thoroughly explored in 1956 and an account of the studies was published. Limbaugh had been shown the publication, which includes a diagram of the cave... and presumably he was familiar with the main features.

There are two submarine entrances to the cave and they join after a distance of some 150 feet in a rather large room which opens through a 60 ft. vertical well or chimney to the outside. Progress along the cave is difficult because of the extreme irregularity of the topography and there are apparently many blind alleys and crevices not shown in the diagram. Fresh water from the mountain flows just under the roof of the cave, while a body of salt water extends along the floor as far as the cavern has been explored. A well defined interface exists between the fresh and salt water. The depth of this boundary and the rate of flow of the fresh water varies with season and the amount of rainfall. ...

Considerable rain fell in the area both before and after March 20 and Clouzot and Poudevigne both agree that the fresh water flow was strong and quite turbid on March 20. Directly beneath the well lies a conical pile of stones. The area above the well is funnel-shaped and diverts debris down into the well; presumably the cone of rocks was formed in this way. ...The cone fills the chamber beneath the well to such an extent that in places there is less than 3 feet of clearance between the sides of the cone and the hole in the ceiling of the chamber. This tends to restrict the amount of light entering the submarine portions of the cave from the well....When the water is clear and the sunlight good it is possible to see light from the well before light from the outside entrance is lost, but on March 20th the fresh water layer was so dirty that the divers had to traverse an area of complete darkness before perceiving the position of the well.

Currents in the salt water underlaying the fresh water stream have not been studied but in any case are weak...the sea was quite calm on March 20th. Poudevigne stated that he thought there was a slight current running seawards from the main tunnel on the afternoon of the accident. ....Poudevigne and Clouzot reported that on the afternoon of March 20 visibility in the salt water layer was about 10 to 12 feet, while in the fresh water stream it was limited to a few inches. Nonetheless, there was sufficient visibility so that Limbaugh was able to photograph in the salt water.

...Poudevigne stated that the topography of the cave surface was such that a swimmer would have a fairly clear and unobstructed pas-

Modified from Bulletin de l'Institut Oceanographique Monaco, No.1131, 1958. By G. Corroy, C. Gouvernet, J. Chouteau, A. Sivirine, R. Gilet, and J. Picard. Redrawn by Steve Kelly Watersport Publishing, Inc., 1994.

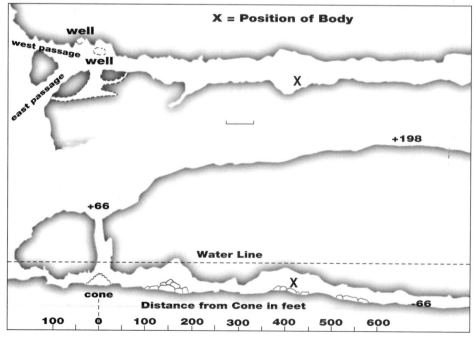

sage for at least a hundred yards if he were to swim inward along the main tunnel from the well. ...The tunnel starts at a depth of about 30 ft. and extends downward to a depth of about 70 ft. at a distance of 170 yards from the well. The top of the cone of rocks lies some 12 to 15 feet below the surface of the water in the well. At the time of the accident the cone extended into the turbid layer. ...Two deep fissures identify the northwest and the southwest bulges of the well at the water's edge and can be used to distinguish the west side from the east side.

The diving expedition got underway in mid-afternoon. Air pressures in the tanks were checked with a gauge and found to be a satisfactory 155 kg/cm^2 (about 2200 psi). Limbaugh was using a 15-liter tank (this would represent about 60 cu ft of air). Poudevigne had a set of 21 liters capacity. The triple bottle rig of Limbaugh was quite heavy and he needed only 5 kg (11 pounds) of weight on his belt. He experimented before the dive to adjust his buoyancy so that he was somewhat heavy, a normal condition where underwater photography is planned. He had borrowed a flashlight from Girault which consisted of a 9-volt C battery powering a 6-volt bulb...It had a new bulb and fresh battery when loaned to Limbaugh and underwater it was about a pound negatively buoyant. Just before the dive commenced, Clouzot reminded Limbaugh that if he became lost he should go to the top of the cave and follow the fresh water stream out.

The boat was anchored near the eastern entrance, the weather was clear and the sea calm. The plan was to enter the cave and proceed leisurely to the well, photographing where possible, surface, and then return to the outside. This was done quite commonly by cave divers such as Poudevigne, Clouzot, and Girault, and was considered a simple and easy maneuver and an easy training dive for amateurs when accompanied by an experienced companion familiar with the cave. Girault has taken his 15 year old daughter in as far as the well. Poudevigne regarded it as such a simple task and had heard so much of Limbaugh's capabilities that he did not consider it necessary to have contact maintained between the two by means of a short rope. Limbaugh and Poudevigne submerged at 1521 and made their way in at the east entrance. Limbaugh and Poudevigne returned outside and re-entered the cave so he could photograph

At about 1600, almost exactly one week after Limbaugh was last seen, Guitay caught the yellow reflection from the tanks still attached to the victim's body. The body was lying on one side on the floor of the main tunnel and was slightly hunched. It was oriented at an angle to the main axis of the tunnel and was almost exactly 100 meters (330 feet) from the well.

a silhouette view of the action. They continued inward, Limbaugh examined the fauna attached to the rock surfaces with considerable care. He seemed to be especially interested in the mussels and oysters in the upper parts of the cave. A direct swim without stopping from the east entrance to the well would require probably a maximum of 5 minutes, but Poudevigne estimated that they took about 15 minutes to reach the well. They surfaced and Limbaugh decided to photograph the upper part of the well, but was unable to keep the camera high enough out of the water to do so. He signaled for Poudevigne to help him, so the latter dove back down to the cone, placed his flashlight on the rocks and then resurfaced and held Limbaugh's flashlight and helped him by holding him up. After the pictures were taken, Poudevigne returned the flashlight and signaled with his hands for Limbaugh to wait while Poudevigne recovered his light. Limbaugh signaled "all right" so Poudevigne dove down, quickly retrieved his light and then returned to the surface. He was surprised to find no one there but assumed Limbaugh had misinterpreted his hand signals and tried to follow him down but had got separated in the murky water layer.

Poudevigne at once submerged to the base of the cone where the water was clearest and started swimming around the periphery, hunting for Limbaugh. He delayed breathing several times to see if he could hear the noise from Limbaugh's regulator, but to no avail. He completed the circuit twice and started running low on air so he turned on his reserve. He surfaced once more in the well, found nothing, so he left the cave by the east entrance and asked Clouzot if Limbaugh had appeared. Clouzot replied in the negative so Poudevigne re-entered the cave by the west passage, penetrated to the cone, but was so low on air he was forced to leave at once by the east tunnel. Meanwhile, alerted by Poudevigne's query, Clouzot had borrowed young Michel's rubber suit and equipment and had donned it and a set of tanks they had brought along as a safety reserve. When Poudevigne returned, he got their only flashlight from him and entered the cave by the east passage at around 1610. He found he was quite overweighted and too heavy. The water was not clear and he soon was unable to see any light from the entrance. He did not pick up any light from the well until he had actually arrived at the cone of stones. He surfaced and called "Limbaugh" three times, saw nothing, so he submerged and left by the west passage, searching for any traces of the lost diver.

When he returned to the boat, they got underway back to Port Miou where they informed Girault of the accident and then notified the police at Cassis, the closest town, some 2 or 3 miles away. They then returned by boat to the cave with their last set of tanks and Girault entered the cavern at dusk by himself. He penetrated by the east passage to the cone, but did not surface for fear of losing his bearings. By this time, firemen were shining lights down the well and cone so there was no point in Girault's checking the surface. Girault started exploring around the base of the cone but quickly decided it was too risky by himself in the dark so he left by the way he had come. It is noteworthy that Poudevigne, Clouzot, and Girault, who were as familiar with the cave as anyone, did not extend their searches beyond the cone without a safety line, presumably because they were aware of the risk of becoming lost themselves in the complexities of the main tunnel.

It is noteworthy that Poudevigne, Clouzot, and Girault, who were as familiar with the cave as anyone, did not extend their searches beyond the cone without a safety line, presumably because they were aware of the risk of becoming lost themselves in the complexities of the main tunnel.

The following four days, 18 dives of at least two men apiece were made by volunteers from the French Navy, OFRS, and Sogetram, searching for traces and clues and exploring the many unknown side tunnels and crevices. On Tuesday, March 22, three teams explored the main gallery back to about 450 feet from the well. In a sand patch about 280 feet from the well, two freshly appearing impressions were observed which were identified as caused by the tips of fins striking the bottom. In a mud patch at the limit of the survey (135 meters from the well) several freshly appearing fin prints were observed oriented randomly as if the swimmer was turning around, searching the different directions.

On Sunday, March 27, Puig again observed the prints at 230 feet, and was convinced that they had been freshly made, since sedimentation had changed their appearance noticeably. Most of the early effort, however, was concentrated on exploration of the maze of tunnels near the well, since all believed that Limbaugh could not have wandered too far with the small supply of air he must have had remaining.

The American investigating team was completely assembled by the evening of March 24. Our purpose was not to participate in the search but rather to observe and collect information and to offer suggestions. The search had been continuous and intensive and had yielded no traces other than the dubious fin prints. The divers from the different participating organizations were willing to continue but just about all the area near the well had been explored and operations further in were extremely hazardous. There seemed to be no logic in risking human lives unduly just to try to find a corpse. Nonetheless, it was considered remotely possible that Limbaugh might have found a hitherto undiscovered air pocket and still be alive far back in the cavern. It was agreed by all concerned that the French company of commercial diving, Sogetram, which had had extensive experience in such situations and had equipment which would make the operation less risky, would be employed to search further into the interior of the cave. The US Navy subsequently supported the Sogetram aspect of the search.

March 25, Drs. Menard and North investigated the cave by diving under the close supervision and assistance of French divers from the OFRS and GERS. Menard found that if left to his own devices at the well he would have made a 90° error in navigation; North was off by about 45° in the opposite direction. After the dive, Menard and North had lunch with Mssrs. Clouzot, Girault, and Poudevigne, to get a firsthand account of circumstances surrounding the accident. Frederic Dumas served as interpreter for the group.

March 26, Sogetram commenced operations. Puig and his crew chief, Francis Guitay, dove in the cave so that Puig could orient Guitay and familiarize him with conditions. They entered by the east passage and intended to explore a little way into the main tunnel. They apparently became confused in traversing the cone, however, because they were soon surprised to find they had made a 180° error and retraced their steps back out through the east passage. Up to this point visibility had been poor and a storm at sea kept the salt water layer stirred up.

March 27, however, found visibility conditions excellent in the main tunnel and Sogetram intensified their search efforts. In the morning Puig and an assistant combed the unexplored corridor and crevices on the west side of the main tunnel and observed the changed appearance of the fin prints in the mud patch 280 feet from the well.

In the afternoon, Guitay, assisted by Jean Havet, dove with the intention of penetrating to the maximum extent allowed by their hoses (250 meters). At about 1600, almost exactly one week after Limbaugh was last seen, Guitay caught the yellow reflection from the tanks still attached to the victim's body. The body was lying on one side on the floor of the main tunnel and was slightly hunched. It was oriented at an angle to the main axis of the tunnel and was almost exactly 100 meters (330 feet) from the well. Both divers saw the underwater camera nearby but did not notice any flashlight. The area was in a very large chamber where the tunnel had widened to approximately 60 feet. The body was lying to one side of the center of the tunnel. The mask was in place and the fins and weight belt were still on. The reserve mechanism on the tanks had been actuated. The breathing tubes were in the normal position and the mouthpiece was held loosely in the mouth, according to Havet, but subsequently freed itself.

The marine biologist now lies interred with plain fisherfolk of the Mediterranean, a fitting place for a scientist who devoted his life to studies of the sea.

The body was transported back to the cone with all equipment attached and the camera was left at the site of the discovery...North identified the body as being Conrad Limbaugh...The victim's underwater watch was still attached. The only evidence of damage was a 3-inch tear in the rubber shirt in the abdominal region...

A complete autopsy was performed on the body on March 29 ...No evidence of physical damage such as cuts, bruises, etc. were found. The watch was removed and had stopped at 5:56. The plastic crystal was severely scratched. ...Death was established as having occurred 8 to 10 days previously and the cause was asphyxiation. A little water was found in the lungs.

A brief final ceremony was held on March 30 at 1100 AM. According to the wishes of Mrs.Limbaugh, the body was interred in the Cassis cemetery. The marine biologist now lies interred with plain fisherfolk of the Mediterranean, a fitting place for a scientist who devoted his life to studies of the sea.

SCIENCE UNDERWATER

JIM STEWART

Among scientific and technical divers, Jim Stewart enjoys the status that Chuck Yeager has among professional pilots. Stewart didn't invent scientific diving in America; that distinction belongs to his predecessor, Conrad Limbaugh. But he organized it, standardized it, and spread that knowledge around the country and around the world. In the process, he made a lot of history and had a lot of fun.

In 1991 Stewart retired after a 30-year career as diving officer at Scripps Institution of Oceanography. His celebration was attended by an all-star lineup of colleagues, former students, and diving professionals whose lives have been influenced by this living legend.

STEWART HAS NEVER BEEN AT A LOSS FOR WORDS, and on that occasion he gave his valedictory address on the history of scientific diving in America. Because he was there from the beginning, and as often as not the center of attention, it is his story as well. From the first diving research expedition in the California Channel Islands to the first mapping of Scripps submarine canyon, from the first 600-foot bell saturation dive to the first dive on the shipwrecks of Truk Lagoon, Jim Stewart was there. He has logged numerous hours under Antarctic ice, and dived in an atomic crater at Enewitok three days after the H-bomb went off. He participated in the rescue of Hannes Keller on his ill-fated 1,000 foot dive, and survived a shark attack at Wake Island. He wrote the book on scientific diving, and worked to see it adopted virtually worldwide.

Jim's diving career began before there was scuba. On Memorial Day, 1941, the teen-aged beach kid first borrowed a friend's mask and put his head underwater. Growing up in San Diego, the ocean was a part of his natural environment, so free diving and spearfishing soon replaced swimming and surfing as Jimmy's primary aquatic interest. Diving in those days meant breath-hold spearfishing, and one's prowess was determined by the pounds of fish he shot. No one had fins then. "We just swam up to the fish and stuck it," he recalls. The weapon of choice was a simple wooden spear, often longer than the diver's body.

Coming out of the ocean at Scripps Pier, 1965.

In the final year of World War II, Stewart was drafted and served with the Army Air Corps in Nome, Alaska. Upon returning home, he was invited to join the Bottom Scratchers, the nation's first dive club An exclusive organization with membership by invitation only, the

Bottom Scratchers in their heyday numbered only 19. Eight are still alive, and Jimmy is the youngest. Initiation requirements included collecting three abalones in 30 feet of water on one breath, bringing in a 6-foot shark by the tail, and catching a 10-pound lobster. Scuba was not allowed.

In those days, most enthusiastic divers competed in spearfishing meets. It was at one of these that Stewart met Conrad Limbaugh, the first diving officer at Scripps. As a UCLA undergraduate in 1949, Limbaugh had seen the first Aqualungs at Rene Bussoz' Westwood sporting good store. Andy Rechnitzer recalls, "Connie

Jim with a white sea bass, La Jolla Cove, 1957.

convinced Boyd Walker (a UCLA professor) to buy regulators from Rene, along with a triple set of tanks and one single tank. In the summer of 1950 we brought the gear to Scripps. Connie and I were graduate students of Carl Hubbs, and he supported the concept.

"Connie and I were the (Scripps) diving program. We explored up and down the coast out of his green Kaiser (automobile). Connie was so enthusiastic that he invited anyone and everyone to join him and try it out. That's how Jim got started." Stewart never took a certification course, learning on the job as did most of the early divers.

As more Scripps students expressed the desire and need for scuba training, Limbaugh developed a diving course. He recruited Stewart as a volunteer in the program, to assist in kelp research and diver training. Although this program was geared exclusively to science, it soon spread to the sport diving community as well. In 1953, Los Angeles County sent Bev Morgan, Al Tillman, and Ramsey Parks to Scripps for training. These three started the the Los Angeles County program.

Stewart earned a degree in botany from Pomona college and obtained a job as a surveyor. His volunteer work at Scripps was upgraded to a part-time job assisting Limbaugh and Wheeler North on their kelp study. Adapting topside surveying techniques, the research team performed the first underwater transects, a method that is now a cornerstone of underwater science.

Among Stewart's duties was fish collecting, both for research and for display at Scripps Aquarium. A major problem at the time was keeping deep water fish alive, due to pressure changes rupturing their swim bladder. Stewart helped develop the technique of removing gas underwater with a hypodermic needle, which is still used today.

His first foreign trip came in 1955, to Enewitok and Bikini, the sites of atomic and hydrogen bomb tests. His assignment was to study effects of the bombs on marine algae. Stewart recalls, "We were diving in those craters three days after the bombs went off. Our radiation protection consisted of a pair of Speedos."

We were diving in those craters three days after the bombs went off. Our radiation protection consisted of a pair of Speedos.

Since then Jim has been diving in most of the world's oceans, including the Arctic and Antarctic. In 1967 he was aboard a research ship that had anchored in Truk Lagoon to hide from a typhoon. An exploratory dive put them on the deck of a Japanese freighter with three zeroes aboard. Subsequent dives revealed three more sunken ships. When word of the finds got out, Truk became the prime destination for sport divers interested in World War II shipwrecks.

Another discovery occurred closer to home, at the tip of Baja California. Stewart, Limbaugh, and North were at Cabo San Lucas in 1959, studying cleaning symbiosis. A storm interrupted their diving, and when it passed it had cut about 30 inches of sand from Lover's Beach. 110 feet below the surface, sand flowed over the rocks like a submerged waterfall, tumbling into the depths. They had discovered the underwater sandfall of Cabo San Lucas, a rare undersea phenomenon. Together they produced the film "**Rivers of Sand**", an award winner at international festivals.

A year later, Limbaugh died while diving in a cave in France. Stewart was named to succeed him as diving officer at Scripps. By this time he was working full time at Scripps, and had participated in some of the pioneer efforts of diving science during the 50s. These included the first diving research cruise in the Channel Islands, aboard the 100-foot vessel Orca. It was on this trip that he and Andy Rechnitzer first recorded the sounds of humpback whales. Jim recalls, "Coming down the slot between San Clemente and Catalina Islands one very dark night, we stopped, threw a hydrophone in the water, and heard these strange sounds. What the hell is that? Now of course we know."

From 1952 to 1960 all diving for the University of California was centered at Scripps, but eventually other campuses started programs as well. The University president's office asked Stewart to develop statewide guidelines governing them. He wrote the first

Teaching Bureau of Reclamation divers, Santa Barbara, 1969.

university diving safety manual (based on Limbaugh's writings), which included rules on training, dive procedures, maintenance, and record keeping. Published in 1966, these rules struck a delicate balance between strong safety standards and enabling scientists to do their jobs. According to Scripps biologist Paul Dayton, "...(at other institutions) the bureaucrats got scared about liability, and hired ex military people to run dive programs. (They were) elitist, macho types. Many scientists couldn't qualify. So they got Jim to come to their institutions in the late 60s to explain the Scripps program... Everywhere I've been I've seen the effects of Jim Stewart selling diving as a scientific tool...Many of us owe our careers to him."

Stewart says, "I inherited a program. In his 1953 letter, Roger Revelle (a distinguished marine scientist and director of Scripps at the time) wrote (UC) president Sproull that scuba should be accepted as a legitimate means of conducting research. I just brought it out of the dark ages. Lots of Revelle's words are still in our regulations...The people that started scuba were water people. We trained the rest.."

As colleges and consulting firms around the country became involved in scientific diving, they too adopted the Scripps guidelines. Today, they form the basis of the American Academy of Underwater Sciences (AAUS) diving manual, the "bible" for the scientific diving community. Stewart was a founder of AAUS, an organization originally formed to combat OSHA's regulation of scientific diving. The ten year effort was successful, and today AAUS is the voice of scientific diving.

The battle began when Stewart and Glen Egstrom appeared before the Department of Labor in Washington to tell them they weren't needed. "But the following year," Jim stated, "there was a new wording: 'employer-employee relationship.' That got us. It took ten years and about a hundred meetings to get out. At one point, OSHA gave us a $5000 grant to come to Washington and tell them how good we were. We collected statistics on 3/4 of a million scientific dives, and our hit rate was .0037. They asked, 'Why are you here?' and we asked the same question.

"The day we got our exemption, the Carpenters and Joiners Union filed an injuction with Fed OSHA, and it took us another 3 years to fine tune it. This program became the guideline for how to do business in scientific diving, so chalk one up for Scripps."

Stewart's training philosophy is to stress personal skills and self-reliance rather than dependence on equipment. For many years, his Scripps students weren't allowed to use BC's until they completed their research diving course. This finally changed when auto-inflating BC's became required by the training agencies. Yet unlike the dinosaur fringe of scientific diving veterans, Jim is open to new ideas. Scripps divers use the full gamut of equipment, from ADV's to back inflation units. When diving computers came along, his only stipulation was that every member of the team should be supplied with one.

In addition to university divers, Stewart has trained National Park Service rangers, California Fish & Game, State Parks and Recreation, Water resources and Cal Trans personnel. He also has developed safety standards for diving submersibles.

Stewart's own diving experiences are rich and varied. One of the best known and most often told is the 1961 shark attack at Wake Island. Stewart was diving with Ron Church, taking out tsunami recorders in waters he describes as "...like being in the shark tank at Sea World." At three feet in a surge channel, one of the sharks moved toward him. It wasn't a really big one, so "...I dived head first at him, he turned and went toward Ron. Ron dived at him also. He started to do an 'S' with his body, went into a mouthing action, and humped his back. This is indicative of an animal with something on his mind." As the two divers inched together the shark became more and more agitated, biting the water, lowering its pectoral fins, and shaking its head. Suddenly it darted straight for Jim's left shoulder, spun 90 degrees, and veered toward his mask. As he instinctively raised his elbow to protect his face the shark hit twice, ripping open the joint capsule and slashing two arteries.

> "Everywhere I've been I've seen the effects of Jim Stewart selling diving as a scientific tool... Many of us owe our careers to him."
> —Paul Dayton

At first, there was no pain, just the shock as blood began spurting from the elbow. Jim grabbed the brachial artery pressure point to stop the bleeding. Church helped him over the reef, and the shark departed as quickly as it had struck.

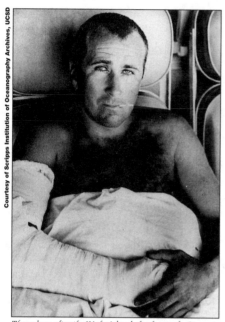

Courtesy of Scripps Institution of Oceanography Archives, UCSD

Three days after the Wake Island shark attack, Stewart rests at Trippler General Hospital, Honolulu Hawaii, March, 1961.

His written report of the incident concluded, "The shark swam away as though he had expected tuna and was was disappointed. I asked myself why he left and came to the conclusion that it was a combination of four reasons. 1, Ron swam to me immediately. 2, The shark met an unaccustomed resistance in the bone of my arm. 3, He had never tasted a man and the unfamiliar taste caused him to leave. 4, I hadn't had a recent shower."

There was no doctor on the island, so a nurse had to tie off the arteries. Stewart was eventually flown back to Hawaii for surgical repair. Today his elbow is a mass of scar tissue, and the takeoff point for another diving story.

During the 60s divers continued to extend the limits of depth. Stewart was an active participant in some of these experiments, sometimes as a support diver and sometimes as the man on the spot.

Hannes Keller was a Swiss mathematician who had some revolutionary ideas about deep diving. Keller claimed that his secret gas mixtures prevented narcosis and drastically shortened decompression times. In the late 50s he had gone to 800 feet in pressure chambers. The Office of Naval Research (ONR) contracted him to make four demonstration dives in the United States. But before he could climax the series with a 1,000 foot dive, the grant ran out. **Skin Diver** Magazine picked up the tab, and things were set to go on December 3, 1962, off Catalina Island.

Keller and British journalist Peter Small descended in a diving bell, supplied with large storage tanks which would allow adjustment of the breathing mixture as depth increased. Keller was to leave the bell at 1,000 feet to place Swiss and American flags on the bottom, while Small waited inside. Their semiclosed circuit full face mask equipment was good for 15 minutes at that depth. But an undetected leak in the deep mix cut it short. While attempting to untangle his communication line, Keller felt the first symptoms of blackout. He returned to the bell and began to initiate emergency procedures. The plan was to close the hatch, drop their masks, and fill the bell with compressed air. Although they would both pass out, they would remain alive until the bell could be winched up to shallower depths, where decompression could begin. Keller tore off his mask but Small lost consciousness before he could do the same. Consequently he was rebreathing inert gas, with no oxygen.

When the bell was winched up to 210 feet, safety divers Dick Anderson and Jim Whittaker noticed the hatch was still open, and a fin sticking out. Decompression would be impossible without the hatch being sealed. Using Whittaker's knife, Anderson shoved the fin back inside and slammed the hatch. He then signaled Whittaker to ascend and have the bell winched upward. When nothing happened, Anderson surfaced to find out why. Whittaker had disappeared.

Stewart, observing the proceedings from another boat, was asked to go down and see what he could do. "When we got the call, Dale Well and I were suited up and in the water in eight minutes. We met the bell at 175 feet and I had to cut a motor block off (which was) used as a balancing weight on that thing. We got sucked up in a boil of water that came up with it...at about 400 feet a minute...With a set of twin 70s, just a shirt and no lead, I came out of the water up to my waist. My face mask was pulled down over my nose...and Well's watch was yanked right off his wrist. That kind of violates the ascent rate."

By the time the bell surfaced, the problem had become a double tragedy. Small was dead. Whittaker's body was never found. Keller recovered completely, but never attempted another deep dive.

Five years later, Stewart was the man in the diving bell. This was Westinghouse's "Project 600", an attempt to extend the bell saturation record to a depth of 600 feet. Stewart and Rick Chesher were housed in a chamber, pressurized to a depth of 350 feet, and mounted on the deck of a barge anchored in the Gulf of Mexico. Breathing a 95-5 Heliox mixture, they made a one-hour excursion at 600 feet. Their water-heated suits were useless, because by the time the water was pumped to that depth its temperature had dropped to ambient. During the 62 1/2 hours of decompression, temperature within the cham-

The shark swam away as though he had expected tuna and was was disappointed. I asked myself why he left and came to the conclusion that it was a combination of four reasons. 1) Ron swam to me immediately. 2) The shark met an unaccustomed resistance in the bone of my arm. 3) He had never tasted a man and the unfamiliar taste caused him to leave. 4) I hadn't had a recent shower.

ber was maintained at 93°. Owing to excessive heat loss while breathing a helium mixture, this is equivalent to only 70° in air. At one point, it dropped to 85° and they almost froze. Stewart wryly recalls some additional problems of that experiment. Food had to be passed through an airlock into the inner chamber. Styrofoam cups were being used. "By the time it was pressurized, we had a very small cup surrounded by a lot of coffee."

Stewart at McMurdo Station, Antartica, September, 1974.

Stewart was an aquanaut in the first cold-water undersea habitat. "In 1963 when we lost the submarine *Thresher*, everybody suddenly discovered we had an ocean. There were people at 1,000 feet and we couldn't have got them out; our maximum depth for recovery was 800 feet. So *Sealab* I went in at 198 feet off...Bermuda. *Sealab* II, as well as all the Cousteau houses, had been in nice clear, warm water. They then looked around for the scroungiest place in the world to put the next one. This was in the canyon off La Jolla. I coordinated a good portion of the diver-related activities and made several dives to the habitat at 205 feet."

Since 1967 Jim has been responsible for all US Antarctic diving, training, and evaluation. Many of his most memorable dives have been under Antarctic ice. He still returns every year or two for research projects. The water there is a constant 28.5 degrees F, just above the freezing point of salt water. Under ideal conditions, this is the clearest water in the world. "The human eye will see about 800 feet in distilled water. It's so clear that a light beam can't be seen, because there are no particles in the water to backscatter.... You feel like you are going to fall to the bottom, there's nothing there...It's too pretty to be real."

Dives have been made there with air temperatures as cold as 65° below zero. Although most divers use dry suits with several layers of underwear, Stewart wears a modified wet suit under the ice. With hood, boots, and cuffs built in, he can last 25 minutes. "People can't believe that I do that, but my hands have never lasted long enough to get my body cold." They were frostbitten in Alaska some years ago.

"Noon in the Antarctic looks like sunset," he remarked. "That's as high as the sun ever gets. That's got something to say about my career as well."

This is uncharacteristic false modesty. Respected as a legend and a major voice in the scientific diving community, Jim Stewart's name may not be a household word to the current generation of sport divers. Recognition, however has come from his peers, as he has received many of the most prestigious awards in the field. Among the more recent are: Undersea Medical Society's Craig Hoffman Award for diver training techniques and safety (1986), NAUI's Greenstone Award for worldwide contributions to diving safety (1986), Southern European Research Diving Academy's Golden Trident Award for lifelong international contributions to research diving and safety (1987), and DEMA Hall of Fame Award (1990). On his retirement from Scripps he was named Diving Officer Emeritus, a distinction that is rarely conferred on non-academic personnel.

Retirement from Scripps doesn't mean the end of Stewart's diving career. He will continue to consult with sport and scientific agencies, train scientific divers for the government agencies, and his Antarctic work will continue as well. But now he will have more time to go camping, hunting, and climbing in the high country of Idaho.

Salty, sardonic, and understated are words that best describe Jim's sense of humor. Sit down with him over a beer, and you will be treated to diving history, told vividly by someone who made it and lived it. But his greatest legacy is his students, and the students of those he has trained. No one else has influenced more diving leaders, directly and indirectly, both in the world of scientific and of sport diving.

CHUCK MITCHELL

When he was in high school, Chuck Mitchell lived a young diver's dream. Hired as a part-time technician at Scripps Institution of Oceanography in the early days of their diving program, he worked with diving legends like Conrad Limbaugh, Wheeler North, and Jim Stewart. Through college and graduate school, Scripps projects took him around the Pacific, from Baja Caifornia to Canton Island. With that background, it was inevitable that Chuck would go on to become a marine biologist. Today he is the president of MBC Applied Environmental Sciences, and was one of the founders of AAUS.

When 15 year old Chuck Mitchell heard about the job at Scripps Institution of Oceanography, it seemed like a nice way to spend the summer of 1955. They were advertising for a part-time technician, at least 16 years old. Chuck was a year too young, and had just graduated junior high. But he kept badgering them, stressing his experience in and around the water, and finally got hired. That part-time job set the course for the rest of his life.

"I was an avid skin diver and spearfisherman for many years. Jack Prodanovich was the custodian at my high school, Point Loma High. He had had already lost his eye in an accident with a speargun. I talked to him about diving quite frequently. He was like a mentor, but I held him in awe from a distance. Wally Potts was our milkman. I was a member of a skin diving club, and he would occasionally let us use his patterns to make spearguns at his garage workshop."

Hired on an NSF (National Science Foundation) grant, Chuck was assigned to the biochemistry department. Wheeler North was part of that group; Ray Ghelardi's office was just down the hall. Chuck took the Scripps diving course with Andy Rechnitzer as head instructor, and was awarded card number 103. "I was the kid, and was subjected to a lot of testing and scrutiny. That's something lacking in diving today. I remember making whole dives with no faceplate, my air being turned off constantly. For a 100 foot card, you had to go to 160

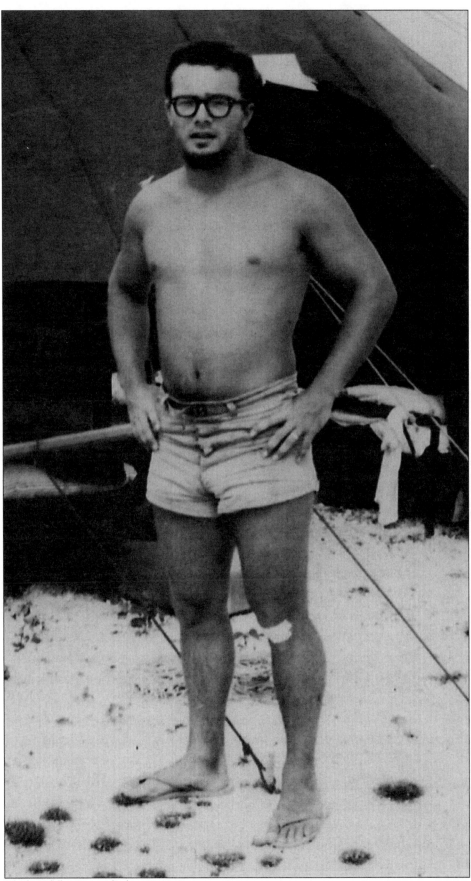

Chuck Mitchell at Canton Island age 20, 1960.

feet on air in a chamber, and 60 feet on pure oxygen. If you convulsed, you failed. The test was done on the *Nereis*, a submarine repair ship anchored in San Diego Bay. I went with two women that day, Nan Limbaugh and Marge Reidell, both excellent divers. They

were the first two women who had ever been in there. That old Navy chief who was with us did nothing but grouse about women in his chamber. He did everything he could to stress them out. We made the descent to 160 feet in less than a minute, temperature was about 105.

Chuck Mitchell and Scott Smith spearfishing at La Jolla, 1956.

"Those were great days. Every place we went diving was new. I thought scuba was great because now you could stay down. You weren't just stringing a bunch of snapshots of one minute dives together."

Diving in those days was cold, with only a navy watch sweater, belted around the waist, to keep the cold water from circulating. When Bill Batzloff was hired to manage the Scripps diving locker, he brought his expertise in making wet suits. Soon all the research divers had them.

At the end of the summer, a project was funded to study kelp forests along the west coast. This meant Mitchell could stay on, working weekends, after school, and vacations. Key scientists on the kelp project were North, Ghelardi , Connie Limbaugh, Jim Stewart, and Pat Cunnison.

One of the legendary Scripps researchers, Carl Hubbs, accompanied the group on some of their kelp forest surveys below the border. On one occasion in 1957, they were camping on a beach and unearthed an Indian burial ground. "That shot the week because Carl took over the expedition and we excavated that site. One team worked on digging, the rest of the party was designated as midden sorters. Carl began digging down by strata; we would identify shell fragments and species. He was throwing dirt out of hole over his head. The only thing that stopped him was hitting bedrock.

"Hubbs was a diver, but not really active. He spent a lot of time paddling around... doing big tidepool poisons and collecting lots of fish, wading with his faceplate. Carl was one of the original workaholics, he would run you right into the ground. (We) were expected to do whatever was necessary, just like he would. He used to drive an old green Jeepster, (on) the roads of Baja at 90 miles an hour...You never knew when he was going to slam on his brakes because he saw a lizard. I can remember him dashing across the desert and diving in the dust because he had seen a snake he wanted to capture. His wife, Laura, was the recorder, like a lieutenant. She would have her notebook out already, it was a running commentary. "

Pain and agony! I fell in the water semi-conscious and really made an impression on the Mexicans.

"I was always in small boats as a kid, a good boat handler, so I frequently got loaned out as a boatman for people on trips. Per Scholander (a renowned physiologist) took a trip just below Ensenada when he first came to Scripps . I was the oarsman and the surf entry person. It was god awful. I kept thinking I was probably gonna die, they had no conception on what it took to get a small boat with people in it through the surf with no motor, just oars."

"In the summer of 1957 we took the Orca, a 113 foot boat, and surveyed all the kelp beds in Baja. We dove in every rocky headland, every kelp bed, and did transect lines. We dove San Geronimo Island, Sacramento Reef, San Benitos Island, Cedros, Punta Eugenia, and Bahia Tortugas..Turtle Bay was a shock. I expected a place with white sand beaches and swaying palm trees, not this thing that looks like a lunar landscape. In those days at Punta Eugenia, there was a substantial abalone fishery with hardhat divers.

"Two incidents come to mind. We had been diving next to some Mexicans in heavy 28-foot wooden skiffs. They rowed them everywhere and used hand-cranked compressors. We were trying to impress them with our mobility and ease. I was the last one out of the skiff, got my knee up on the gunwale, slipped, and landed right on my crotch. Pain and agony! I fell in the water semi-conscious and really made an impression on the Mexicans.

"Two days later we stretched a transect line on the bottom to count plants one and a half meters on either side of the line. After laying the line, we came back to the boat to get fresh tanks. Some of the beds were so thick and dark it was hard to read your slate. A Mexican hardhat diver found our transect line and was using it as a convenient track to go down. He carried a short machete and was chopping down kelp plants along our line. We were chasing him and at the same time counting plants as they were drifting up, so we wouldn't have to run the transect line all over again.

"The (southernmost) scraggly plant we found was at the mouth of Magdalena Bay. But the last of the real kelp beds was Ascuncion, near San Ignacio Lagoon. Then we dove the canyon in Cabo San Lucas just for fun, going to La Paz to lay over and refuel."

A year later, Limbaugh found the Cabo San Lucas sandfalls by accident. "They were down there on a boondoggle of some kind, camping on the beach and sleeping on cots. The waves from the Pacific side came in overnight and inundated the camp. A lot of stuff got washed away. They recovered most of the dive gear, but lost things like canned goods. So the next few days were spent trying to recover those supplies. It was Connie who noticed that some of the stuff got washed over on the lee side. There were some canned goods half buried in the sand, and they were moving. Suddenly he realized the sand was moving, chugging away." When they followed the sand with scuba gear, they found it spilling over the rocky face at 110 feet. A year later, Limbaugh, Stewart, and North returned to shoot their award winning film about the phenomenon, **Rivers of Sand.**

When the tanker *Tampico* ran aground south of Ensenada in the late 50s, North began a long-term study of the effects of the massive diesel spill. "Actually, it's not done yet. A few months ago, NOAA wanted the data. Wheeler still has the data and has never published it. There's at least 12 or 15 years of annual surveys.

"We used to load everything in three- ton stakebed trucks, fill the back with 50-60 tanks and food, and drive on down the road. Nobody had four-wheel drives. We would drive into all these god-awful areas and spend the week diving. Jim Stewart, Pat Cunnison, Earl Murray, Ray Ghelardi ...a whole bunch of people contributed their time just to dive."

After high school graduation, Mitchell enrolled at San Diego State as a zoology major. Continuing to work part-time at Scripps, he was hired in the summer of 1960 by physical oceanographer Bill Van Dorn, to help install tsunami wave recording stations in the central Pacific. "Just before we got there, the big tsunami hit Hilo and just about wiped out the town. All the cars, buildings, and warehouses were washed off with it. People were very receptive to us."

Chuck's task was to install connections and instrument cables at 140 to 160 feet. The next stop after Hawaii was Canton Island in the Phoenix Group. Its main claim to fame was that Amelia Earhart is supposed to have crashed there. At the time it was under joint US and British protectorship, and a tracking station for the space program was under construction. Workers were imported from surrounding islands: Tonga, Samoa, and the Gilberts. One of Mitchell's jobs was to drive to the Gilbertese village every day and pick up three laborers for the tsunami project. Unclear on how much to pay them, he asked the British commissioner. He suggested $1.80. "So we paid them that per hour. A couple of weeks later the commissioner came to our tent in a bit of a huff. We had turned the island's economy upside down. It was supposed to be $1.80 a day. We had to reduce their pay to the prevailing level.

It startled everybody; the shark would instantly shoot away 60 feet, then immediately came back closer to see what it was.

"It was a great introduction to the South Pacific. Everybody free dived, so there was always informal competition. They didn't have goggles. Even with my corrective lenses in, they loved using my faceplate. I had my wife send three of them, and they went crazy over that."

After living in a tent on Canton for six weeks, the group moved on to Johnston Island. It was a hell hole in 1960; recovering from a lot of bomb testing. Barracks buildings were everywhere on the barren island, along with bunkers that stored gas and explosives from World War II. "But the diving was incredible. There was tiered table coral, humongous reefs with heads 20 feet in diameter. I was 20 years old, and divemaster for this group of six, making fish collections for Scripps. I was also the shark watcher. It would get bizarre, watching a dozen sharks circling at one time.

"Jim Froman made a shark repellent device out of a fire extinguisher handle with a venturi and a short wand. Acetic acid was the active ingredient (but) it didn't work...If the shark came too close, you would give it a hit with this wand, there would be a big blast of bubbles. It startled everybody; the shark would instantly shoot away 60 feet, then immediately came back closer to see what it was. I used it for a about a week, then reverted to just poking them with it when they came too close. They were there all the time but we never had a problem..

"Another device he invented released cyanide into the shark. I wouldn't let him bring it on the boat, because cyanide can be absorbed through the skin. I've had sharks come in real close, had them bite fins and things I was working with, but I've never been aggressively attacked.

"The next station we were going to install was Wake Island. I had to go back to school, so Jim Stewart came out to take my place. That's where he got his arm chewed." (See Stewart story pp 118-127.)

In 1961 the kelp program came to an end, and Chuck took a position with the Bureau of Commercial Fisheries. They were studying tuna behavior, going up and down the coast of Baja on fishing boats and diving in the nets while the tuna were being caught. "Sharks associate with tuna schools. They get hung in the nets, and eat a lot of that tuna. One of the most unnerving things is to jump into the water with lots of big ones, like 13 foot tiger sharks. You knew they were there, but might not see them for the rest of the dive because of all these tuna."

Another failed experiment utilized underwater speakers broadcasting white noise, which sounds like frying bacon. In the Revillagijados Islands, the sharks ate the speakers.

They also collected sharks, trying to come up with a repellent that would work for the tuna fishing industry. Mitchell shot a lot of underwater movie footage of the sharks reacting to various chemicals. One was nigrosine dye, which had been used in World War II to "protect" downed flyers. The sharks would eat the bricks of dye. "I've got a lot of great footage of sharks swimming off with black smoke coming out of the gill slits. I think the dye was used so the people couldn't see the sharks." Another failed experiment utilized underwater speakers broadcasting white noise, which sounds like frying bacon. In the Revillaggeados Islands, the sharks ate the speakers. Seal control bombs, resembling M-80 fircrackers, were also used. But nothing worked.

Another project involved camouflage nets for the tuna industry. The idea was to develop a net that was harder for the fishes to see. This involved blue water diving, at depths of 150 feet with no surface tether and no BCs. Because of the dangers of losing depth orientation, and because of sharks, they made a shark cage.

"One day there were three of us in the cage. We decided to take underwater pictures of different pieces of equipment working. First we shot a plankton net. Then we decided to try a bathythermograph, a torpedo-shaped thing that records depth and temperature. The tow boat passes overhead. One guy was in the cage, I was sitting on top of the cage, waiting for this thing to come by. All of a sudden there is a strange whirring noise, we can't tell what it is. Suddenly my faceplate gets ripped off. The boat has put out way too much cable, it is caught on the shark cage and the boat is going 10 knots. I look down into the blue abyss and here is this "torpedo" coming right at us. It hits the bottom of the cage, sticks in the chain-link fence material, and we are heading right up. One person is still inside, plastered against the wall. Luckily we went only about 15 feet; the thing broke loose and went between us. It must be the same sensation that combat pilots get when they see a surface-to-air missile coming up from below."

Mitchell countinued working for the Bureau of Fisheries through graduate school. In 1966, he left to become a biologist for the California Department of Fish and Game. With Chuck Turner and Ron Strachan he was assigned to a project studying the biology, ecology, and behavior of coastal marine sportfishes.

Mitchell and Turner shared a common interest in underwater photography. Shooting with a Rolleimarine, Turner shot fish portraits and behaviors in the 50s and 60s that still look good today. He also did some of the first surveys of marine outfalls and harbor construction. Unfortunately he died before his time, of septicemia in 1968.

It must be the same sensation that combat pilots get when they see a surface-to-air missile coming up from below.

Mitchell had a large stockpile of movie footage he had shot during the previous years, using a Bell and Howell in a Sampson-Hall housing. Some of it was used in an early television documentary series, *Encyclopedia of the Sea*, produced by Bruno Velardi. Mitchell describes himself as a frustrated artist, and recalls hours spent in darkrooms with Ron Church, a friend since high school days. "Ron was a pro photographer for Convair (and) would show us all the pictures he had taken of rockets taking off. The diving stuff was just a hobby."

In 1969 Chuck left Fish and Game to rejoin Wheeler North at the California Institute of Technology, researching methods to restore kelp beds. While there, he started his own company, Marine Biological Consultants (now MBC Applied Environmental Sciences). North was a minority partner. "I needed three people to set up a corporation, and asked him to be vice president. He wanted to invest in the company, but I had $1,000 and didn't need any money. In the end, he put in $100, I put in $900. That was all the capitalization; everything else was generated out of retained earnings. Wheeler still owns 10%. He put in a hundred bucks (and got) a good return on the investment."

Chuck was instrumental in the formation of AAUS, the American Academy of Underwater Sciences (see Lee Somers story pp 246-253). It began in 1977, when federal OSHA came out with emergency guidelines for commercial diving. The requirements included such things as a chamber at every dive site, which would have wiped out research diving at universities. Diving officers at California schools formed an organization to voice their concern. "Dick Bell, Lloyd Austin, Jim Stewart, Glenn Egstrom, Bob Given were the prime movers. I wanted to make sure the consulting companies were included under the umbrella. We went back to Washington to testify, and the Department of Labor told us this was just a draft. We believed them, but DC is a treacherous place. When the final regulation came out, the scientific diver was still included. Then we had to backtrack to California OSHA. We raised so much hell with them, they let us write the California regulation for scientific diving. It was a long hard process, (that) took us a year and a half. Cal OSHA said these are wonderful, we love them. Then somebody up there proceeded to take the commercial regulations and decided to make those a subset of our regs. They took two stacks of written material, shuffled them into one stack, and it came out awful. We were were placed in the position of having to testify in public hearings against the very regs we had written.

> Graduate students today are struggling with the same problems underwater. We look back and say, 'It didn't work in '55 and it ain't gonna work now.'

"There had now been a change of administration in Washington, and they realized they had screwed up. The head of federal OSHA talked directly to the head of Cal OSHA and said, 'Don't implement these regulations because we are trying to get research divers out.' After eight years, the situation was finally resolved. AAUS had proved to the government that the safety record of scientific diving community was excellent through self-regulation. "I think the primary reason our accident rate was so low is that the original people were water wise, and gave us a core of experience. Graduate students today are struggling with the same problems underwater. We look back and say, 'It didn't work in '55 and it ain't gonna work now.' "

Mitchell served two terms as AAUS president, and for many years subsidized the organization's secretarial and mailing services through MBC's offices. Those functions have recently been taken over by the Smithsonian Institution.

Mitchell continues to be an active diver and boat skipper, and is working on a private pilot's license. MBC is involved a number of projects dealing with the marine environment. Among the most significant are kelp restoration from Orange County to Santa Barbara for Fish and Game, an eco-system model of northern Pacific fisheries to look at the impact of gillnets for NOAA, and a five-year monitoring program on the impacts of generating stations' sea-water intakes on larval and juvenile fishes.

Looking back on his career, Chuck says, "Before the job at Scripps, I'm not sure I even knew marine biology existed. I stumbled on an occupation that would allow me to do all the things I thought were fun, every single day."

SECTION 4

WOMEN UNDERWATER

DOTTIE FRAZIER

Nobody could have been more qualified to be America's first certified woman diving instructor than Dottie Frazier. By the time she took the course, she had been a free diver nearly twenty years, a swimming instructor, a commercial fisherman, and a commercial diver. She overcame prejudice to train more than 2,000 divers and run one of the nation's first wet suit factories. Today an active 72, this tiny, feisty lady is still an inspiration for those who follow the path she blazed.

DOTTIE FRAZIER GREW UP AROUND THE WATER. When she was a year and a half old her parents divorced, and she went to live with her father aboard his sloop in Long Beach Harbor. "My first dive was when dad dropped the coffee pot over the side. He handed me a weight and said, 'Go get it.' It was in 15 feet of water, I was 8 or 10 years old."

Her father was head of the harbor commission and the realtors board, president of the chamber of commerce, and of the Port of Los Angeles. "He made our first mask out of fire hose; it just killed your face. Dad put a piece of home made glass in it, gooped around a sealer, and put a strap on it. He had never seen another mask, just got the idea from a glass bottom box. He (also) dreamed up this piece of garden hose that we used as a snorkel. When the first Churchill fins came out, I scoffed at them. Who needs them? (But) we both turned to the use of them.

"For years we used a glass-bottom box to get abalone from the back of the boat, with a long 20-foot sectional spear. I was on the oars and dad would spear them. The only ones you could get were on the sides of the rocks, so you could get your spear in, twist it, and get them off."

At the age of ten, a broken back almost ended Dottie's diving career before it began. She was competing in the finals of the Junior Olympics in the high dive. "I was in the middle of a swan dive and

Dottie in Bel Aqua dry suit, 1954.

some guy on the platform above hit me feet first (and) broke me in half. I was in a cast for 18 months and they told me I'd never walk again." But she recovered, eventually becoming an instructor at the Long Beach Bathhouse, a famous indoor pool. She won championships for seven straight years as a competitive swimmer, became a Red Cross Water Safety Instructor, and served many years on the Long Beach Chapter's Water Safety Committee. So even without diving, Dottie's aquatics credentials were firmly established.

Dottie and 12½ pound lobster at Salt Creek, February, 1954.

FREE DIVING

"We started (free) diving for lobsters when I was 13 or 14. (They) were very abundant, but if you just used your hands...you had to be fast. You had to wiggle your fingers to keep them busy at one side while the other one came in from the side and made a grab. I got more than my share. My biggest bug was 20 pounds...I only weighed about 89 pounds then. He almost pulled me over backwards and ripped my dry suit. I've caught numerous big bulls...(but) wish we'd left them, then there would probably be more lobsters. We never took our full limit because we were living on the boat. We had what we called our food aquarium over the side...(kept) lobsters and abs in there. If it became rough or dirty, we just reached over the side and decided what we wanted for dinner."

Free diving was a popular activity along the California coast even before World War II. Dottie recalled the Diving Derbies, a series of contests running from San Diego to Santa Barbara, with prizes for the the largest fish, abalone, ray, and shark. This was when she started meeting other divers. They included Jack Ward, Lee Jamieson, Dr. Nelson Mathieson, and Herb Sampson, later members of the Long Beach Neptunes. Dottie was a charter member, the only one still living.

By the late 40s equipment had improved. Dottie was using Duck Feet fins and a real snorkel, the Bel Aqua. "We were still diving with a wool sweater and socks...all winter long....I could stay as long as anybody, a half hour to an hour. Then everybody would come in and build a fire on the beach.

"When Bel Aqua called and asked me to model the first dry suit, I started using it (but) didn't particularly like it. It would get a hole and fill up with water. When wet suits came out, it was great.

"I started teaching skin diving in the YMCAs in San Pedro and Long Beach, and at the Balboa skin diving shop (later Hoskins Water Sports in Newport Beach). We specified good swimming, floating, treading...and a good ocean checkout. My kids were born in '40 and '41; they would go to a lot of the classes with me. No other women were teaching in those days."

Dottie and husband Jake with family in 1954 after an hour's diving at the foot of Orizaba.

Dottie's father put her through a secretarial college, but she hated office work. After three months on the job, she quit to become a commercial fisherman. "A friend was leaving on a cruise; his deckhand had an appendix burst. So he called me. I was between jobs, got a housekeeper for my kids, and did it. I was gone for three or four months at a stretch. We got Mexican clearance, fished, and brought our catch back to San Diego. During the early part of the war, Castanola and Van de Camp and Chicken of the Sea had barges all around Catalina. We'd take our stuff in there and I could come home more often, a three or four day job.

"I bought this house in 1943 and paid it off in (four years) just from my fishing. We had a crew of three...the old skipper, Red the deckhand, both retired Navy. So I was a deckhand, cook, and stood watch in the crow's nest and at the wheel. They did the harpooning, I cut up the sharks. ...Before they had synthetic oils, we had to harpoon sharks, cut out the liver, can them, and take them in. When the broadbill, longfin, or albacore came out, we worked them. It was very lucrative, one just moved right into the other. I did that eight or ten years. Every time we'd get near an island, I'd go over the side and get dinner."

Widowed in the war, Dottie raised four boys. She continued to free dive, but like a lot of her contemporaries, considered scuba to be sissy equipment that allowed a lot of unqualified people to enter a territory that had been exlusively theirs.

Integrating the Instructor Ranks

Jim Christensen, a good friend from the Diving Derby days, came over one day in 1955 and asked, "Dotty, why don't you get into this

new scuba instructor class that's starting?" She protested that she didn't know anything about scuba. Jim said, "I'll teach you." Dottie still has the letter from Al Tillman that reads, "We received your application for UICC, but I think you want a regular course. We will refer

Dottie as instructor to all male students, whom she called "her boys" in 1959.

you to the YMCA. If there is a mistake we will be glad to accept you."

"They returned my application. At this time I'd never been scuba diving in my life. I'd never have gone into it if Jim hadn't insisted. Who needed it? I could free dive 50 to 60 feet. Jim said, 'You're going.' "

There was quite a bit of antagonism at the time against a woman instructor. Dottie credits Christensen with getting her through the course. "I learned how to scuba dive in 4 UICC. Jim towed me through everything. When I didn't want to go any more, he'd say, 'You're gonna go, you're gonna do it.' It was militaristic (and) I was really resented. After a few meetings it was all right, but I could hear the undercurrent: 'What's she doing here? This is for men.' I felt like walking out...Jim would pull me back...There were 20 to 30 in the class; he and I took the two top honors. I got tops in the water work because of my free diving experience. Jim questioned me on all the technical stuff: 'No that's wrong, say it this way.' They finally accepted me but I don't think anybody knew I hadn't really been (scuba diving) before. I had access to a pool because I was teaching skin diving. Afterwards, I would go in and practice scuba.

"On the day of the ocean ditch and recovery, there was rough surf and a lot of surge. People were bailing out. When Jim and I went down, he pulled a great big knife and put it into a place which held us down, and he'd hold me down, otherwise I couldn't have done it. We were the only ones who really passed that day. He was fantastic."

Tillman later sent Dottie another letter, inviting her to a part-time position with the county setting up programs for teaching women. Shortly afterward, Barbara Allen became the second woman instructor, and Zale Parry became the third.

PENGUIN

Becoming an instructor was easy compared to selling the diving public on being taught by a woman. "I walked into Penguin Dive Shop in Long Beach and asked, 'Do you have an instructor?' They said no. I said, 'How about giving me a try?' 'No, if we're going to, we're going to have a guy.' I said, 'Well at least give me a chance. You don't have to tell them I'm a woman. Just say D. Frazier is your instructor. If they don't like it, you don't have to pay me.'

After a few meetings it was all right, but I could hear the undercurrent: 'What's she doing here? This is for men.'

"It was at a private pool. There were about 12 students, all doctors. I knocked on the door and said, 'I'm your diving instructor.' (The man's) face dropped about this far and he said, 'There's got to be some mistake, we don't want a woman.' I said, 'At least let me talk to them. I'm the only woman in the field and you've got to give me a chance. Let me teach the first half of the class and if you're not satisfied I'll walk out.' I knew if I could get the skin diving part of it, which I'd been teaching for ages, I was gonna just wear those guys down. And I did. I upped my class to 60 hours (from 30) and I worked their (buns) off, all of them.

"I was a First Aid instructor, but to teach doctors...this was ridiculous. I assigned all my diving medicine topics to the doctors. 'You are going to lecture on aerotitis media, you on this and this....' They had one week to look up and learn the material before giving these lectures. They turned to me and said, 'Is this right?' I'd say, 'You're doing fine.' (while) writing all this down for my next class. They dug up stuff that the county didn't even know. I later gave a lecture to the county instructors. 'Where did you get all this information?' I'll never tell. After that, I was so busy (from referrals) I couldn't handle all the classes. But they'll never know...they were giving me the instruction.

"Penguin was a complete retail dive shop owned by Lyle Anderson, who also had a beautiful pool out in Park Estates...We used that after the doctors' class. He had a 40-foot cruiser which I used for all Catalina dives. We would stay over at his home in Avalon, dive Saturday and Sunday. A good setup."

Eventually, Dottie bought the shop from Anderson. She made custom wet suits, and set up a network of 48 dealers throughout the United States. "I made the suits for UDT in Terminal Island, Honolulu and San Francisco. I tailored every suit myself, gave 100% guarantee as long as I took the measurements. Our suits were just glued, I never sewed a suit, and we had about five assemblers. My son, Darrell Gath, the youngest instructor ever certified by the county, managed the shop when I was out playing. I worked seven days a week, teaching every night or doing ocean dives, for about 18 years. I got out when they started sewing everything...the machines were really expensive. I'd never had a zipper come out or had a suit come apart. Then I got very sick, and sold out because of illness around 1970. I later worked for Healthways, was the only woman foreman they ever had. I also designed a suit for US Divers and for Healthways, based on my Penguin models."

I knocked on the door and said, 'I'm your diving instructor.' (The man's) face dropped about this far and he said, 'There's got to be some mistake, we don't want a woman.'

ADVENTURES

Dottie's most embarrassing moment came at the Sportsman's Show. "I dove into a tank and my suit filled up with water. I didn't have anything on underneath, and came up stark naked in front of thousands of people. Fortunately the water was so murky that nobody noticed until my suit floated to the surface and the MC said, 'Dottie did you lose something?' They threw me a big towel and let me wrap it around myself."

Dottie recalled her two most frightening experiences: when she got the bends, and when she was alone in the water with a gigantic shark. She and her friends were diving a World War II torpedo bomber that had crashed at Anacapa Island during a World War II training flight. It was well preserved, lying on a stretch of ocean bottom at 120 feet. "It was my second dive of the day, and my watch had broken. I told my buddy, 'Don't let me go over, I want to make sure I get up in time.' We got back to the boat, his watch had stopped. Before we got back, I hurt all over. The chamber up here was in use; they tried to get me into the one at Scripps. I ended up at the hospital and hemorrhaged. My hands were totally numb...you could prick me with a pin and I couldn't feel anything. They thought I was going to die. I never got into a chamber. They were treating the hemorrhaging, (and kept me) in the hospital four days. It took almost two years for me to get feeling all the way back. They refused me treatment at the Navy. They said it was all in my mind, I was a girl, and girls don't get the bends. Yet all these guys I was diving with told them I had to get into a chamber. The doctor said that my recovery was pure luck.

"Gradually I got the feeling back. I was continuing to dive...even when I broke my leg in a snow skiing accident. (It was a) spiral fracture, all the way up into my crotch. After two years in a cast, I told the doctor I would dive with the cast on if he didn't take it off." For the last six months, she had a full brace, and a full-length leg zipper on her wet suit. The guys would remove the brace, zip her up, then pour her over the side and hand down equipment. Dottie did all her kicking with one leg.

The shark experience took place on a trip to Baja. "Six of us flew down to Bahia de Los Angeles, and hired a panga to go out diving. It had cable for an anchor line, and a horrible looking grappling hook. We went out to Smith Isle, had all been out in the water. I had a load of lobster, Doc Mathieson and the other guys had lots of fish. On my way back to the boat, somebody yelled, 'Dottie, shark, shark!' The boat was about 100 feet away. Then I saw a fin that was, so help me, so big it looked like a submarine. It had to be a white. I didn't know what to do...they said, 'Go underwater, don't stay on top.' So as the thing kept circling, I dropped my speargun and lobsters, and kept going down, watching it. Underwater it looked ten times bigger. I couldn't get closer to the boat. The anchor was lodged in the rock, there was nothing to cut the cable with, nobody had any big guns, and nobody would come in the water after me. This must have gone on for 15-20 minutes; I'd been out in the water two hours already. I started cramping up. Finally I said, 'This is it, I've had it, this is the way I'm going to go.' (The shark) turned around and got almost to the boat, so as hard as I could I swam right at his mouth. The water is crystal clear and the guys could see this. They told me later, 'We thought you were absolutely insane.' It kind of startled him, he shot out away from me. When I got close enough, those guys just totally lifted me into the boat. And I cried and carried on just like a dumb female. They said, 'Dottie, don't ever pull that again. The next time he's just going to open his mouth and you are going to swim right in.' I figured that was it, I was going to get it over with real fast. I'd never seen anything that big in my life. They claim it was at least 20 feet long. I mean, all these guys were top notch divers, but there was no way they could come in. That was the closest call I've had."

Dottie also tried her hand at hardhat diving for a while. She took the course at a commercial diving school, and worked with towboat and barge companies. "I've taken metal cable off screws, recovered fenders off tugs, taken boat trailers out of Marine Stadium that were lost during launching. Then I worked for an insurance company. Peo-

Finally I said, 'This is it, I've had it, this is the way I'm going to go.' (The shark) turned around and got almost to the boat, so as hard as I could I swam right at his mouth.

ple would claim they lost their boat (and) the company would send me to check it out. I found boats with holes drilled in the hull...big cruisers. I recovered papers, purses, jewels." Her biggest problem

*Dottie and son on the set of **Beyond The Reef**, shot from Movie in 1961.*

was findiing a suit that fit; even the Japanese version was too big. After quitting the business, she transformed her helmet into a lamp.

TODAY

"After I sold the shop...all these years I've been managing my father's hotels, apartments, and flats. I do all the plumbing, hiring gardeners, hanging doors, and minor painting." Dottie has been diving in Australia, Japan, New Zealand, Hawaii, Canada, the Caribbean, and Mexico. "I have all my gear, but I don't scuba much any more. It's too hard to haul tanks around, and my equipment is so antiquated.

"I'm 72, and think about the 80s coming up. I think I still hold the record for being the oldest female racketballer at City College. Right now I'm playing at least three to four days a week at the YMCA, all with guys. I still ride a motorcycle, water ski, backpack, and skin dive. Now maybe I'll have time to enjoy my four sons, and teach my 12 grandchildren and two great grandchildren how to enjoy all the sports I still love.

"There's no age limit. I don't want to quit for a while."

Al Tilman and Dottie, the stars of **Introduction to Skin Diving,** get ready for the first scene.

WOMEN UNDERWATER
ZALE PARRY

The first well known woman diver in the United States was Zale Parry. For two decades she was Hollywood's leading underwater stunt girl, doubling for actresses from Carol Baker to Sophia Loren. Zale is perhaps best known for her work in the classic Sea Hunt television series. But her underwater credentials were genuine. She was one of the first female diving instructors, and the first woman to dive below 200 feet. Her example influenced countless men as well as women to take up diving in the 50s and 60s. Currently Zale is working with Al Tillman on a history of diving in America.

EXCERPT FROM ZALE PARRY'S
LOGBOOK: "Feb 9, 1957

"Met Bill and Bob Meistrell at 6:30 AM at the Dive n Surf shop, and after a wakeup cup of coffee at a local restaurant, we donned our diving suits and placed our gear in the small outboard...boat which was hitched to the truck. (We) launched a few blocks away with great organization and system, and before we could say Robinson Crusoe...were...putt-putting to the diving grounds straight out to sea. Never in my whole diving career have I seen such a fantastic rockpile. Never in my life have I seen so many lobsters... The nylon shopping bags were filled. Each of the boys got 10 while I proudly got 7. (Note: The limit in those days was ten.) What a morning!"

ONE FACT SHE ADDS TODAY is that the boys made her sit on the center thwart and face the sea, because they were taking bearings and this was their secret spot. In those days before the feminist movement began, any female diver had to be one of the boys. This beautiful, petite blonde could keep up with the boys and then some. Zale Parry's break in Hollywood came through a neighbor in the industry, but she was a big name in the diving fraternity long before **Sea Hunt** was a spark in a script writer's imagination.

Like many women after her, Zale took up diving because of a man. He was Parry Bivens, an engineer at Douglas Aircraft where she was working as a secretary. They first met on a blind date. Bivens had been diving for many years, both free and surface-supplied,

Zale Parry glamour shot in the late 1950's.

before buying one of Rene Bussoz' first Aqualungs. Zale's first lesson was in a swimming pool with his regulator and a heavy fire extinguisher tank. "I asked, 'Is there anything I should know?'" His reply was the standard, "Just don't hold your breath."

Thus ended the first lesson. "It was just heaven. It worked, it was wonderful, but it was very, very heavy." This was 1951, just two years after the first Aqualungs had been imported into the United States.

Zale began tagging along on Bivens' weekend dive trips. "He always had his buddies with him; the girl friends just sunbathed." Tanks were hard to come by, and there were never enough to go around. Fortunately for Zale, wet suits were still a few years in the future, and the boys usually got cold before running out of air. "I was just a sort of tag along; and could use any air that was left in any of the tanks... We had a gauge that had to be put on with a wrench. If a tank had 500 pounds, I'd use it. It was a long time before I ever dived a fresh bottle. I probably made the most free ascents in the world; they were just part of the sport to me. No fear, I just did it." These experiences later proved invaluable when portraying underwater damsels in distress for movies and television.

Zale had always felt comfortable in the water, growing up in the lake country around Milwaukee, Wisconsin. At the age of 14 she was offered a summer job in a water show that did exhibitions for sportsmans shows and county fairs. Zale performed synchronized swimming and surface diving for four summers, until she moved to California in 1951. During after-hours at Douglas Aircraft she attended Santa Monica City College, and taught swimming to polio victims at Santa Monica's Cabot Kaiser and Chase Hotel indoor pools.

As diving became a greater part of her life, she bought a small boat in partnership with Parry Bivens. "Parry was a UC Berkeley grad, a structural engineer, really a brilliant mind. He wanted to get into diving medicine, so he quit his job with Douglas and went on to med school. On the few days off he worked on the boat, which I funded for gasoline. We weren't married yet, just good friends." They eventually married in 1955.

Diving in those days wasn't as fashion conscious as it is today. "We didn't have wet suits. We went to the Army-Navy surplus stores and bought khaki underwear and wool sweaters; it didn't matter if they had holes in them....I mean we looked like ragpickers. For a weight belt, we just melted lead and put it on an Army khaki belt. There wasn't such a thing as a safety release. You just wanted to make sure the belt was secure, it would slide off your hips if you didn't have it on right."

In 1954, Bivens formed a company called SURE (Scientific Underwater Research Enterprises) and started building recompression chambers. These were the first operational chambers for the treatment of civilian divers in Southern California. "One was in our garage for years, and if Parry wasn't available, I operated it. Abalone divers who were bent would come to us, asking, 'Can I sit in there a little while?'

"Within a very short time, equipment was coming to us for testing from US Divers and Healthways. We would take one of my pots from the kitchen, place the gauges or watches inside, covering them with water. Then we put the pot in the small chamber. We were the first hyperbaric testing lab."

In August 1954, Zale set a women's depth record on scuba of 209 feet. The claimed record at the time was 180 feet; Zale had already been to 150. "You have to realize that if you put your head underwater in those days it was a record."

Zale's record attempt was sponsored by some big names in the diving industry at the time: Northill regulators, Hope-Page nonreturn valves, and Bel-Aqua suits, among others. The idea was that if a woman could go 200 feet using this gear, anybody could do it. The Coast Guard was called in to officiate, and a small fleet of boats gathered three miles off Avalon to watch the auspicious occasion. One radio station even had an announcer on the scene to deliver a blow-by-blow account.

As far as Zale was concerned, the buildup was bigger than the event. "I didn't need a record...For the dive, I had a new dry suit from Bel-Aqua. It was nice as long as you were on deck. Once you got into the water, you had a free flowing waterfall from your neck down to the toes...So we went down to 209 feet." Why 209? Because that was the bottom. "There was nothing to see down there, just a piece of bull kelp and a beer can." (Nine months later she reached 307 feet, breathing air, on an experimental chamber dive.)

But it was a big deal to the media. Newspapers and magazines picked up the story, **Argosy** Magazine did a film on it, and she eventually wound up on the cover of **Sports Illustrated** (May, 1955). The fledgling sport of scuba diving was hungry for a sex symbol, and Zale Parry was it.

By then Zale was already on television. A neighbor, Jerry Ross, was the publicity agent for Jack Douglas, an early producer of adventure travel documentaries. His shows, **Seven League Boots** and **Golden Voyage**, would begin with Douglas at a studio helm, saying, "Good evening ladies and gentlemen, boys and girls...." A frequent guest on the program was Colonel John D. Craig, an ex-military diver and adventurer, who was one of America's first underwater film makers.

Craig and Douglas were launching a new show called **Kingdom of the Sea**. Craig would show and narrate an underwater or sea adventure film, and the final 5-minute segment would be devoted to a demonstration of water safety and seamanship. "They needed somebody who could swim. Jerry said, 'The kid next door is always in the water, but she's a girl.' They replied, 'Send her in, we'll look her over.' When they saw me, I didn't have to do a stroke, didn't have to get my hair wet. They hired me."

Zale's segment of the show was live, with no opportunity for retakes. "I sometimes worked in a large tank full of water; the fire department would come in and fill it. It was cold." These short safety spots were basic, low budget, but educational. They centered around swimming and self-rescue skills. Once Craig found the fuselage of an airplane, rigged it up on a tripod, and Zale demonstrated how to go underneath and breathe out of the air pocket. But when it came to simulated ice diving, she drew the line. "John had the idea of pouring paraffin on top of the tank. I told him, 'That's fake, I wouldn't do that number for anything.' "

In 1955 Craig and Zale opened Marineland on live television, with Scott HydroPaks and microphones mounted in the full-face masks. As they swam around the big fish tank, they explained what the viewers were seeing. Craig's show was the first syndicated underwater program, and it lasted nearly five years.

During this time Zale enrolled in the Los Angeles County program, and became its third female underwater instructor. "Dotty Frazier was the first, Barbara Allen was second. Other members of my class were Mel Fisher and the Brauer Brothers (producers of an early underwater television show)." She was also attending UCLA at night, working toward a degree in theater arts.

In 1957 producer Ivan Tors sold the TV moguls on a new concept for a weekly show. Entitled **Sea Hunt**, it would follow the adventures of diver Mike Nelson catching bad guys and rescuing damsels in distress. For the starring role, Tors hired an obscure actor who was mostly playing villains in westerns: Lloyd Bridges. As far as damsels were concerned, plenty of starlets were available to portray them. But none of them could dive. So he hired Zale Parry for that job.

The **Sea Hunt** team included some names that today are part of the lore of diving: Tors, Bridges, Lamar Boren, Courtney Brown, Rico Browning, Al Tillman, and Jon Lindbergh. The son of Charles Lindbergh, Jon worked as a stunt man on **Sea Hunt** four years. He later achieved recognition for his work with diving submersibles.

Zale was technical director for the first two episodes, later replaced by Tillman. Boren was the underwater film director and Brown doubled for Bridges. "Lloyd was a very athletic man, easy to teach. Courtney taught him how to use the equipment, then watched how Lloyd kicked and copied his leg movement when doubling for him. Bridges is a very mellow fellow, quiet unless he is approached, very cautious in what he says.

Zale and Lloyd Bridges on the set of **Sea Hunt.**

"I was the gal on topside maybe 12 times on **Sea Hunt**, but underwater it was a whole lot easier to have Zale be everybody. The fellows wore wet suits but the girls almost always wore swim suits. I rarely got cold. To this day I can take cold, but can't take the heat.

"It got awfully complicated, because they had to get one film in the can per week. " Locations for the underwater sequences included Hawaii, the Bahamas, the Keys and Silver Springs in Florida.

Zale recalled one particularly close call while filming there. "At the bottom of Silver Springs was a very large cave, used by many photographers because the backlight was really good. We were 60 feet down at the bottom of the spring, quite a few feet in. If you went further into the tunnel you would be under the parking lot of the springs resort. Lamar Boren was the photographer, Paul Stader was director. The girl was following Mike Nelson into the cave to search for a villain. They jerry-rigged my double hose regulator, setting the clamp extremely loose so that it would come off at the right moment. While I was getting into position I had to hold it on; it was that loose.

"There was a lot of debris and branches of trees. Oh, Mike Nelson knew how to get through the debris, slippery as a noodle. And the girl, of course, the dummkopf, gets caught. She knows she's stuck, and I had to be very careful because once that clamp goes I've had it. The girl is reaching for his fin, trying to get his attention and he's just out of reach. The crisis gets worse, the hose comes off and it's flailing like crazy over her head. She's struggling, she's had it, and

Zale and Lloyd Bridges playing house for a TV special.

I'm breathing water with my air. The intake came off just after an exhalation. I was really in trouble.

"At that point I swam to Lamar and he gave me his mouthpiece, handed the camera to his assistant, and held me down. I said, 'No, it's OK.' But they didn't think I could swim out of the cave and free ascend from 60 feet, choking like that. So it took quite a while, but I finally caught my breath. We had to shoot the scene over again."

During this period Zale also did stunt work for Hollywood movies. "MGM was filming a picture in Hawaii, called **Underwater Warrior**, the life story of Commander Doug Fane of UDT. Dan Dailey played Fane, a tough cookie. I was his wife underwater.

"That was an exciting time for me. I had a chance to go into the Pacific sub base training tank at Pearl Harbor, to be checked out. No woman was supposed to be on any Navy ship, because women were going to sink the Navy or put some voodoo on it. Fane took me to see the admiral of the Pacific Fleet. I was never so frightened in my life. He was a very official looking guy, with all the gold and epaulets. 'I think she'll be OK,' he said, 'but we'd better put her in the tank because she's going to dive off Navy ships.'

"The young navy guy on top of the tank said, 'I want you to be in this bullet position: feet first, arms straight overhead. Then see how far down you can go. About 25 feet and you pass.' He winked at me, because sub base candidates have to go a little bit deeper. Well, he couldn't keep up with me. When I got to 60 feet (the depth level is written on the inside walls) he pulled me by my bathing suit strap, and said 'That's it, level off, we're going up.' He told his officer, 'Did you see that? She's OK.' "

Another memorable Hollywood assignment was doubling for Sophia Loren in **Boy on a Dolphin**. "They cut my hair and dyed it. I had to wear three brassieres that were especially made for my size.

They were rubber, and when I got out of the water and squeezed my elbows, I was laden with water. Sophia's character ends up on a ledge admiring this dolphin statue. The ledge breaks off and she falls. She had bare feet, and her dress was gathered between her crotch and tucked under her belt. One of the tricky things I did underwater was to fall. A lot of the stunt maneuvers that looked simple really were quite complex." For this shoot, Zale wore special underwear with thin lead weights shaped like corset stays, so that she could descend faster in drowning scenes.

When I got to 60 feet (the depth level is written on the inside walls) he pulled me by my bathing suit strap, and said 'That's it, level off, we're going up.' He told his officer, 'Did you see that? She's OK.'

She also doubled in Blake Edwards' **Peter Gunn** television series. "Blake liked to shoot at night for the light and shadows. I was drinking hot soup and breaking off pieces of the styrofoam cup to see which way the current was running. He didn't get to me till three in the morning. I hear about my pals dying of cancer and I think it's because of the stress you have to go through for motion picture stuff."

Sometimes real-life adventures were more exciting than the make-believe ones. On an off-day during a film project in Baja California, Zale and a couple of friends decided to go spearfishing. One of them shot a big roosterfish, and Zale volunteered to swim it back to shore. Placing it on a surf mat, her major concern was to minimize bleeding and not attract predators from below.

The challenge, however, came from the sky. A huge pelican was looking for an easy meal. Shore was about 1000 feet away, so Zale crept forward on the mat, covered the fish with her body, and kicked for the finish. But the big bird wouldn't leave. It flew away to gain some altitude, then dive-bombed just inches away. "He appeared on the other side, kept pace with me, with his grotesque sagging pouch and beak clapping near my head. This was the Air Force and the Navy combined.

"My pals saw the show and came to my rescue, or was it the safety of their catch? But the bird was still determined. Finally one of the men grabbed both of its webbed feet and pulled it underwater. Only then did the fish get ashore."

Searching through trunks full of pictures with Zale was like a trip through diving history. Each photo triggered a story or a memory.

"Here's Lloyd Bridges and I playing house underwater for the CBS Easter Special. Lamar Boren shot it. I was wearing an apron, Lloyd had on a suit and tie, and I'm holding a pot with a live lobster.

"Dan Dailey was so funny. We were on a submarine, the deck

seemed about 600 feet long, and level at 10 fathoms. We hung on as the sub was about to surface, and Dan was doing the soft shoe with fins on.

"Here are Chuck Nicklin and I, measuring kelp for Dr. Wheeler North's project at Point Loma. He also had us bopping urchins with hammers and giant wrenches. The seals would watch us and all the fish would come in. We'd laugh our heart out because it was a simple job but it had to be done.

"This was the first Santa Monica film festival. In '54 I acquired a Rolleimarine and learned photography from Parry and Lamar Boren. A lot of our friends had very good pictures that were just stuck in dresser drawers. We decided it would be wonderful to have just one show, and have everybody bring their stuff. It went over really well. For the next 17 years Al Tillman and I were instrumental in organizing these festivals.

"This mermaid costume was for a swim with dolphins in the film **Danny and the Mermaid.** I had to work with them for three days because their sonar was picking up on the sequins and ruining the shots." (Zale had more cooperative dolphins in her earlier work on CBS and NBC specials.)

"Every time we went with Mel Fisher it just put a wet blanket on my dive, because Mel always had a new map and was going to find treasure in Spanish wrecks. They were just looking for a rockpile that looked abnormal, and never found anything. I thought he was a treasure hunter only in his mind, until he moved to Florida and found his first dubloons.

"Here's a party at the Navy's annual Arts Ball in Coronado...Dr. Roger Revelle came as a sea lion. Commander Fane came as the Creature from the Black Lagoon. I was carried into the sea of fantasy on a surfboard borne by six Navy frogmen.

"Here's my daughter, Margaret Zale Bivens, age three, in one of the CBS holiday specials. She was one of the first kids they ever put in the water with dolphins. I was a safety diver but it wasn't necessary, because the dolphins swam on either side, protecting her." Recently married, Margaret today is a veterinarian in Northern California.

"Zale Parry to me is like another person, isn't that strange? I didn't think this would ever happen." As the 60s drew to a close, she gradually phased out of stunt work and began a less celebrated but more lucrative career, portraying ingenue parts in television and motion pictures, and acting in television commercials. Parry Bivens died in 1963. Zale is presently married to Bob Neuman, a commercial pilot who isn't a diver. For a time she ran a motorcycle shop with Bob, taking over the operation when he went back to flying. The two of them still enjoy weekend rides on his Harley Davidson.

Zale's daughter Margaret Zale Bivens, then 3-years-old, posing with famous dolphin "**Flipper**" for CBS TV special. Margaret is now a veterinarian.

Now in her 60s, Zale is trim, fit, and enthusiastic. She works out regularly in the pool, teaches swimming, and does charity work. She is a member of the Fire Department's emergency response team, and still dives occasionally, but only for fun. Her major project today is a book on the history of diving in America, which she is writing in collaboration with Al Tillman. No one else is more qualified to do this, because Zale and Al lived and made more than their share of that history. I for one can't wait to read it.

How would Zale Parry like to be remembered? "As someone ultimately involved, someone who made a difference, and encouraged thousands of people, men as well as women, to experience the underwater world. "

What's a lovely girl like you
— by Zale Parry

"What's a lovely girl like you doing in such an abominable sport as this?" asked the prop-man. The scene was a motion picture set located on a floating barge off the coast of Santa Catalina Island. Before I could answer, he continued his work of gathering equipment for all of us actor/divers, while saying loud and clear, "Never saw such a sport in my lifetime of work as a property master for the great studios of Hollywood. First, these people sprinkle baby powder in their costumes; they breathe it, it's all over the deck, it lands on me and in my hair. Then they walk to the rail to choose the tanks and regulators I prepare for them. Who knows where the mouthpieces were last, or who breathed out of them? Then they spit in the faceplate, and with a few swipes of their fingertips, wash the inside of the glass until they can't see out of it, finally dipping it in a communal pail of sea water and immediately fit it to their face. Worst of all, I'm here on deck, watching as each tank is emptied and replaced, and never once have I seen any one of them — not even you — use the head. Disgusting. Now tell me, what's a nice girl like you doing with such a sport anyway?"

DEMA Hall of Fame 1993. From left to right, Frank Scalli, Bob Straight, Zale Parry, Bob Meistrell, Scott Carpenter, Dick Bonin, Eugenie Clark, E.R. Cross (behind Eugenie), Jim Stewart, Glen Egstrom, Jean Michel Cousteau.

The man had a point. He had been working for many years on western movies. All he had to do was hand the cowboys and cowgirls their holsters, guns, and spurs, while the Indians were handed the bows, arrows and tomahawks and such things. I thought the powder dust would be a pleasant fragrance compared to the earth dust that he used to bring home after a day's filming.

Zale Parry to me is like another person, isn't that strange? I didn't think this would ever happen.

"Well, Mr. Blaine," I replied, "I'm here because I love what I'm doing. Aquatics is my life. I never get tired. At the end of the day, I am rested, refreshed from being in and out of the sea, and I really feel bathed and very clean. I'm very curious and I'm following my bliss. This is a very happy place to be."

He shook his head, helped me get into the tank harness like a true gentleman, and handed me my swim fins.

Zale Parry and Jim Stewart at the DEMA Hall of Fame, 1993

WOMEN PIONEERS
NORINE ROUSE

Norine Rouse is one of the first high-profile woman instructors. An environmentalist before it became fashionable, she is noted for her understanding and gentle relationships with creatures of the sea..

IF YOU WERE A 40 YEAR OLD SUBURBAN HOUSEWIFE suddenly finding yourself divorced, what would you do? If your name is Norine Rouse, you learn to scuba dive. The year was 1965; Jacques Cousteau's film, **World Without Sun**, was the inspiration. Norine wasn't exactly an aquatic neophyte at the time. She had been active in swimming, serving as a volunteer Water Safety Instructor for the local Red Cross chapter.

"I was living in New York. My first dive was in Zack's Bay. It was 32° out and 42° in the water (and) there wasn't a thing to see down there. I thought 'How can I like this when there is nothing to see?'

"One of the reasons I wanted to be a diver (was) because I was a mother and a housewife, but wanted an identity. Now I have one. I'm a diver."

Seeking clearer water, Norine headed for the Underwater Explorers Club in Freeport, Bahamas. Al Tillman was running the operation at the time, and Jack McKenney was one of his dive guides. Norine looked so comfortable in the water that they didn't realize how limited her experience had been. Certified as an instructor on her ninth dive, Tillman then hired Norine as the first female instructor at UNEXSO. "Al said it's time to show even a woman can do it. My age was an asset because parents would rather let their children dive with an older woman than some 18 year old beauty.

"Jack McKenney...got me into feeding everything. One day he gave me a conch to feed a moray, and it jerked it out of my hand. He

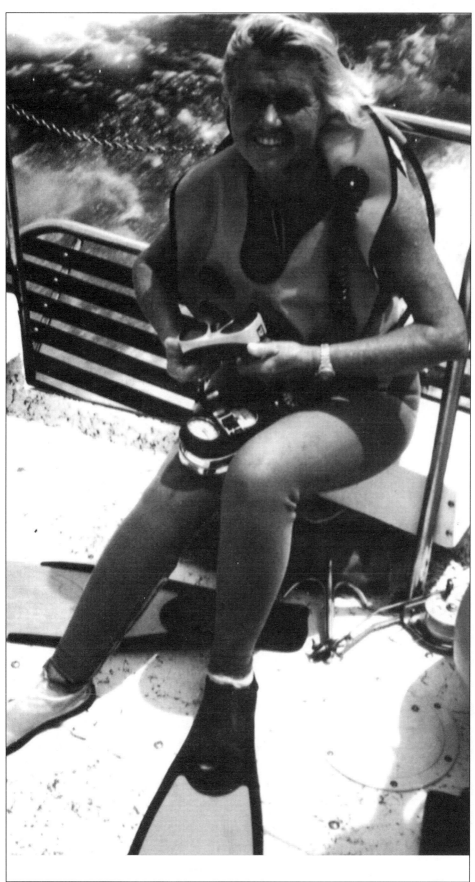

Norine after a day of diving.

took his snorkel, hit the moray over the head, took the conch back, then handed it to me to feed him. This got me into relating with fish. I had a moray I'd been feeding...went down one day and somebody had cut its head...I never fed anything again."

Norine and pet moray eal.

UNEXSO was going through a period of slow business. Salaries were declining, so Rouse moved on to West Palm Beach, Florida. There she met John D. MacArthur, one of the richest men in the world, and eventually convinced him to back a diving operation, the Colonnades Undersea Center. Construction was going well, when a well known instructor stuck his nose in and told MacArthur he would never make it if he didn't offer spearfishing. Norine's option was clear. "I had my choice of taking out spearfishermen or quitting and I quit.

"They made a major mistake. They had a big banquet and never acknowledged MacArthur....They kept the underwater world from having a lot of the money that he would have left. I get goosebumps when I think of it."

> One of the reasons I wanted to be a diver (was) because I was a mother and a housewife, but wanted an identity. Now I have one. I'm a diver.

A former student suggested Norine start her own dive operation, and offered to back it. That was the start of the Norine Rouse Scuba Club. "I got the idea from UNEXSO. We had a deep training tank, (used) different progressions of levels. We tried to make it a family sport...stressing education and conservation. I never allowed a speargun. I used to chase spearfishermen off the property (and) wouldn't sell air to people who had spearguns in their boat. I still hate them. The older I get the worse I get. I just know how much the ocean lost because of (them).

"At that time, 1972, we were the only ones taking regularly scheduled divers out of West Palm Beach. Now there are 22 boats, and...the club (which she is no longer associated with) is the only one that won't take spearfishermen.

"We started giving free dives to anybody who would turn in their spearguns. One guy owned a shop, and his small spearguns cost less than a dive. So he would bring me a brand new speargun and I would open the box, take it out, bend it, and put it on our statue of bent spearguns. It's still in my back yard."

Norine is best known for her interaction with marine animals, especially turtles. She explains, "You can learn a lot by watching marine life. I learned about currents by observing fish swimming into them...

Norine and her pet turtle Robert.

"I don't want anything to be unhappy...I will not pick up a pufferfish. The little pufferfish you picked up is (terrified), otherwise he wouldn't be puffed up. It's a much greater accomplishment to pet them on a rock... I try to think like the creature.

"I realized we were seeing one big turtle quite a bit (and) got to looking for him. If he was asleep I didn't want him to be scared. I put my hand in front of his nose and talked to him through the regulator. And he knew it was me. He never bolted, he would come out and swim. That was Rajah, the one that Jack McKenney made the movie of in **Florida Diving.** Every year he came back a little later. Meanwhile another one was also coming and that's the one I've been petting up to now. He hasn't come back yet this year and I'm very upset about it.

"Turtles like to be cleaned. The scientists didn't think they had any feelings through their carapace, but they obviously do, otherwise they wouldn't like it. (**National Geographic** photographer) Bill Curtsinger calls me the giant yellow cleaner fish. You have to have permit now (to do that) because the turtles are endangered, and luckily I have one."

When asked if there is anything about her that attracts animals, Norine replied, "Good thoughts. I've had turtles swim across a reef and single me out. Fish too. Maybe it's the yellow suit. I don't know, I was the first to wear all yellow. But even when I used to dive in a T-shirt in the summer they did this.

"Once there was this big amberjack that had about 100 feet of fishing line hanging out of his mouth. I went up and cut it, trying to swim in the current to keep the pressure off. He looked at me, opened his mouth and let me cut it. I petted him twice and he swam away. This kind of thing makes me feel at least I haven't hurt the ocean."

Norine can be feisty, and her opinions are sometimes at odds with the mainstream diving establishment. Take for example, deep diving. "We all did it as pioneers, why should we do something we don't let other people do, as long as we teach them how to enjoy it? Palm Beach has deeper diving than most because our reefs don't start until 80 feet. I quit teaching because (the agency) wouldn't let me do an 80 foot checkout. The same people that preach this stuff are the first ones to say it's so nice to dive with a group that knows what they're doing. If you go five feet here and five feet there, you've put too many fears in them."

Phillipe Talliez, Norine, and John Fine.

Norine has led trips to some of the world's most exotic places, but West Palm Beach remains her favorite. "Nothing is more exotic than swimming in the current when the Gulf Stream is near and there are big creatures going by." How about an example? "There had been a small whale shark in the area. I saw some spots, swam over there, and it turned out to be a 13 foot tiger shark I signaled everybody down, because we can't go back to the boat with our kind of currents It was a mess, tiger sharks all over the place. The remoras let go of them and we kept hitting them to get them off of us. There were lemon sharks all over the bottom. We drifted through and came on up. We went back in the afternoon, but most of them were gone. I went to show somebody a turtle, but its head and all four flippers were bitten off. That's when I realized in retrospect it had been a dangerous dive."

Nothing is more exotic than swimming in the current when the gulf stream is near and there are big creatures going by.

Her most memorable dive was in the Sea of Cortez. "The year before, Michelle Hall had freed a manta from the line and got to ride it. I saw this manta ray, held on with one finger, and rode it for 20 minutes. It took me down through the sharks, and the fish feeding, and I never felt so at one with the ocean. Everything likes the feeling of touch if you are gentle...I rubbed it very gently, and it made no effort to get rid of me. I got off because I had to decompress. I've ridden a whale shark, and it's not like being close to something that's of a size you can relate to."

Today, Norine is still running trips, both local and international, out of The Aqua Shop in West Palm Beach. Her advice to divers: "Respect the marine life. That's their home and you're a visitor. You are there by reason of technology, you're not a part of the environment, and you don't have a single enemy down there. Not even the shark."

SECTION 5

ART UNDERWATER

ART UNDERWATER
JOHN STEEL

*Divers of the pioneer era may not recognize the name John Steel. But they will remember his paintings: on the covers of **Skin Diver** Magazine, in advertisements for Voit and Swimaster, on boxes of dive equipment, and on the covers of magazines like **Westways** and **Outdoor Life**. Steel was the first widely published underwater artist. His striking paintings of underwater scenes delineate the early period of diving history.*

UNLIKE ARTISTS WHO ARE ONLY CASUAL DIVERS, Steel's work vividly attests to countless hours spent underwater, especially in the kelp forests of California. No other artist has captured the essence of California diving like John Steel: the angle of the kelp leaning in the current, the muted quality of light filtering through the canopy, the feeling of depth and space, the forced perspective and natural action postures of man and fish. Now 72 years old, he is still an active diver, traveling six to eight weeks a year to exotic destinations like Fiji, the Red Sea, and Papua New Guinea

All of Steel's early diving art is in the hands of collectors. In the past 20 years he has turned his talents to wildlife, from Alaskan bears and elk to African lions and Indian tigers. His limited edition prints and paintings are displayed in galleries throughout the country, bringing up to $6,000. He still occasionally paints underwater wildlife, concentrating on sharks, whales, and sea otters. An accomplished photographer, Steel's paintings are based on his own photographs, both terrestrial and underwater. For whales and white sharks, he has used the work of Flip Nicklin and Al Giddings, for sea otters, Steve Rosenberg.

Steel was always interested in art, but made no serious attempt to pursue it professionally until World War II. Serving in the Pacific Theatre, he was on the island of Pelelieu in Palau, site of one of the bloodiest battles of the war. There he met combat artist Tom Lea of

John Steel spearfishing, 1960s.

Life Magazine, and showed him some of the sketches he had done. Many were of dead enemy soldiers. The artist encouraged John to send them to **Leatherneck**, the Marine Corps magazine. "They sent me about 70 pounds of equipment and wanted me to send more sketches. But my commanding officer said I couldn't be released from my assignment. I didn't want to carry all that stuff around, so I left it in somewhere in the Pacific."

> I never graduated from art school, because of an argument with the president's girlfriend, who taught painting. They told me I wasn't capable and ought to open a hamburger stand.

To this day, Steel refuses to talk much about his military experiences. He served in three wars: World War II, Korea, and Viet Nam, the latter as a combat artist and photographer. He was wounded in two of them, and carries a metal plate in his jaw along with several decorations.

After being discharged from the service in 1946, Steel enrolled in Pasadena's Art Center on the GI Bill. An avid swimmer since his youth, he was immediately attracted to the ocean. He bought his first faceplate on the Redondo dock, along with a spear with a detachable head. When he speared a halibut in five feet of water on his first free dive, John decided this would be a good way to cut down on family grocery bills for his wife and infant daughter. "What the government gave us to live on wasn't quite enough, so in order to get food I started diving for abalone. I ate abalone every day for two years. I finally became allergic to them so I started trading them for hamburgers...Today I can't be in the same room with an abalone. My wife prepares them now, I just get them for friends.

"I never graduated from art school, because of an argument with the president's girlfriend, who taught painting. She told me I wasn't capable and ought to open a hamburger stand." Instead of heeding that advice, John went to work for North American Aviation as a technical illustrator. "I started back in night school, and worked at home every night, every weekend, every sick leave and every holiday, practicing drawing and painting. Free diving was my first love. So I did four underwater paintings of guys in eel grass, getting abs and lobsters and stuff. I took them over to Voit Rubber and they bought all of them. Paid me a hundred bucks apiece and I thought that was a lot of money."

In the course of his diving activities, Steel met Chuck Blakeslee and Jim Auxier, who had recently started a magazine called **The Skin Diver.** Most illustrations in the magazine were topside photos of divers posing with fish they had killed. Underwater photography was still in its infancy and couldn't capture the scope and the beauty of the underwater world. That would require a painter who combined diving experience with artistic skill. "My first **Skin Diver** cover was a picture that Ron Church had taken of Mel Fisher using a rebreather. I speared a cabezon and put it on the edge of my drawing board. I painted the fish and put Mel in the background. His spear was pointing directly at the viewer."

Steel has moved from illustration into fine art. This is one of his contemporary paintings.

Editor Jim Auxier described the painting this way: "Undersea artist John Steel repeats his excellent June cover painting this month with another outstanding scene...a mechanized diver stalking a Cabezone (sic) in a kelp forest off Palos Verdes, Calif. The master-brushman has included in this one painting action, life, marine animals to scale and undersea beauty as only a diver can see it." Actually, the painting described was Steel's second cover. The first, **Skin Diver's** first full-color cover, came a month earlier in June 1955: a free diver spearing a moray eel. This was four years after the magazine had made its debut.

Steel recalls one early dive with associate editor Chuck Blakeslee. "We were diving at the Portuguese Bend Club, Palos Verdes. We looked under this one big rock, and about 10 feet back inside you could see a bunch of black and orange legs. Chuck told me to get my spear. He stuck it in butt end first and rattled it around in there. We went back to the surface and watched. Pretty soon seven bugs, all of them over ten pounds, came walking out. We just kept going down, bringing them up, and throwing them in the boat."

Another diving buddy of this era was Ron Church, who was establishing himself as one of the first great underwater photographers. "He used to pose for me for covers. One time he shot a white sea bass. I did some sketches from memory, then I got him to come over and pose and stuck the fish on myself."

Eventually Steel turned his own attention from hunting to photography. "I speared some kind of bass. Another fish that looked just like the one I speared kept following my tube with the stringer on it. It was probably the mate of the one I killed. That was when I decided to quit spearfishing."

Like many of the early divers, Steel began using scuba almost reluctantly. "I made friends with Voit public affairs director Herb Larson, after doing some freelance work for them. He gave me a

tank and a regulator. Mel Fisher had a compressor, so I got my air fills there. I never took a course but had read a lot of Jacques Cousteau stuff and knew enough to be careful. I never went very deep, but always preferred free diving. It's not because I was chicken, but I like to do everything on a breath of air. I didn't like wearing all that gear around me."

Steel was still a technical illustrator at North American. When they discovered he was selling paintings on the outside, they transferred him to the company's commercial art group. He was assigned to do most of the public relations art for the Strategic Air Command. "They sent me to

Another one of Steel's contemporary paintings.

Colorado Springs, had me do paintings of pilots running to the airplanes, stuff like that.

"I was also doing stuff for Voit and Swimaster...like Johnny McCarroll bringing up a big turtle." **Skin Diver** covers brought $200 each, which was big money in those days. He also did covers for **Westways**, the Auto Club magazine which paid only $150 despite a much larger circulation.

A typical painting would begin with sketches, which he submitted to the editor for approval. Then he would get a friend to pose, shoot photos of him, and combine that with backgrounds from underwater photos that he had taken. Nearly all the human figures were posed on land, a surprising fact considering the realistic action and perspective that typify Steel's work of that era. "A typical painting would be a combination of very many things. It would start out in my head before I got down to painting by the numbers. It would be about 40 hours of work, just painting, spread out over some three to six days, depending on subject matter. I worked in gouache (a water based paint) or in casein (which is milk based). I work mostly in oils now, and also some acrylics."

Steel got into exotic dive travel in the early 60s, long before it became fashionable. Garrett Airesearch hired him to paint calendars, and would send him to a different place each year, including Australia, Tahiti, and even Viet Nam. "In 1962 I was staying on Bora Bora with a family of Tahitians. I'd go out fishing with the husband. First we would get a plant they called whiskey; it looked like sugar cane. We would twist it so the juice would come out, let the tide wash it into coral holes, and all these lobsters would march out drunker than hell. We would just pick them up and throw them in the outrigger."

Steel's last **Skin Diver** covers were published in 1966, before he returned to Viet Nam, this time as a combat photographer and artist with the Marine Corps. By the time he came back, the magazine had changed editors and was featuring underwater photography instead of paintings on the covers. "Afterward, (art director) Art Smith tried to get me in there, but...I was getting $1000 to $1500 from other outfits." These included **Outdoor Life**, Random House Books, Disney, calendar companies, and Revelle models.

> Pavelka prefers Steel's contemporary paintings to the older ones. "His old work is very basic compared to what he does now. The man is just a phenomenal painter... and... wildlife photographer.

"When I turned 65 in 1981, I decided to paint what I wanted to paint, got out of illustration and into fine art. I love to paint animals and underwater scenes. I used to shoot photographs before elk and deer hunting season in Wyoming and California. By the time I quit illustrating I had quite a file of photographs. So I painted wolves and deer and other animals. Some friends took me to a reserve in Montana, where they keep a wolf pack for scientific study. I've gone to Alaska and shot pictures of Kodiak bears, been to Africa and India shooting lion and tiger pictures." Limited edition prints of these were published by Wild Wings Company, Binson's, and Hadley House Publications. "I've only got about a half dozen paintings that haven't been sold, except what my wife has kept."

Steel's technique has evolved and matured since the 50s. Then, heroic male figures, clad only in swim suits and fins, were battling the monsters of the deep. His paintings from that era look almost primitive compared with his exquisitely shaded photo realism of today. Yet they remain as artifacts that reflect the macho era of diving, a simpler time before the age of environmental consciousness. Steel's change in subject matter from man as predator to the celebration of wildlife mirrors that of our society.

Despite a coronary bypass four years ago, John is still an active free diver. On doctors' advice he doesn't scuba dive deeper than 25 feet any more, but he aways preferred breath-hold diving anyway.

His Santa Rosa, California neighbor, Ron Pavelka (west coast sales representative for Dacor), reports, "He's amazing...very active, walks about four miles a day. He just got back from eight days salmon fishing in Alaska (and) those trips are pretty strenuous. Even though he is 72 years old... John is still a pretty tough cookie."

John Steel today doing what he does best.

Pavelka prefers Steel's contemporary paintings to the older ones. "His old work is very basic compared to what he does now. The man is just a phenomenal painter...and...wildlife photographer."

When asked about his current activities, Steel replied, "I'm not diving locally any more because it's too damn cold and there's too many people. My wife and I take at least two dive trips a year. We've been to Bonaire, the Bahamas, Roatan, San Andreas, off the coast of Nicaragua, the Red Sea, East Africa, Fiji...we've done our share.

"I've been lucky. I know a lot of better artists who haven't been as lucky. I've had nine lives, still got about two left...I'm happily married, got four kids, and live in a beautiful spot. I paint every day and wouldn't trade with anybody I know in the world."

Note: *The cover of this book was specially commissioned and painted by John Steel, 1993.*

Steel's paintings were featured on **Skin Diver** *magazine covers from 1955 through 1966.*

ART UNDERWATER
CHUCK NICKLIN

Many pioneers are retired, but Chuck Nicklin is still at the top of his profession, shooting movies for Hollywood productions, Imax specials, and documentaries for **National Geographic***. Renowned for marine mammal photography, he is credited with the first major shots of sperm and blue whales. Beginning as a breath-hold spearfisherman before the introduction of scuba, Chuck opened one of the west coast's first dive shops, the San Diego Diving Locker. He learned from some of the early legends: Jim Stewart, Connie Limbaugh, and Ron Church; then helped the next generation get started. Some of today's leading underwater photographers, including Howard Hall, Marty Snyderman, Steve Early, and his son, Flip, got their start working for Chuck at the Diving Locker.*

WHEN CHUCK NICKLIN WAS DISCHARGED from the Navy in 1947, his future seemed to be mapped out for him. He would enter the family's grocery business and eventually take over management of the store. But he had always been fascinated by the ocean waters off La Jolla. His first look underwater was through a borrowed Japanese Ama diver's mask. "I stuck my head in the water at La Jolla Cove, and said, 'Wow, this is for me!' "

Although the first Aqualung units were two years away, free diving equipment was starting to become available. A relative in the Navy bought Chuck a pair of black Owen Churchill UDT fins. His Sea Dive mask came from a local sporting good store; its hard rubber edge had to be sanded to make an effective seal. An old Navy sweater provided thermal protection during free dives for lobsters and abalone.

Like many of the early divers, Nicklin tinkered with war surplus equipment in efforts to extend his bottom time. "The first time I ever went underwater and breathed off anything, (it was) a gas mask and a little bottle of oxygen...I went to Mission Bay with my father and he put a rope on me. I said, 'If you see me stop moving around, pull me in.' I turned this thing on to take a breath, held it, turned it off. This was repeated for every breath... for maybe five minutes. I thought there's got to be a better way.

"I spent all my free time talking diving. In the back room (of the grocery store) I had...pictures of diving on the wall, I had scrapbooks,

Chuck Nicklin poses with his camera during a shoot.

and was gung ho for diving." Chuck tried scuba for the first time in the early 50s, as a member of Delta Divers. With no classes available at the time, they just taught each other how to use the equipment at the La Jolla Shores beach. "I was in the small grocery business, too poor to buy one of these fancy (Aqualungs)...The first day of abalone season, it was a tradition to go to Bird Rock in our wool sweaters. I scammed a short Pirelli (dry suit), with a band around the waist. Over the top of that I would wear a long john top and bottom. It looked weird, but was necessary to protect the thin suit.

> We knew we should be decompressing, but weren't quite sure how the whole thing worked. So we would take little 38s and lie down at the bottom of the pool at Buena Vista Gardens, thinking we were decompressing. This was probably 45 minutes after we got out of the water.

"We did some weird things, makes we wonder how we got through it. I remember being on the bottom with a bag of ten abalone, the legal limit in those days...I was starting to breathe hard, kicking away and starting up, and all of a sudden my feet hit the bottom. I hadn't moved at all...was scared to death and dropped the abalone. I couldn't drop the weight belt, it was a cartridge belt with lead in the pockets.

"We used to dive in the north canyon and shoot rockfish at about 140 feet...deep enough so their eyes would pop. We knew we should be decompressing, but weren't quite sure how the whole thing worked. So we would take little 38s and lie down at the bottom of the pool at Buena Vista Gardens, thinking we were decompressing. This was probably 45 minutes after we got out of the water."

Like most divers, Chuck was a hunter in the early days. The last black sea bass he speared weighed 376 pounds. "They would dive down and wrap themselves in the kelp, you're free diving 60, 80 feet to cut them out...get that line wrapped around you, you're in a lot of trouble. I did all that and feel sorry about it now."

In the mid 50s Jim Stewart, Conrad Limbaugh, and Wheeler North started San Diego's first instructional scuba program. It was based on the pioneering Los Angeles County program, and Chuck eventually became an instructor, his first formal certification.

Nicklin had been introduced to Connie Limbaugh by Homer Rydell, the Gallo Wine distributor. After a few trips down to Mexico, the two became good friends. Limbaugh, Stewart, and North were partners in a part-time consulting business, doing their research out of a garage. In 1959 a contract on testing the offshore sewage outfall brought in enough money to expand the business into a dive shop. The problem was that they all were graduate students, and had neither the time nor the retailing expertise to run the shop. Rydell recommended Nicklin. "I was in a small business, knew when the checks would clear and all that stuff; that's good training for running a dive shop. They had a choice of me or Ron Church...and decided I would be the manager, and Ron would work with me."

photo by Bob Casebolt

Chuck Nicklin and Jacques Cousteau.

It was the area's second dive shop, preceded only by San Diego Divers' Supply. The entire budget of $5,000 was spent on a Rix compressor. But because of Limbaugh's reputation and his connection with Rene Bussoz, the manufacturers stocked them on credit.

"During our first class, Jacques Cousteau was in town. The class was in the back room, and we introduced (him). He said, 'This is your introduction to the ocean, I hope it's as good for you as it is for me.' Every once in a while someone from that class staggers through the door and asks, 'Do you remember ...when Cousteau welcomed us to the ocean?'

"Jimmy (Stewart) and Andy (Rechnitzer) and those guys did more than just help running the store. Their reputation made our store a sort of scientific headquarters. Anyone in San Diego on a scientific mission went to the Diving Locker, and that helped us get started. Many a day we had a lot of empty boxes on display...because we just didn't have the capital we needed. When Bev Morgan was closing his surf shop, he came down and taught me how to make wet suits. I was a one-man show for a while, made my first suit on the floor of my house.. I would sell them the suit, cut it, glue it, try it on them, and take their money.

"I still use a rubber-in suit. When gray whales are coming through I can't free dive in a dry suit, so I use a rubber- in suit to keep warm. To do whales, you've really got to free dive."

Ron Church was a professional photographer for Convair Aviation, and had set up a darkroom at the Diving Locker. Although at first he resented Nicklin being in charge, they soon became close friends. Church had a Rolleimarine housing, which allowed only 12 pictures on a roll of film. He and Nicklin would go to the edge of La Jolla

Canyon and take turns, each shooting one picture at a time. While waiting his turn, the one without the camera would scout the next picture.

When Limbaugh died in a cave diving accident in France in 1960, his widow, Nan, gave his cameras to Chuck. "So all of a sudden I had

photo by Bob Casebolt

a fairly sophisticated 16mm camera and a Rolleimarine, and all the things were starting to fall in place. I had a base, the Diving Locker, I had Ron to help me, and could get away, because after a couple of years there were other employees.

"It was a big advantage to be able to get away...When a job came up, a lot of other fellows couldn't do it because they worked five days a week. Convair would call with their submarine stuff and I would get involved ...At first it was scraping money together to buy a roll of film, then it was, 'I just sold a picture so I can buy

Like many early photographers, Chuck began as a spearfisherman.

some more film.' "

Chuck won a gold medal at the Santa Monica Film Festival and that got peoples' attention. But his big break came one day in the early 60s, during a diving day off La Jolla on Al Santmeyer's boat, *Duchess.* Heading across the bay, they spotted a whale spouting. It was a Bryde's whale caught in a net, the ropes digging into its flukes. Weak from trying to breathe, the animal was barely struggling. Nicklin and Bill De Court jumped in, dived to 20 feet and cut the whale loose, shooting pictures in the process. "It was just one of these things that hit at the right time. Nobody knew anything about whales then. Our pictures were in the paper, in **Time** Magazine; people were calling from everywhere to interview us because we rode a whale. So this got a lot of publicity. I was getting a lot of calls, 'You're the guy who shot the whale, can you shoot this?' So the first thing you know, I was doing more of that kind of thing.

"I did the first diving on the Deep Submergence Rescue Vehicle built by Lockheed. Until they turned it over to the Navy, I did a lot of the photography. When they made their first deep dive, everybody got a dive on it and a plaque stating that they had ridden in it. On my plaque, they put "outside the DSRV" because I had always been on the outside to shoot it."

Nicklin has worked on a number of big-budget Hollywood productions including **The Deep, The Abyss,** and some James Bond films.

But the first was a B film for Warner Brothers. called **Chubasco.** An acquaintance of Wheeler North had asked for help, and he recommended Chuck. "They wanted shots of local tuna boats...at water level, in the net with the tuna and sharks. I said, 'Yeah, I can do that.'

Chuck Nicklin in a current photograph.

They said, 'Bring diving gear, we'll supply the camera, meet us at the boat in San Diego.' So I got on the boat and they said, 'Well, this is the camera.' I said, 'Oh my god!' It was the first big Panavision 70mm, about the size of a steamer trunk...(it) weighed 300 pounds, they had to put it in the water with a crane. And I had been shooting 16mm. I had no idea what it was, how to load it...(and) had never seen a roll of 70mm film. They introduced me to my camera assistant. After the producer walked off, I asked him, 'What do you know about this thing?' He said, 'I know everything.' I said, 'You're my friend; we are going to be a great team.' So all I had to do was take it in the water and point it.

"At one point I was in the net with the camera, all sorts of skipjack screaming around. A stunt man (was supposed to) fall in and the other actor was going to jump in and save him. So I'm in the water, the guy falls in, sinks about (two feet) and panics. He can't swim. He wanted the job so badly and figured he would learn to swim when the time comes. So Christopher Jones wound up doing the stunt. That film still shows up about 3 o clock in the morning on TV."

Chuck's first assignment with **National Geographic** involved shooting Dr. George Bass' expedition on iron age shipwrecks in Turkey. The photographer originally was supposed to be staffer Bates Littlehales. He and Chuck had become friends during an earlier gray whale shoot in San Diego. When he ruptured an eardrum on assignment in the Bahamas, Littlehales recommended Nicklin to take his place. At the time Chuck was shooting with a Bronica 2 1/4. "They flew me back to Washington, said to throw away all those 2 1/4s, handed me a Calypso, a Seahawk housing with a Leica and a 20mm lens, and a couple of Edgerton strobes that hardly ever worked. For three days in Washington they gave me Nikons with black and white film, and I'd go off and shoot. They'd process that night, then tell me (what they liked). They gave me the little booklet on how to shoot for **Geographic:** You need a sunset, you need a scenic with a little animal or a person, you need so many close-ups...a long list.

"So I went off to Turkey and shot this story. We had a bell and a submersible decompression chamber... (We) swam into it at 20 feet, then they brought you up to 10 feet for the rest of your decompression. We also decompressed on a line. They had a bucket with books in it. As long as you kept the books wet they would hold together and you could read. We also did that on **The Deep** because we had such long decompression."

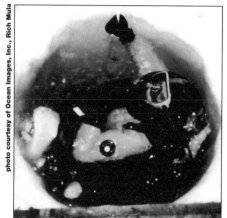
Chuck ice diving in the Antarctic.

Most of Nicklin's Hollywood film work was done in collaboration with Al Giddings. His low-key, self-effacing personality is a counterpoint to Giddings' drive, so they hit it off from their first meeting in the early 60s. Giddings had been contracted to make a film in Cozumel under the sponsorship of US Divers. He invited Chuck to come along, but he reluctantly refused because he was still running the grocery store as well as the dive shop. Soon afterward Giddings returned to San Diego for a film festival. He announced, "By the way, we are going to make a film in Cozumel and Chuck Nicklin is going with me" By this time the grocery business was for sale, and against his better judgement, Chuck went along. That was the start of a relationship that has lasted over 30 years.

The relationship worked because Chuck was content to accept a secondary role and let Giddings get the glory. "I didn't want to produce films, it was never very profitable. In the old days you put $5000 into a film and showed it at festivals for $100. ...Al and Stan Waterman and I worked together on **The Deep**. Al and Stan were the co-directors underwater; I was just an underwater cameraman. Peter Yates, the director, would say, 'Al you get the long shot, Stan you get the eyes, and Chuck, get something good.' So I had a lot of time to go anywhere I wanted, shooting through holes and when the rushes came up I'd get a lot of comment because my shots were so different. One night we came back from the rushes, Yates and Peter Guber (producer) were standing in the lobby of the Southampton Princess Hotel when we got off the bus. They told Al and Stan (to) come right back down.. to talk about the shoot tomorrow. And I had a date with Jackie Bisset that night. Maybe there is something to just being a cameraman.

"Al and I worked on *For Your Eyes Only*, we did *Never Say Never* (it was Jordan Klein's film, but we did part of it). I've also done a bunch of funky little things where we did one or two scenes, falling into a pool or a raft. You get paid, it's part of the job, but nobody ever hears about it."

Nicklin received lots of help in the early days and he in turn has helped a new generation of photographers get started. Howard Hall, Marty Snyderman, and Steve Early worked at the Dive Locker, inspired and encouraged by the work of their boss. "When we did *The Deep*, we needed somebody to bait the sharks in. Howard and I had been doing that kind of stuff and I told Al (to) get him. Al asked, 'Who's Howard?' So he got his first taste of the real film world at that time.

I didn't want to produce films, it was never very profitable. In the old days you put $5000 into a film and showed it at festivals for $100.

"If I helped people get started, it's by being one of the founders (with Ron Church and Bill DeCourt) of the Underwater Photographic Society. It started because Ron ...wanted to start a photo club and promote business for (our) shop. So he started this club in the back room. Others who came in (included) Emil Haabecker and Chet Tussey...Chet was really into film for a long time, he was one of the early backbone people of UPS." Today he manufactures a line of premium camera housings.

While Chuck traveled the world shooting film and stills, the Dive Locker continued to grow and expand. He bought out his partners, and today the business is in the capable hands of his son, Terry.

His other son, Flip, has become one of the world's top marine mammal photographers. The first underwater photo he ever shot was with a fisheye Nikonos borrowed from Bates Littlehales. This got the 18-year-old interested in photography, so he bought a used Oceanic housing. Chuck gave him a Nikon F and a 28mm lens, which didn't work. He found that out when everything on his first four rolls of film was out of focus. "The old 28mm wouldn't focus through the dome port without a diopter. I didn't know it either because I never used it underwater. Flip kids about it now, saying,'My dad tried to stop me.'"

National Geographic photographer Jonathan Blair came to San Diego to upgrade his diving, on the way to an assignment in the Leeward islands. He was concerned about tiger sharks. Flip built a cage and was invited to go along as an assistant, agreeing on the condition that he be allowed to take pictures. A couple of them were published in the article. While handling the lights for Chuck's Imax film, **Nomads of the Deep**, Flip shot some stills of humpback whales. He showed them to **Geographic**, then returned to Hawaii at his own expense for a couple more months of shooting. They liked what they saw, reimbursed his expenses, and put him on assignment to shoot a feature on humpbacks. That was the first of many marine mammals assignments for Flip. One of them covered 18 months and 150,000 air miles, ranging from the Arctic to the tip of South America. Today Flip is recognized as one of the best of a handful of elite photographers specializing in large marine mammals.

My conversation isn't about what I did last week, but what I want to do next.

Chuck continues to shoot marine mammals as well. He filmed the first extensive documentary on sperm whales and blue whales, off the coast of Sri Lanka.

"I still like to shoot pictures. I'm in love with video, because I can do so much more with it than with a movie camera. Giddings has also turned to video now; most of his topside is shot with it. I'm going to New Guinea soon, on a new 72 foot boat out of Walindi. Then I've got the **Explorer** II to the northern reaches of the Coral Sea.

"My conversation isn't about what I did last week, but what I want to do next. The youngsters sometimes look at us gray haired guys and wonder what's he going to do? But then there's a current and they are busting their neck and you're down there passing them by and waving...

"I have a friend who lives his life about what he's done. I want to live my life about what I want to do next."

SECTION 6

CAPTAINS OF INDUSTRY

CAPTAINS OF INDUSTRY
BILL & BOB MEISTRELL

Although Bob and Bill Meistrell are the only people in both the diving and the surfing Halls of Fame, they are best known today as the men behind Body Glove. Long before Body Glove they owned one of the nation's first dive shops, were part of the first group of underwater instructors, and taught movie stars to dive, including Lloyd Bridges. How a pair of twins from the midwest built a multi-million dollar empire from a wetsuit logo, and had a lifetime of fun and adventure doing it, is a story worth telling.

ALTHOUGH THEY GREW UP IN MISSOURI, the Meistrell twins were always intrigued by submarines. Bob, the more gregarious of the two and who represented the family in this interview, recalled, "We put boxes together and made periscopes. I wanted to be a deep sea diver." At the age of twelve, they made their first diving helmet. Bill is the engineer of the pair, but both of them worked on the project. "I got a five gallon oil can, cut out the bottom, and had a guy solder shoulder pads on it so it didn't cut into you...Put a piece of glass on the front and used tar as a seal. We had enough sense to put in a check valve (made from a marble and a spring), so the air wouldn't come out when they stopped pumping. (One of us would) wear this thing in the swimming pool, sit down on the bottom and read magazines, while the other would pump from the surface with a tire pump. That pump would get so hot we would have to dip it in the water. You'd feel the water coming up to your nose...I don't know how many times we bailed out of that thing...It's a wonder we didn't get air embolism. We also used it to march around in some of the lakes out there, at depths of about 15 feet."

When the twins were four years old their father died, so their mother had to raise seven kids alone. Older brother Joe was a lifeguard at the local pool; Bob and Bill followed in his footsteps and became accomplished swimmers. "We joined the Boy Scouts every year just to swim for them, then would quit after the meet."

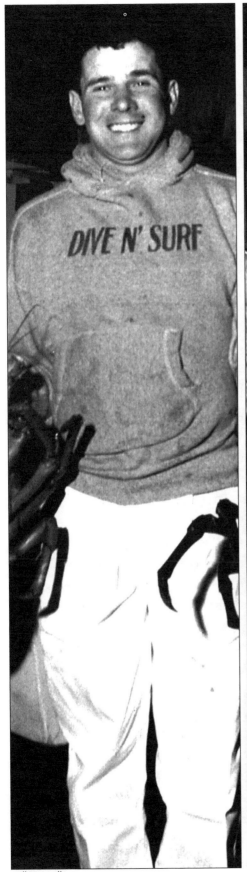

Bill Meistrell.

Bob Meistrell, 1950's.

Joe moved to California, and Mrs. Meistrell followed with the rest of the family in 1944. They settled in Manhattan Beach, and enrolled the twins in Redondo Union High School. After a year and a half, they transferred to El Segundo High to play football and swim.

Billy Jr., Pat, and Randy, 1958.

The Meistrells fell in love with the ocean, despite a few problems. "At Manhattan Beach you couldn't swim because it was so polluted. There were even condoms in the water; we used to call them El Segundo Whitefish." They got into surfing just when light boards were starting to catch on, and were among the first to apply fiberglass to protect the nose of the foam-filled plywood boards.

Later they bought a genuine diving helmet for $25, after the owner was killed using it. "We...marched all over the breakwater with that thing, one at a time with the other pumping. There were no wet suits in those days; we used to shiver and shake. It was just good for looking around, you couldn't lean over and grab anything. Maximum depth was 20 feet. There was clear water with a white sandy bottom, lots of fish...a whole other world."

At El Segundo High School, the Meistrells swam for legendary coach Whitey Saari. They also went out for football, but Bob broke his back on the first play of the first game. Consequently, he couldn't dive into the pool, and had to start his races from a pushoff. "We played a trick on Whitey once. Our team had to win the final relay and I couldn't dive. Bill swam the first two laps, I was supposed to swim the last two. I sneaked down to the shower and he came back to swim the last leg...we won by a hell of a long ways."

After graduation they became full-time beach lifeguards, but Bill was soon drafted into the Army. Bob, thinking he would be deferred because of his broken back, got married. Two months later, he too was a soldier. "They said, 'You're warm, you're breathing, you're in.'" Bill went to Korea where he was awarded a Bronze Star, while Bob stayed in the reception center in Monterey. It was the only time in their lives the twins were separated. "I hitchhiked back and forth to Santa Cruz and surfed almost every night by car light...without a wet suit. There were no other people, but a little seal would sometimes jump up on my board and surf into the beach with me."

The Meistrells' diving career began in earnest after they got out of the service. Bill had bought an Aqualung, so Bob's wife, Patty, bought one for him. "On my first dive off Sapphire Beach I almost drowned because we didn't have quick release weight belts. My dry suit had a hole and filled up with water. I used a cartridge belt for weight and

The Meistrell twins on Compton College swim team, 1948.

couldn't get out of that damn thing. The only thing that saved me was our eight-foot hand spear. I kept poking that spear into the bottom and pushing myself to shore...Bill was there, but wasn't paying any attention to me. The buddy system wasn't in force in those days."

DIVE N SURF

Attempting to combat California's cold water, they tried electrically heated flyers' suits from war surplus, but those would burn up. Wool sweaters worked only as long as they were dry. Finally in 1953, they found some insulating material called Neoprene, and made the first practical wet suits. At the same time in Northern California, Jack O'Neil discovered Neoprene and began making suits. Meanwhile at Scripps Institution of Ocenaography, Dr. Hugh Bradner adapted the same stuff from a cold-weather suit used by the Navy in the Arctic. No one knew about the others, but by the end of that year all three were in the wet suit business.

The Meistrells got in by borrowing $1800 from their mother and buying two-thirds of a struggling little shop called Dive N' Surf. It had been opened just two months earlier by surfer Hap Jacobs, who later pioneered the modern surfboard, and diver Bev Morgan. Morgan, a Los Angeles County lifeguard, went on to manufacture a successful line of commercial dive gear. The store wasn't doing well and Jacobs wanted out. So the Meistrells bought in, with Morgan staying on as a 1/3 partner. They moved into a little building in Redondo in late 1953, but held onto their lifeguard jobs.

"Business started out slow. The first day we owned the shop, I sold a 15 cent magazine. My mother was skeptical about our investment. I figured if it could just do $100 a day it would be a nice little business and could quit lifeguarding. Eventually it got over $50,000 a day. Now people say we ought to sell the dive shop... I'll never sell the thing we started with."

Dive N' Surf shop in 1953. From left to right, Dale Velzy, Hap Jacobs, Bill Meistreill and Bev Morgan.

1 UICC

Bev Morgan, Al Tillman, and Ramsey Parks went down to Scripps Institution of Oceanography in 1954 and took Connie Limbaugh's diving class. Morgan then talked Los Angeles County's recreation department into sponsoring an instructors' class, the first such certification course in the country.

"Al Tillman was in charge. Bev wrote the LA county instruction manual, Dive N' Surf produced it. Charlie Sturgill (one of the first great spearfishermen), Tommy Rice, Rex Guthrie, Julie Orenstein, Rusty Williams, and I took the class for the county lifeguards...Some didn't know how to scuba dive. Limbaugh taught them diving and how to be an instructor (at the same time).

"Charlie had problems with ditch and recovery. When you turned on the air the mouthpiece would freeflow and Charlie would rush to the surface. Connie (who taught the course from the deck) would say, 'Mr. Sturgill, you're not supposed to come up that fast.' We had to do a ditch and recovery at Marineland. Most guys couldn't do it because the water was so rough, but they passed them anyway. I don't think anyone of the 26 people failed that course."

Some other members of 1 UICC (the first Underwater Instructors' Certification Course) were Andy Rechnitzer, Bill Walker, E.R. Cross, and Herb Barthels. Bob Meistrell's instructor number is 13. He and Limbaugh later became good friends. "Connie said you always swim against the current and swim in kind of a teardrop, that way you won't see the same place twice. He had an uncanny ability to get back to the boat. Me too. I watch the sunlight and the current and a compass.

"I used to teach in the pool with the worst equipment I could find. I'd take every clamp off the regulator mouthpiece...and would have them put the faceplate on the step with their eyes closed. I'd splash water and knock the regulator off the mouthpiece."

In 1955 a second Dive N' Surf store was opened in La Jolla, with Morgan in charge. But things didn't work out, the store was closed, and the Meistrells bought out Morgan in 1958. Bev had just gone through a divorce, and took off on a sailing and diving trip around the world, on a boat called the *Cherokee*. Along the way he wrote a memorable series of articles for **Skin Diver** Magazine, detailing his adventures.

> Now people say we ought to sell the dive shop... I'll never sell the thing we started with.

Meistrell valued Morgan's involvement in Dive N' Surf, and learned a lot from him. When Bev became bored with servicing regulators and building wet suits, Bill took that over. When he got tired of retail sales, Bob assumed that responsibility as well.

BIRTH OF BODY GLOVE

Morgan's wet suits carried the brand name Thermocline. The Meistrells hired a marketing consultant, Duke Boyd, who told them that name wouldn't sell. He asked about the characteristics of their suits. "Billy said that it fits like a glove (so) Duke came up with the name Body Glove. We paid him $200 to get a logo designed. He found a guy who did it for $35. Years later, that guy's son came into the store and said 'My dad did that.' He was living in Hawaii, and we sent him a whole bunch of Body Glove stuff."

The brothers also did freelance commercial diving on the side. Los Angeles sanitation department hired them to inspect outfall pipes in the 60s and 70s. One day at 175 feet, Bob and Don Siverts were diving double tanks inside a pipe. Bob was sucking hard, when suddenly there was no air. Two metal tips on the diaphragm had collapsed. He gave Siverts the trouble sign, and buddy breathed up to 40 feet, while being stung by jellyfish all the way. "I went to U.S. Divers that day, and they were in a state of shock. They had a lot of regulators out there with that tin part. This was before the days of recalls."

Diving for fun and food was part of the agenda. Bob set up an artificial reef of toilet bowls to attract lobsters at a secret location. "We put out 300 of them in a big circle, had them stacked up in 110 feet of water. I was diving with Hugh O'Brien, the movie star, at that time. I'll bet there were a thousand lobsters on it. We just took a couple and then would leave. Somebody later went out there, put a chain or a rope through them and towed a whole bunch of them to another place, because there's a whole bunch of broken ones out there.

"Bill and I always wanted to own a submarine. In 1970 Bill, Don Siverts and I salvaged a boat called the *Emerald*, a 55-foot yawl. We sold the boat to Don but never bothered to collect the money. He'd built a two-man, 1000 foot sub and we bought in for what he owed

Instructor Bob Meistrell, 1956

us. He also built a one-man sub, and we are part owners of both. We do pipeline inspections and instrumentation recovery, plane crashes and body recoveries... I've (been as deep as) 535 feet... I saw the biggest black sea bass ever in my life once in Redondo Canyon...also five 150 pound broomtail groupers, and a sevengill shark, about 8 feet long. All hang out there." They are now in the process of tearing down the submarine to replace it with one that has 2,000 foot capability.

THE HOLLYWOOD CONNECTION

Bob has taught diving to a number of movie stars, including Gary Cooper, Jill St. John, Charlton Heston, Richard Harris, and even Lloyd Bridges. When Jill called, Bob didn't know who she was. "She had claustrophobia and couldn't swim. My wife taught her to swim and I taught her to dive. A good little diver, a very smart gal. When she got married she called and said, 'Mission accomplished.' She wanted to learn because her future husband was a diver."

Bob has fond memories of Cooper. "He was a neat guy, very shy to talk to. We dove a lot. His doctor told him he couldn't go deeper than forty feet. I never sold him a depth gauge, and lied to him about depth when he asked.

"I taught Lloyd Bridges after he did the **Sea Hunt** series. Rico Browning did most of the diving for him. We built all those gray suits for Lloyd...wiped them down with toluene and spray painted them. We charged them $100...My nephew had to stand there wearing the suit for three hours. They thought it was too much and tried to do it themselves. They tried spraying it with Lloyd's stand-in in the suit, and he couldn't put his arms down before the paint was dry. They had to cut the suit off of him. After that they let us do it. Lloyd really wanted it to look good. I taught him and his two kids to dive.

"We were at a party at Hugh O'Brien's. My wife and I didn't know anybody. In walks Gary Cooper and his wife, they immediately spotted us and came over and sat with us. Lloyd Bridges and his wife walked in. I said, 'Why don't you invite him to come over to our table?' Gary says, 'I doubt if he'd remember me.' I says, 'Well, you did **High Noon** together,' But he's a very bashful guy, just a real good-old cowboy, that's all he was. He asked me to go over there and invite him. So I went over and Bridges said, 'I don't know if Coop will remember me.' "

The whole gang, 1991. From left to right, Bill Sr., Randy, Ronnie, Julie, Billy, Robbie and Bob.

"We did a movie together, in the early 60s, **Wreck of the Mary Deare**. Cooper and Heston did all their own stunt work. I was in charge of the underwater part. Nobody knew I was in charge till they asked Cooper to come up from twelve feet without exhaling (and) I yelled at them."

A major influence on Bob was another scuba student, Ed Janss. A multi-millionaire, Ed's father had developed most of the San Fernando Valley. "He was the most fantastic man I ever knew. When I taught him to dive I asked 'How did you find out about me?' He said, 'I had you investigated. Found you were totally honest but a bit confused.' This was 1962. and we had a good business going (but) he was amazed that we were doing this well.

"Bill and I never had a father; Janss was that role model for me. We'd go down to Mexico, I would (offer) him $1,000 for expenses. He would say, 'I've got a lot of money, and I can never spend it all. If I didn't want you here I wouldn't have invited you.' He became an award-winning underwater photographer, and the Meistrells traveled with him to the Galapagos, Hawaii, Japan, and Micronesia. In 1989 he died after a series of strokes left him crippled. Although Bob maintains he had the entrepreneurial drive all along, Janss clearly was an important influence.

GROWTH OF BODY GLOVE

Bob credits his son, Robby, for the recent growth of Body Glove. "When Robby took charge of the company he started spending so much money on advertising, we thought we were going to go bankrupt. He kept saying, 'Dad, I know what I'm doing.'...He would give away hundreds of emblems and decals just to get the logo into the public eye...In 1989 he talked to an advertising club and asked them to guess how much we spent on advertising. Guesses were up to $7 million. The actual amount was $250,000. We had so many covers of magazines you couldn't believe it. You seldom run into anybody who hasn't heard about Body Glove."

"In the mid 80's, Body Glove came out with swimwear made of

neoprene. It has been featured in **Sports Illustrated** swimsuit issues and in numerous magazines and covers."

Today the Meistrells handle all the business, including licensing within the family. They have expanded into other areas of clothing; athletic shoes, jeans and jackets, a kids' line, even undergarments. Foreign licensees are located in Australia, New

All the Meistrells are introduced to the water at an early age.

Zealand, Thailand, Hong Kong, Canada, U.K. and Europe.

Bob isn't worried about the fickleness of fashion. "We've been around a long time...Good service, good products, free advertisement. Randy (Meistrell) is in total control of quality. Anything they build has got to get past him.

With success came the inevitable rip-offs. Someone made a t-shirt logo with a middle finger extended. The Meistrells, who now employ a full-time lawyer, sued to put him out of business. "At the Action Sports Show, the first time we really became big, there were 17 body somethings there: body heat, body bag. Everybody capitalized, there's (little) we can do."

Despite their success in other areas, they have no plans of selling the dive shop. "The shop was always good… Dive N' Surf was built on service. You satisfy somebody, they are going to tell 20 or 30 people. If they are dissatisfied they will tell hundreds."

Body Glove wet suits are manufactured in the Meistrells' South Bay factory. SAS wetsuits are made in the same building, but have a separate sales force. They also produce orthopedic goods, like braces and protectors, with the Body Glove logo. It doesn't hurt sales to see them on the knees and elbows of NBA, NHL, NFL, MLB players and AVP and WVPA volleyball players. Other products include bags, hats, key chains, and wallets. About a dozen patents hang on the wall of Bill's office, attesting to his skill as a designer and inventor. This is despite the fact that neither the twins nor any of their children ever went to college. (That doesn't include a semester they spent at Compton Junior College just to swim on the team.) Bob says the grandkids will have to be the family pioneers in higher education.

The Meistrells are the only persons in both the surfers' and the diving halls of fame. "We were among the first surfers, (spent) years and years along the beaches. (We were selected) not because we were great surfers, but the ones that brought out the wet suits. Without them there would have been a lot more drownings."

We had so many covers of magazines you couldn't believe it. You seldom run into anybody who hasn't heard about Body Glove.

At 65, the brothers show no signs of slowing down. They still dive regularly and oversee the family's business empire. On most weekends, they cruise the coastline in their 70-foot powerboat, the *Disappearance*, decorated with a huge Body Glove logo. Despite the farm boy facade, everybody now knows them as shrewd, saavy, and above all honest businessmen. Bob sums it up: "Billy and I don't have goals, we don't know what the hell we want to do yet."

DICK BONIN

Dick Bonin co-founded Scubapro and for nearly thirty years led the company to a premiere position in diving. Behind the scenes, he was a founder of the Diving Equipment Manufacturers Association, and later its president. From his service with the Navy's Underwater Demolition Teams to his experiences in the formative years of the diving industry, to the success of Scubapro and the new Ocean Futures organization, Bonin has helped make diving what it is today.

CHRISTMAS SEASON 1962 was ruined for Dick Bonin and Gustav Dalla Valle before they much chance to enjoy it. On December 26 they were informed that their employer, Healthways, was filing for bankruptcy. Like many diving manufacturers of the time, Healthways had barely been hanging on. They survived by selling cheap gear, much of it made overseas, through discount houses and department stores. In an attempt to upgrade their image they had recently hired Bonin to form a new division of the company, that would produce an upgraded line of products to be sold only through professional dive stores. The new division was to be called Scubapro.

Bonin and Dalla Valle considered their options. They could type up resumes and seek new jobs in the diving industry, or they could proceed on their own and form a new company, building on the concept they were working on at Healthways. For the sum of a dollar, Dalla Valle bought the rights to the name. Bonin recalls, "Gustav bought Scubapro for a dollar and got me with it. He still thinks he paid too much."

The two friends were an unlikely pair of business partners. Gustav, the son of an Italian count, had inherited a lot of money and proceeded to blow it. Educated as an architect, he dabbled in painting on the Left Bank in Paris, raced cars, and was an all-around bon vivant. Eventually he settled in Haiti, running the first diving and snorkeling business in the western hemisphere. Life was good for

Dick Bonin is still an active free diver and spearfisherman.

Gustav, part owner of a casino and a renowned spearfisherman, until Papa Doc Duvallier came into power. Realizing the future for diving in Haiti had lost its luster, he left for the United States. Through his contacts in Europe, Dalla Valle had obtained import rights to European lines of equipment including Cressi and Beauchat. When Healthways hired him as director of research and development, he brought those along.

Lieutenant JG Dick Bonin, U.S. Navy, 1955.

UDT

Dick Bonin's introduction to scuba came in the Navy. At the outbreak of the Korean War, he had enlisted and was sent to Officer Candidate School in Rhode Island. A native of Chicago, Bonin had been a successful high school swimmer at Fenwick under legendary coach Dan O'Brien. The commanding officer, watching him perform in an intra-squad swim meet, suggested that he volunteer for underwater demolition training. Prior to then Bonin hadn't even seen the ocean, but he followed up on the suggestion. Only 19 out of 137 candidates passed the grueling course at Little Creek, Virginia. Dick spent the following three years as a frogman, ultimately becoming submersible operations officer, the forerunner of today's SEAL teams.

"We did a lot of commando work...I liked diving right from the beginning," he recalls. "I was curious about what was under the water...dove from the Arctic to the Caribbean, and I was always entranced with it."

Although he never got into combat, some of Bonin's activities were classified and he cannot talk about them to this day. The ones he can discuss are interesting enough. In the Arctic, his unit was involved in the building of the Distant Early Warning Stations. All supplies were brought in by landing craft, so channels had to be blasted to make the bottom smooth enough to bring them in. "Ecologically I don't think they would agree with it these days, (but) I blew all those approaches...We always had a couple of our people with M-1s on a small craft. One day while we were in the water, a polar bear charged us and they had to shoot it." Dick's unit was scheduled to go to Korea when peace was declared.

In 1954 he was involved in a search for the Civil War ironclad, *Mon-*

itor. A man claimed to have found the wreck site, and obtained a contract with **Life** Magazine. There weren't many divers around at the time, so **Life** contacted the Navy. They assigned Bonin and another UDT member to the project. "**Life** rented a spotter plane. We would sound for it and just dove on everything we could find. We were pretty close, but didn't have the electronics they have today." It took nearly 30 more years to find the *Monitor.*

Gustav bought Scubapro for a dollar and got me with it. He still thinks he paid too much.

Bonin's most exciting experience occurred on a deep-water test in 1955. "I may hold the record for free ascent. The Navy was already using three open-circuit units: the Aqualung, the Scott, and the Northill. The Ships Bureau in Washington decided we should have open water deep tests on them. We went down to a submarine anchorage off North Carolina to conduct deep dives to 250 feet with all the units. Lines and decompression stages were set up. The chief took the Scott and I took the Northill...I was down at the bottom of the line, about 250 feet, when it started leaking water. We found out afterward that the exhaust valve (which was in the middle of the diaphragm) inverted and popped through it, leaving a hole for water to pour in. I cleared it out, cleared it out, to the point where I couldn't clear it any more, so I made a free ascent up that line. We were well trained and had done emergency ascents in the escape tower at New London. There were masks hanging down at the decompression stages. I made it to the stage; it was really no problem, just a mental discipline. While decompressing, about sixteen hammerheads came in and circled the stage. The ASR (submarine rescue vessel) had thrown garbage over the fantail. They kept circling, but would go away whenever I pounded on the stage. That was exciting; I've never heard of anyone making a free ascent from a greater depth."

Early Days of the Diving Industry

Upon his discharge in 1956, Dick figured his college degree in economics could lead to a successful career as a salesman. A Navy contact led to his first job. A Chicago firm called Divemaster was using an instructional course, written by former Navy diver E.R. Cross, to help sell its line of diving equipment. They asked the Navy to check it out, and it was passed on to Bonin by his executive officer. Divemaster remembered and offered him a job when he got out. "I decided if I was going to sell, I would sell something I liked. I went there and ran that operation for about two years. They were a dive shop and wholesaled to other shops."

At the time, there were only three other dive shops in Chicago. Training was done primarily through YMCAs, and Bonin began teaching classes at the Oak Park Y, where he also formed a club. This was before national instructor certification, but as an ex-frogman he was more qualified than most contemporaries.

Dick in UDT gear, 1950s.

"We dove the lakes in Wisconsin and Illinois, the quarries from Racine to Lemont. It wasn't like the Caribbean, but it was diving...We dove in Lake Michigan recovering weapons and deceased people when the police asked for volunteers. They would call the dive shops and we had our network. The sheriff's recovery teams evolved out of that." When problems arose with the city regarding access to Lake Michigan, Dick and Vern Pedersen called a meeting of dive clubs. This was the start of the Illinois Council of Skin and Scuba Divers.

After two years Bonin left the midwest for California. "Swimaster, a rubber company in Los Angeles, bought a company called Spearfisherman from Bud Brown, a brilliant guy in Huntington Beach. Brownie was an engineer who left Ford Motor Company and developed Duck Feet fins, Spearfisherman snorkels, and one of the original dry suits. Swimaster bought his tooling, but after a year they weren't going anywhere. They hired a marketing consultant who went around the country, and wound up picking me to run the company."

I decided if I was going to sell, I would sell something I liked.

For a small company, Swimaster had a big impact on the fledgling diving industry. They introduced Duck Feet to the sport market, where they became the premiere fin for many years. They also introduced the first flexible snorkel and the first American spearguns, based on those Jack Prodanovich was making. "Bill Hardy, one of my customers, brought me down to San Diego where I met Jack and Wally Potts, saw their guns, and was just wide-eyed. With the two of them we produced the Swimaster guns, which later became the Voit guns, which are now the JBL guns." They also adapted one of Brown's ideas to make a wide-view mask with a big purge valve and a Neoprene seal. These products built Swimaster into a top line despite the fact it produced no breathing apparatus. In those days there were no large staffs; it was just Dick and the production manager running the show.

"At Swimaster I introduced the philosophy of marketing solely through professional dive shops. Before that it was generally sell everybody, including Sears. We sold strictly to stores that could supply all services, had to teach diving lessons so people bought gear through a responsible source. That philosophy has guided my whole career, and it started at Swimaster."

Scubapro test dive team, early 80s.

Dick got to know a lot of the pioneer shop owners, including Bob and Bill Meistrell of Dive n Surf, and Mel Fisher of Mel's Aqua Shop. As far as he knows, the nation's first dive shop was Watergill in Venice, California, owned by Bob Lorenz. "A Mark V helmet with full dress suit was hanging outside the shop. When Bob retired he gave me the helmet, because I had always admired it. It's now in my living room."

The forerunner of DEMA started about this time. Mike Kelly of Voit, a giant of athletic goods in those days, suggested starting an association in diving like they had in sporting goods. The founding members were Kelly, Harry Rice at US Divers, Randy Stone at Healthways, Sam Davison Sr. at Dacor, and Bonin. That was basically the diving industry in 1957. Called the Organization of Underwater Manufacturers, it met regularly for a number of years and eventually evolved into today's DEMA.

Swimaster was sold to AMF Voit, and Dick moved to Sportsways. There he worked with Sam LeCocq, a brilliant, controversial engineer who made several significant contributions to diving technology that are virtually forgotten today. He was the first to apply the o-ring sealing principle to diving equipment. His Sportsways Waterlung was the first successful single hose regulator, and was ultimately responsible for making museum pieces out of two-hose models . He also produced the first submersible gauge, the SeaVue, and the first breathing valves engineered specifically for diving. The ones before that were primarily medical valves. "LeCocq also came up with the first 3/4-inch sealing tank valves; before that they were 1/2 inch. So Sportsways introduced a lot of things that are still standards today. I was vice president in charge of products and sales. Sam was one of the genuine creative personalities that came along in this business." But there were also serious problems, many of them financial, so Dick left Sportsways. Within a few years that company was defunct.

photo courtesy of Peterson Publishing

Dick Bonin, 1974.

The next stop was Healthways, where we began this story. Healthways was essentially a barbell company trying to make a go of the diving business, but was trapped with an image of inferior imported gear. Bonin was hired to start a prestige division of the company that would upgrade their image, but it was too late. Within four months Healthways had gone belly up.

SCUBAPRO

Bonin and Dalla Valle were on their own now and risked their meager savings on their new company, Scubapro. Based in a rented shed in Gardena, Dick's income had dropped from $13,000 a year to zero. "We went through hell. We didn't take salaries, couldn't pay the bills, bounced a check for taxes, they even cut off the phone one time. We borrowed cash against invoices, something you do when you're desperate." Gustav's credit was still good in Europe, so he bought whatever he could over there and Dick sold it to dive shops. "Our original products were either mediocre or had been around for a long time. I told them, 'We don't have much now, but if you stick with us we'll develop a line you can be proud of.' We waded through it and turned the corner. When we started to have some success, we developed our own products."

Scubapro's first home grown product was the Mark II regulator, a workhorse, piston first stage with a downstream second stage that Bonin describes "...as close to maintenance free as has ever been done. Some are still being used in the Caribbean." Everybody in the company was a jack of all trades, so the design was a joint effort of Dick, Gustav, and Dick Anderson.

One of the most successful Scubapro products came in over Bonin's strong objections. On one of his European trips, Dalla Valle purchased the rights to a funny looking French fin with vents. Bonin's reaction: "That's the ugliest fin I've ever seen. We won't be able to give these things away." Gustav replied that they had better try selling some, because the order had already been placed. They were displayed at a sporting goods dealer show, and a few shops bought them out of curiosity. Soon calls starting coming in from dealers, asking for more. Up to that time nobody at Scubapro had even tested the product, but they quickly realized that the new Jet Fins were a big hit. The first vented fin and the first serious fin with adjustable heel straps, it spawned a generation of imitators.

That's the ugliest fin I've ever seen. We won't be able to give these things away.

Gustav retired in 1975. Now in his 70s, he owns a winery in Northern California and recently became a father. By that time Scubapro had became a major force in the industry. Their innovations included the balanced adjustable second stage, the first silicone masks, quick-release power inflators, jacket-style BCs, the AIR II, and the Shotgun Snorkel. Bonin's philosophy was to surround himself with good people and to stress professionalism.

Not all Scubapro products were winners. Hidden away in a catacomb are a few items that Dick wishes had never seen the light of day. One was the Scuba System, a back-inflation unit with a hard shell and an integrated weight system. It was extremely unstable as the air shifted around, giving the diver the feeling of being in a swamped boat. "We should have listened to our customers; it was a bomb," he admits today.

Dick continues to be an active diver but rarely uses a tank. "Free diving is the one activity that takes my mind away from everything. When I go spearfishing I'm completely absorbed...the physical part of it is an athletic pursuit. When I met Prodanovich and made his guns, some of the top spearfishermen of those days started coming around (including) Terry Lentz and Jim Christensen. Jim introduced me to diving the breakwaters, which I never knew were worthwhile. He usually told me to go one way and he went the other way. I got involved in the blue water part when our engineers, Mark Lamont and Jim Dexter, got into it. It's always a thrill to remember your first yellowtail, which I got under a kelp paddy. My first white sea bass was a long time coming; after 3 or 4 years I thought I was never going to get one. That was a tremendous thrill.

"Where I really got into the challenge of free diving was in UDT when we would take candidates in the escape tower at New London. In those days we did a lot of free ascents under controlled conditions from 110 feet; they don't do it any more. The water is warm and crystal clear, you don't worry because there are locks you can get into. We practiced ascents, ditches with open and closed circuit gear...it's amazing how good you could get in just a day or two."

Ocean Futures

Bonin retired from Scubapro in 1991, but not from diving. When DEMA experienced organizational difficulties, Dick was asked to

take over and guide them through the crisis. Today he heads up Ocean Futures, a nonprofit organization formed to represent the diving community on issues of access and the environment. "A year ago when the gillnet controversy came up in California, I brought in

Test diving in the Mediterranean.

Scubapro and DEMA. I found out diving isn't organized (and that) the environmental area is a minefield."

The gillnet issue in California could have been lost if the state's dive shops hadn't supported a major petition drive to get the proposition on the ballot. As a result, gillnets were banned. Another recent example of diving's political clout was the question of access to marine sanctuaries. It could easily have gone the other way if the diving community hadn't been there to participate. "We found out you are pretty much all by yourself fighting against a much bigger organization. The diving community needs a voice before somebody else speaks for us.

"It was time for DEMA to give something back; we owe something to the sport and to the sea. I suggested we start a foundation and get organized. We sell memberships to individuals and to businesses, primarily pro diving dealers. Ocean Futures is a nonprofit environmental organization from a diver's perspective, dedicated to preserving what we have and leave a heritage for the divers to come...not just protecting the reefs, but development of reefs, educational programs,...a tremendous opportunity to do a lot of good and also represent us when it's necessary. If it all works I see an international organization, because the problems are worldwide. The marine environmental movement in the US is ahead of other areas. Lots of people from overseas signed up because they have the same problems. The potential is immense."

Ocean Futures can be contacted at Suite 603, PO Box 2705, Huntington Beach, CA 92649.

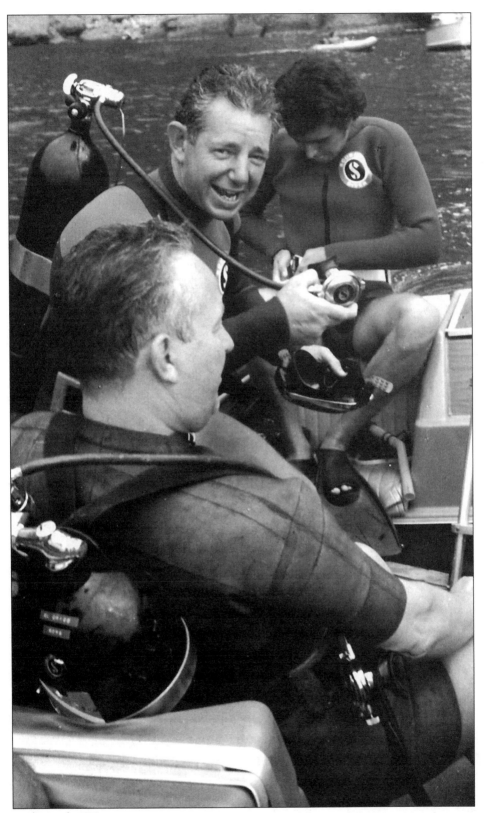

Test dive in Italy, 1970s.

CAPTAINS OF INDUSTRY
BOB HOLLIS

A renowned inventor, photographer, adventurer and entrepreneur, Bob Hollis today heads up Oceanic, the fourth largest company in the diving industry.

"HERE I AM 35 YEARS OLD," said Bob Hollis, "losing my investment in this operation, losing part of my business because I've been away so long, almost losing my life, and what for? To bring up a pot of dirty clothes and garbage."

The date was August 1973, the place a surface recompression chamber on the trawler *Narragansett,* anchored over the wreck of the *Andrea Doria.* Hollis and Jack McKenney were in there after a near disastrous night dive that almost cost them both their lives. Two colleagues, Don Rodocker and Chris De Lucchi, were in saturation aboard an underwater habitat on the deck of the ship, 160 feet below the surface. McKenney and Hollis were assigned to bring down a transfer capsule containing hot meals, clothing, and a can of CO_2 absorbent. The problem was that the 65 pound capsule was far more negatively buoyant than expected, and the combination of exertion, depth, and 43 degree water exacerbated the effects of nitrogen narcosis. Even with inflated Fenzy BCs, the two divers had to struggle down the descent line and roll the heavy pot to the habitat, where the supplies were exchanged for used ones. The hard part was yet to come: bringing the transfer capsule back to the surface.

As they pulled themselves up the line with one hand, holding the pot with the other and kicking furiously, McKenney's regulator began to draw hard. He was low on air and couldn't reach his infla-

*Bob Hollis suiting up for **Andrea Doria** dive, 1973.*

tor valve to add buoyancy. At 80 feet he sucked his last breath. Knowing Hollis was better at conserving air, Jack let go of the pot, inflated his Fenzy, and shot upward to the decompression tanks hanging at 30 feet. Left with the full weight of the pot, Bob lost his grip on the line and began sinking back into the pitch-black void. Kicking desperately, he groped for the line in total darkness and luckily his hand fell on it. Continuing to kick and pull himself with one hand, he somehow made it to the 30-foot tanks where safety diver Bob Coffey relieved him of the capsule. Totally exhausted, Hollis shot to the surface on the air in his BC. Helpful hands stripped him of his gear, yanked McKenney to the surface, and had both of them in the chamber within 11 minutes. These events are described in dramatic, first-hand detail in McKenney's autobiography, **Dive to Adventure** (Vancouver: Panorama Publications, 1983).

A veteran of three expeditions, Hollis has logged more hours on the *Doria* than any man alive. Although he is known today primarily as the president of Oceanic Products, the spirit and pursuit of adventure has been the major motivating factor in his life.

Bob Hollis grew up in Orland, a rural Northern California community, and wasn't introduced to the ocean until dropping out of college and moving to the bay area. He was employed by Standard Oil as a welder involved in the manufacturing of refining equipment. While working there he earned a degree in mechanical engineering through a correspondence school, and eventually became an engineer.

In the mid 50s Bob began free diving along north coast, spearing fish and hunting abalone. He bought his first two-hose regulator in 1956. Like most divers in those days, he never took a course because they weren't available. Every weekend was spent in and under the water.

In Monterey he met photographers Nate Lawrence, Karl and Helmut Stellrecht, who were shooting with home-built underwater housings. Using the materials available at the time, Bob made his own from Plexiglas. By 1958 the first electronic strobes came out, and he made housings for them. Then as now, there were problems getting them to fire reliably. He used military connectors, filling them with high density silicone grease. After a long swim to the bottom, as often as not the strobe wouldn't fire. The routine was to go back in, take it apart, re-grease the connector, and swim back out. "We would do that three to four times a day. If I had to do that now, (I'd ask)...where's the boat ?

"1956 through '60 was my introduction to photography. I bought an old rigid UDT raft, rugged as hell, and got involved into offshore diving out of Monterey, Carmel, Golden Gate, and Half Moon Bay. We would load ten or twelve tanks and three guys in the rafts. I designed a planing board, towed it with Signal Corps wire. A diver would ride it and send messages back, using codes for fish, rocks, and pinnacles. Planing down to 200 feet on scuba in Carmel...was incredible. We found some sponge banks that had never been dived on. We did planing operations all the way to Big Sur, camping overnight or sleeping in the raft...even sleeping in our wet suits when it was cold. My buddies were the Stellrecht brothers, Kyle Loveley, Nate Lawrence. In the early days of underwater film shows, they were the big winners."

> The boat skipper said the shark was a least 20 feet long; it had to be the same animal. It was a pleasure to see him, but I don't want to see another except in a cage.

Hollis bought an old whaling boat which he used to tow the raft to the Farallon Islands for the weekend. "We anchored in Fisherman's Bay, as many tanks as we could cram in, a couple inches of waterline, hoping for no swells going out. On one dive we found a cave that turned out to be a hole in an old ship and found amphora-type bottles and a small chest. We were convinced there was treasure there, but could never find the opening again. The bottles were in Al Giddings' Bamboo Reef dive store for a number of years."

The Farallons, a rookery for sea lions and elephant seals, sometimes attracted white sharks looking for an easy meal. Photographer Leroy French was attacked by one in the early 60s and rescued by Giddings. Shortly afterward, Hollis' boat was anchored to a buoy out there. "During the night a horrendous storm came up. The next morning another boat came in. Some of those guys were spearfishing; we didn't like that. Our chain had broken, and we decided to look for the anchor. Doing a circular search pattern... a great white was right under me on a ledge, so big its dorsal was laying over. After looking about 30 seconds, I motioned to the other guys to get back on the boat. As we came up, the other ship was gone. While we were underwater, a guy got hit...500 stitches, was in the hospital for six months. The boat skipper said the shark was a least 20 feet long; it had to be the same animal. It was a pleasure to see him, but I don't want to see another except in a cage."

Hollis began traveling to the Sea of Cortez in 1957, camping in San Carlos Bay near Guaymas. "It used to be boiling, alive with fish. (In the) early 60s we sailed across to Tortuga Island off Mulege.... At

80 feet, about the limit of free diving depth, the fish were getting larger....We got tanks and dropped to around 120-130 feet. There were 300 to 500 pound sea bass, 40 to 100 of them, hovering above the sand. There was a current. All you had to do was put your heels in the sand and slide; these fish would part just like going through a herd of cows and let you through ....I was pretty young, had always been a hunter....I drilled a 400 pound fish (and) the line pack came off like a rocket. I grabbed hold of this thing, that fish took me... from 130 to 190 in seconds. I pulled the line under a rock. It caught and snapped like it was nothing. That gave me a lot of respect for a big fish. Giddings was also a hunter in those days. He shot a 260 pounder; the biggest one I ever brought back was 140 pounds."

I came as close as I'd like to think to being trapped underwater... had to take the tank off and make an emergency ascent. That ended my commercial career.

By the early 60s Hollis had become heavily involved in underwater photography, and founded the Underwater Photographic Society of Northern California. An early active member was Dewey Bergman, who was running a travel agency in Berkeley. He later sold it and formed See & Sea Travel. "In 1965 I organized a group of friends from the Photo Society and booked a trip to Cozumel through Dewey. That became the first See & Sea trip (and) the first organized dive trip there. I led most of the See & Sea trips the next two to three years, all to Cozumel.

"We made the first trip to Chinchorro Banks (where) Dewey and I found ancient cannons. It's against the law to take antiquities, and Pablo Bush Romero (founder of CEDAM) heard rumors. He was connected with the Mexican government and had a museum in Mexico City. Pablo asked Dewey, who played dumb. Pablo said he would come back a half hour later in case he had a change of heart. Dewey came to our room and said, 'We have a problem.' I said, 'See if we can't trade him three for three.' He finally (agreed to) write that it was a CEDAM expedition, see that we get credit, and kept the legal authorities out of it. Of course he had to take possession of the cannons immediately. He put one in his museum, treated all of them, and two wound up at the Smithsonian. Later he told us these were the earliest cannons ever found in these waters."

About that time, Bob started a short-lived part time commercial dive operation, cleaning boat bottoms, doing salvage and mechanical repair. "Strictly for money. I hated it. A boat sank under the San Rafael Bridge. I was hired to put a line on it...got all tangled up, there was no visibility. I came as close as I'd like to think to being trapped underwater...had to take the tank off and make an emergency ascent. That ended my commercial career."

In partnership with Ray Collins, Bob opened a sporting goods, surfing, diving and fishing store called Anchor Shack One in 1966. (There would eventually be two more stores.) It was an instant success, enabling him to quit his job with Standard Oil. With a pool and classroom in the complex, they were teaching the bulk of students in the Bay area at that time.

photo by Sandy Skaar

"We started heavy marketing for the store. Within a year we were teaching NAUI and NASDS classes, as many as three a night, five nights a week. We wrote our own advanced classes: marine biology, underwater photography, spearfishing with targets in the pool. We started out teaching extension tube photography. We were the first to come

Bob Hollis, early 60s.

out with two tubes, combined ratios, (and) also used extension tubes in housings." Beginning underwater photographers were initially taught in tide pools, with umbrellas used to cut down sunlight and parallel underwater conditions.

At the same time Bob was making underwater photographic equipment and selling it by mail order under the Anchor Shack label. The first successful product was the Hydro-strobe, an aluminum housing for the Honeywell Stobonar. Before the era of submersible strobes, most serious photographers used them. "Paul Tzimoulis wrote a seven page article on the Hydro-strobe one time. The photo of him using it showed water inside the lens, and nobody ever caught it. We sold at least 6,000 of those all over the world."

With partner John Clark, Bob incorporated Oceanic Products in 1971, primarily to expand on the Anchor Shack line of photographic products. Their plant was burned down by an arsonist within a few months of opening, but that was only a temporary setback.

The product that put Oceanic on the map was the Hydro 35, an aluminum housing for Nikon and Canon professional cameras. Designed in 1968, it quickly became the standard of its time and remained that way for 20 years. It wasn't the first. That distinction belongs to the Niko-mar, designed by Al Giddings, but only about

250 of those large, cylindrical housings were ever sold. Patterned after the Rolleimarine, the Hydro 35 fit the motor-driven cameras like a glove. About 3,500 were sold, making it the most successful metal housing ever produced to that time. They still bring a good price on the used market and are the housing of choice for many pros, despite having been out of production since 1988.

Housings were also designed for Hasselblad, as well as for motion picture cameras from super-8s to Arriflexes. The latter were custom made for clients like Stan Waterman, Jack McKenney, and Survival Anglia. A full time camera technician was hired to convert 16mm movie cameras for housings. They also made lighting systems for movie work, and built the underwater scooters used in the early James Bond films. Even a video housing was produced, but at three feet in diameter it was considerably larger than the compact marvels of today.

Carl Roessler, just starting out in underwater photography, was on one of the Chinchorro trips. He introduced Hollis to Bob Croft, a Navy UDT instructor who was training to break the world record for breath-hold diving. Bob, Dewey Bergman, and Al Giddings produced a film for CBS television on the project, depicting Croft becoming the first human to breath-hold dive to 250 feet.

Hollis had begun shooting movies in the early 60s using military gun cameras he bought from surplus. They were compact and easily adaptable to housings. "I was more interested in stills, but started gaining skills. Putting a film together and editing was too much work. I was involved in other things, (and wasn't) going to be a slave to this crap. I still have aspirations of doing that someday, but you can only do so many things at one time." Bob later put these skills to work on the Andrea Doria documentaries.

He was an investor on a portable saturation complex being built by Chris De Lucci and Don Rodocker in San Diego, commuting down there almost every weekend to work on it. The long term plan was to use it diving on a series of wrecks around the world. The habitat was first used on the 1973 Doria project. "Don and Chris were the principal guys. We were in saturation five days on the side of the ship. We were saturated on heliox, but made the open water excursions on air, because we didn't have enough heliox. No accurate decompression schedules existed for exposure to both air and heliox (so) no one knew what was going to happen medically."

Commenting on the incident that opened this story, Hollis recalls, "Jack gave me that line with that pot, I could have shot him. I was freefalling in the water...and away he went."

McKenney and Hollis returned to the *Doria* in 1981 when the ship's safe was recovered. "Peter Gimbel raised the money for that one. He spent a number of years organizing it. Nick Caliyonis and I and Jack and Peter went to Commercial Dive Center (now College of Oceaneering), training for saturation. They did oxygen tolerance tests, medicals, scans to make sure we were OK to do another sat dive. We spent six weeks out there diving it; I was in sat 17 days.

"We made the first and possibly the only night dives on the *Doria*. I probably have more time on the *Doria* than anybody still alive: 91 tank dives in addition to 21 total days of saturation. I did all the filming when they were cutting the safe out. Jack and I made some wonderful excursions into the chapel and over the parquet floors, penetrations as far as our 250 foot umbilical would allow us to go...the dining rooms, down to the C deck, where we were looking for an experimental Chrysler car that was supposed to be on board...Wonderful memories, a great adventure that I'll never forget."

Putting a film together and editing was too much work. I was involved in other things, (and wasn't) going to be a slave to this crap. I still have aspirations of doing that someday, but you can only do so many things at one time.

Because of his relationship with Dewey Bergman, Hollis was traveling for fun as well: from the Carribbean to the Red Sea, including such places as Rangiroa , Bora Bora, Tuamotos, Marquesas, and beyond. "Talk about live-aboards, at that time you were lucky to get a dugout canoe."

Back home, realizing they had to branch out beyond photography, Hollis bought out his partner in 1974. The first general diving product was an underwater light. "With a limited amount for tooling, we decided to use one tool for a whole series of products: the handlight, the 2001 series of strobes, also some movie lights...five different products. The handlight was the driving force behind Oceanic. I sold it as an OEM (original equipment manufacturer) product; it was the Scubapro handlight for all of Europe. They bought five to six thousand lights a year."

Oceanic was small but profitable, and by the mid 70s they were into more general diving equipment. Farallon was becoming insolvent, and was about to sell their product line to Scubapro. In eleventh hour negotiations, Hollis made them a better offer. "Farallon had never made any money in its history. We made it profitable within 90 days. We laid off some people, reorganized, re-engineered the product lines (the return door was bigger than the shipping door). That was really the turning point when Oceanic took off and became a full line manufacturer.".

As early as 1979, Hollis realized that the future of diving was going to be in electronics. They were buying movements for gauges from an OEM company, but quality control was poor. "We wound up sending people there to show them how to make their own gauges. Our state of the art was far advanced over (theirs), so we formed Pelagic Pressure Systems." An OEM company, it makes instruments today for Oceanic, Sherwood, US Divers, Dacor, Tabata, Survivair, Union Carbide, and Litton contracts. He emphasized that Oceanic and Pelagic are separate companies. "All the electronic stuff, all the surface mount technology, all our own programming is done in house.".

Bob Hollis with the experimental Electrolung – an early attempt at computrerized mixed-gas scuba, 1972.

A third spinoff company is ROMI Enterprises, which makes regulators for Oceanic and other companies. "That stands for Robert and Mike, my son. ROMI is a machine and engineering group... Oceanic is basically a marketing company, Pelagic makes the instrumentation, other vendors make mask, fins, and snorkels, ROMI makes the regulators. Oceanic Europe was established in 1990."

They are also involved in space. Astronauts at the Johnson Space Center train underwater. The government plans to build a pool in Houston the size of a football field, 60 feet deep, to simulate assembling a space station. Each astronaut has about eight support people underwater, and at that depth they would be approaching decompression times. NASA contracted Hollis to develop a system that would transmit data from the tank to a topside computer, and to a wrist-worn computer carried by the astronaut or a diving support technician .

Taking advantage of his proximity to Silicone Valley, electronics plays a major role in Hollis' vision for the future. "I'd like to be able to go deeper and stay longer. We are working on a sport diving rebreather, with electronic controls to mix the gases. Nitrox has been used for the last 50 years...a Heliox unit (could be made) for deep diving. I expect to catch some flak on Nitrox, but 50 years ago Cousteau and Gagnan probably caught flak for inventing the regulator. It's no different now. Who is to say compressed air is the perfect breathing medium? We are looking at a better breathing gas with state of the art electronics to control partial pressures, so divers will be able to explore greater depths, and stay longer at a fixed depth without decompression issues.

> Why should there be these rules saying that people shouldn't do this? It's a free society, people should be given the opportunity to and go out and (explore).

"A certain risk is involved, but it's like climbing a mountain. There is another frontier out there, (and) there is always a group of pioneers. Why should there be these rules saying that people shouldn't do this? It's a free society, people should be given the opportunity to and go out and (explore)."

Bob's personal goal is to continue that search for adventure. "My long term plans call for buying a 70 to 80 foot motor sailor, sail for eight to ten years, write and take pictures. I'm going to do that come hell or high water. I'd love to do a Newbert type book.

"Diving has come a long way. Not just macho any more, it has become a family sport. I enjoy the thrill of watching my nine year old twins being introduced to the underwater world." In his vision for the future, Bob sees smaller, lighter, user friendly equipment. "A person needs to be free in the water, (so) eliminate multiple hoses. (I see) underwater propulsion vehicles that are small and compact....video, computers, heads-up displays, disk-based images, editing. Rebreathers, for those who can afford it, to explore areas that have been inaccessible.

"One of the things I can say about diving is the reward of meeting a lot of wonderful people. Out of all the activities I've done, I've never had the feeling of camaraderie, the opportunities for travel and adventure, and sharing (that comes with diving). Nothing is better than making a dive and sharing those moments."

SECTION 7

EDUCATORS

FRANK SCALLI

Frank Scalli was one of the founding fathers of sport diving in the eastern United States, but his influence extended throughout the nation. He helped originate the first national program for sport diving instruction, that of the YMCA. He was also a founder of the Boston Sea Rovers, and one of the originators of their annual clinics. These forerunners of today's film festivals and consumer shows continue to provide instruction and entertainment for new generations of divers. Frank was also instrumental in introducing scuba instruction to colleges and universities, teaching at Harvard, MIT, West Point, and Annapolis. For many years he was sales manager for US Divers. A measure of his stature in the diving industry is that he is the only person to have served on the board of directors of NAUI, PADI, and the YMCA diving programs at the same time.

LIKE MANY OF THE EARLY PIONEERS, Frank Scalli's first introduction to scuba came in the military. He had been an Army paratrooper, and with three months left in his tour of duty was sent back to Fort Campbell, Kentucky to await discharge. As the ranking NCO he was given a choice of two or three assignments, and chose that of aquatics supervisor. Frank had no previous professional experience in aquatics, but the Army has its own way of doing things. So they put him in charge of lifeguards at seven swimming pools, a rock quarry, and an officers' lake.

Why aquatics? "I wanted to get my Senior Life Saving and WSI (Water Safety Instructor) certifications. They were planning to start the program after I took over; I always loved the water and it would be fun to have when I got home. WSI was the most difficult thing I had ever done in my life; jumping out of planes was easy by comparison."

While making his rounds, he noticed the guards had a certain technique of cleaning pools. "One day a lifeguard was underwater, picking up hairballs and bobby pins. He had a gas mask with a hose to the surface. When he came up I asked what he was doing. He explained. I asked when he was going to do it again. He said this afternoon at the lake. He let me try it in five feet of water, and that was that. No instruction, I just put it on and went at it. That introduced me into looking at sand instead of tiles and I said, 'This is fun.' "

Three months later he was discharged. The transition from an

Frank Scalli lobster diving off the Northeast coast in 1959.

active military life to a sedentary civilian one convinced Frank of the need for physical activity, and diving seemed a promising candidate. For once he would be able to use his negative buoyancy to advantage. There weren't many places selling gear in 1953, and nobody was offering instruction. So he took his new mask, tank, and regulator to the local YMCA pool. Everything worked fine, except his ears hurt and he couldn't figure out why. The next time he tried it, he ruptured an eardrum. "I went home and said, 'There's something wrong with this, I really enjoy it, but it hurts too much.' So I researched it at the library. They talked about equalizing but it wasn't clear. (The book was geared toward hard-hat diving and didn't explain the process.) I figured maybe it was just a bad day. Went back three weeks later and did the same thing to the other ear. Now I figured that this was a bad activity. But nobody would buy the equipment, so I went back and did some more research."

This finally led him to Woods Hole Oceanographic Institution. There he met chief diver Dave Owen, described by Frank as the east coast version of Jim Stewart. Owen explained the problem, and supplied him with some reading material as well. Scalli asked why more people didn't know about this new sport. Owen explained, "It's not a sport yet."

By the summer of 1954, the YMCA had received requests at two other pools from people who wanted to try out their equipment. There were no standards, so Frank wrote out a list of do's and don'ts. Frank was not an educator or a writer; he was a sheet metal worker by trade. But the Y people liked what they read and adopted it.

By this time Scalli was getting into open water diving. All of it was done alone and without instruction, because he didn't know any other divers. The ocean temperature off Gloucester, Massachusetts is 48 degrees in the summer. "I did my first dive outside the pool in September of '54...no suit, damn near froze to death. Saw some beautiful things on the bottom...and got so carried away that I started shivering and had trouble making it back to shore. (There were) no suits, no BCs, and I was negative buoyant. (I had) an army cartridge belt filled with nuts and bolts...no quick release, I couldn't undo it because my hands were so cold. I thawed out driving home, and thought there has got to be a way to stay warm."

Frank heard about Neal Hess, a Harvard student from Southern California. Later one of the founders of NAUI, Neal was a Los Angeles County instructor who had some experience with wet suits. "That made me realize somebody else knew a lot more than I do.. Up to that time I had plans to wrap myself in tight clothing. He told me about neoprene" His first wet suit was a kit that he had to put together himself. Frank recalls, "The arms and legs were built like boxes. They were easy to put on, but when you took them off all the seams opened up. So you spent the next day re-cementing them with Black Magic (neoprene cement), which wasn't magic at all. That made all the difference in the world. I made two great dives on the suit before it fell apart.

> I was crawling up to the beach and everybody rushed in to see what I was doing. The police weren't sure whether to rescue me or just help me. The fire department wanted to know if I needed resuscitation. I spent the next two hours explaining to people what I was doing underwater.

"We used cotton work gloves, but my hands got so cold I still had trouble on the beach getting my gear off. ...I realized you shouldn't have to use two hands for a weight belt, so I took the old army cartridge belt, drilled a hole through it and put in a pin for a quick release. Now I was fairly comfortable underwater, but still had trouble with long swims on the surface, especially with a bag of lobsters. I probably came near drowning a few times.

"The next challenge was to swim easier on the surface without dropping everything. We played around with the Navy life jackets, but they weren't meant to be used in seawater. The seams opened and they corroded."

About this time, Frank introduced himself to Jim Cahill, a former Navy frogman who had just opened a dive shop in Beverly, Massachusetts. It later became New England Divers, the nation's first mega-dive shop. Jim was teaching a class at the YMCA, but his entire diving background had been with the military. So he and Scalli went to a pool and showed each other what they knew about diving. "That's when I first realized you could take the mouthpiece out of your mouth...before that, it was a part of my anatomy."

On the east coast in the mid 50s, divers were almost as scarce as astronauts. An excursion off a public beach sometimes became a public sensation. Frank recalls, "When I came out, there were about 60 people on the beach, two police cars, fire and rescue. I was crawling up to the beach and everybody rushed in to see what I was doing. The police weren't sure whether to rescue or just help me. The fire department wanted to know if I needed resuscitation. I spent the next two hours explaining to people what I was doing underwater. The following Saturday there were about 60 more people on the beach waiting to see a diver go in and come back alive."

By 1954 there were about fifteen divers in the Boston area. Although they were usually diving alone, they eventually got to know each other. In August of that year they formed a club, the Boston Sea Rovers. "We started with seven divers, after two years we had twelve."

Frank Scalli and Joe Linehan's dive boat the KAY-G, the best dive boat on the east coast, 1958.

Among the first was Walter Feinberg, an innovator who first suggested the annual shows and clinics.

"Bob Ballard came by the Y one time when I was teaching. He was Naval Reserve, showed up with twin aluminum tanks, said he had to be checked out for some position he was looking for in the Navy. I invited him to be a member of the club. Paul Tzimoulis came on the scene in 1958 through the YMCA program."

At this time there was no true nationwide program of scuba certification. The YMCA ran its first national instructor course in 1959 in Chicago. Frank was one of fourteen participants, the only one from New England. Since there were no certified instructors prior to this, they certified each other.

Frank's assignment was to go back to the east coast and run instructor training programs. Tzimoulis was one of the first instructors. Others included Cahill, Fred Calhoun, Frank Sanger (founder of Parkway) and Jerry O'Neill (head researcher in saturation diving for Westinghouse).

Scalli was instrumental in writing the first lesson plan outline on scuba diving. In 1955 he wrote a very basic three-page instruction guide for the YMCA, consisting of just five two-hour sessions, split between the pool and the classroom. National aquatics chairman Bernie Empleton asked to distribute it nationally. "I took some time and improved it, made it more wordy. The five pages became twelve pages. Nothing really changed. It was survival; the activity was to survive and get home every evening."

This was the lesson plan used in the Chicago instructor institute. When it came time for the YMCA to publish its first full-scale textbook, Empleton turned to Scalli and the Sea Rovers for help. **"The Science of Skin and Scuba Diving**, published by the YMCA, was the standard text on scuba into the mid 70s; a revised edition, **New Science of Skin and Scuba Diving**, is still in print. I was on the national committee with CNCA (Council for National Cooperation in Aquatics) when they adopted that book."

At this time Frank was still a full-time sheet metal worker, building respiratory equipment like iron lungs. In addition he was devoting about 50 hours a week to writing and teaching scuba, and working on the Sea Rovers clinics. These were the first events to spread information and education about underwater activities to the general public. "The first one was in 1954. Two years later we had Jacques Cousteau as a guest." How did it get started? "Walt Feinberg felt we should share our knowledge with the community. We brought in Dave Owens from Woods Hole, Harold Edgerton from MIT, local people that we felt knew what had to be done. The Navy sent people from the submarine training tower at New London (including) George Bond, who became the father of saturation diving.

> **In the beginning my main concern was safety. It was amazing to see people come up from their first dive with no pain, no tears in their eyes or blood in their nose.**

"The Sea Rovers did more than just go diving; we felt we had to go out and spread the word. Admission was 99 cents, because the YMCA said if we charged a dollar we would have to pay taxes. It stayed 99 cents for about three years, till we outgrew the YMCA and had to rent a facility. At first we had about 180 people in five rooms and an auditorium. Now everybody runs these programs, and we started it. In the beginning my main concern was safety. It was amazing to see people come up from their first dive with no pain, no tears in their eyes or blood in their nose."

It was inevitable that Frank would become professionally involved in the diving industry. That happened in 1959. "I convinced one of my students who had money that he should open a dive shop and I should run it. I did that for a year, in Everett, Mass, in my home. I was still working my real job, about 40%, screwing around trying to find out if I could make a living in diving. One of my students opened a shop in Natick, Mass and I left my job in the sheet metal trade and became full time in February 1960. The shop was aquatics and sports, we built an indoor pool ...for teaching. The aquatics end did real well and we made money. The winter ski equipment didn't do well and the shop went bankrupt."

Frank wasn't unemployed very long. "Cousteau had an interest in ...promoting more people to get into diving through training and education. Because of his association with Harold Edgerton, he had heard about me...and got word to the company that I should be considered as east coast promotion director. I accepted the job three days after I lost the dive shop, an easy choice. They had just hired Bill Barrada on the west coast; he was my first boss at US Divers.

Frank presents a Boston Sea Rovers award to Melville Grosvenor, president of National Geographic Society, 1973.

"He called and asked if I knew what the job entails. He said, 'I don't know either. Here's what I am going to do. See if we can get a diving program started in universities, places that we can say, 'yes it's being taught here.' With my connections in the Sea Rovers I was able to begin teaching basic diving at Harvard, at MIT (with the help of Harold Edgerton), and most of the major universities. I did that for a year and a half...(I taught at) West Point, Annapolis...I encouraged a friend to start a program at the Coast Guard Academy. We were really moving out, and now diving became respectable because you could have classes at the university. This didn't take it out of the YMCA, but opened it for other people to get into the business. Now people were anxious to take diving."

NAUI was founded in 1960, and in an effort to spread nationally, they appointed Jim Cahill to their Board of Directors. Two years later Jim ran the first ITC in New England, utilizing the same instructors that had participated in the YMCA course three years earlier: Tzimoulis, Sanger, and Scalli. There was no inter-agency rivalry then. "We worked together, we were the same people. NAUI's appeal was that they had financial backing, they had the expertise of the forerunners of the whole thing, the west coast. A great intertwining of knowledge, personalities, ethnic backgrounds." A few years later Scalli was a consultant to John Cronin when he and Ralph Erickson founded PADI. His role was to assure that lesson plans and textbook material conformed to national standards.

Next to instruction, Frank's major underwater interest has been wreck diving. He describes it as, "... one of nature's love tokens to divers." His first wreck dive was on the *New Hampshire.*, a copper bottom Navy gunship, the sister ship of the USS *Constitution* (*Old Ironsides*). After being decommissioned in 1937, she was towed to Portland, Maine for salvage. Lightning from a storm in the Bay of Massachusetts set the ship afire and burned it almost to the waterline. In the mid 1950s, a commercial diver found fragments of posts and beams, along with copper and brass fittings, in 20 to 30 feet of water

off Manchester, Massachusetts . "In 1957 I had a dive boat with Joe Linehan, and we located it. Not much wood was left, but there were copper spikes and bronze drift pins that had originally held the whole thing together... Some were like brand new copper pins from rolling around in the sand. A lot of them had

Sea Rovers awards ceremony, 1964. Left to right: Philippe Cousteau, Paul Tzimoulis, Frank, Dr. Joe MacInnis and Al Giddings.

a marking on it: 'US.' In the Library of Congress, we found most of the fittings were made in Paul Revere's shop in Boston. He was granted the first trademark of the US government. 'US' meant the inspector that inspected these 10 or 12 inch copper spikes and bronze pins would pick out every tenth or twentieth one, then take the U and the S stamp and hit it. We knew there were two stamps because we found three or four of them that were 'SU.' It probably was close to lunch time for the inspector. Before we realized the value, we had sold about 500 pounds to keep our dive boat going. Got about twelve cents a pound for junk. The going rate for one of those spikes now is four or five hundred dollars. We had given up a fortune for gas money for the boat."

The going rate for one of those spikes now is four or five hundred dollars. We had given up a fortune for gas money for the boat.

Not all of Scalli's wreck dives were in shallow water. In 1967 he dove the *Andrea Doria.* with Joe Hohmann, his buddy from the Sea Rovers. "The highlight of my wreck diving career. It was still in very good shape, with rows of portholes as far as the eye could see. We didn't get much off of it except a lot of good memories. After Peter Gimbel and the Cousteaus, we were about the fourth or fifth group to dive on it. I still love to dive with my brother Don (a dive shop owner and instructor). I'm now content just looking at the wonders of being underwater."

Training for the *Andrea Doria.* was conducted in local quarries, some over 200 feet deep. This is also where Frank trained police to do body recoveries. Until the mid 60s, he and other Sea Rovers were doing recovery operations on a volunteer basis. "We trained the police to do that kind of work at US Divers' expense so sport divers could ease out of it, and rightfully so."

Frank Scalli, 1992.

The Sea Rovers came to the attention of **Time** Magazine in the early 1960s. They wanted a photo of a group of ice divers in a hole in a lake. "Jerry O'Neill, our divemaster, had a home on a lake, covered with 14 inches of ice. I asked him to cut a hole so we wouldn't be in too deep water. He cut the hole 6 by 6 feet, submerged the ice block, slid it over, and six of us were ready to go in. With the safety line I slipped in first, and my feet hit the bottom; I was waist deep. Jerry had cut the hole right over a sand bar. In order to salvage the photograph I got all the divers on the bottom without fins, and we got on our knees. That's the way it was published."

In 1962 US Divers transferred Frank into the sales department. Ten years later he became national sales manager, remaining in that capacity until his retirement in 1985. He took the job under the condition that he could continue to operate from his home in Massachusetts. "My first love was promoting, bringing people into the sport safely, convincing others it's a good activity, and it's worked....After the regulator, I can't think of anything making diving more comfortable than the wet suit and buoyancy. If you are comfortable and know you're safe, you can put up with a leaky mask, a slow leaking regulator, fins that might not be the most comfortable. When all is said and done, the thermal protection and the buoyancy are the major breakthroughs. Electronics may make it but I have to wait and see."

Frank combines diving with charity work on the Seamark Program, an annual fund raiser for the Cotting School for Handicapped Children. This is a social event at the New England Aquarium in Boston, featuring keynote guest speakers including Bob Ballard, Stan Waterman, and Jean Michel Cousteau. With the support of the diving community, they have raised over $250,000 for the Seamark

Vision Clinic. In recognition of his fifteen years of effort on behalf of these children, the clinic has been dedicated to Frank Scalli.

In 1992 he was awarded the DEMA Reaching Out Award, for long and meritorious service to the diving industry. Pat Barron, current west coast sales rep for US Divers, sums up Frank as "A guy beloved by the whole diving industry. He attacks any problem he sees, can talk to any audience at any time with a story, an anecdote, a funny joke. He just has a zest for life and a zest for people."

UNDERWATER EDUCATORS
DAN WAGNER

Although American scuba diving got its start on the coasts, the heartland produced its own rugged brand of pioneers. Lacking the clear waters and rich marine life of the oceanic environment, they pursued their sport in lakes, ponds, and quarries, diving for junk while their coastal brethren were spearing big fish. Midwestern pioneers were largely self taught. The story of Dan Wagner's first open water dive is perhaps the epitome of this school: a body search in a frigid quarry at night, without a protective suit. He survived this experience to become an early leader in dive instruction in the Chicago area, initiating programs in several YMCAs, and heading up the Illinois Council of Skin and Scuba Divers. In the 60s, he moved to Florida and began a second career that eclipsed the first. Beginning as an instructor, he eventually owned and operated three live-aboard boats in the area. Wagner chronicled Mel Fisher's expeditions on film before anybody heard of the treasure hunter. Today he produces features on video, while his wife and stepson operate their third boat, the Dream Too.

WHEN IT COMES TO EXCITEMENT, TRAUMA, AND COMEDY, nobody has a first dive story to top Dan Wagner's. He survived the experience to become a leader in two diving communities, and an award-winning producer of films and videos.

It began 1954, when the south Chicago native saw the movie **The Frogmen,** and got excited about the underwater world. When his sister's boyfriend needed some quick cash, the opportunity arose to do something about it. Wagner bought his war surplus scuba equipment for $40. The tank was 38 cubic feet, with a home-made valve system; the fins were black UDT Churchills. The regulator was a surplus oxygen rig of the freeflow type, from an airplane. Dan had some second thoughts, but heard about a man at the Harvey YMCA, who went diving with his family every Tuesday night. This was autumn, and open water diving was strictly a summer activity.

Wagner headed for the Y and met Bill Jacobs. "I asked him, 'What do you think about this (regulator), it doesn't look like what you've got.' He said, 'You ought to take a sledgehammer and go at this thing real quick, because it's dangerous...You can use my equipment; see if you like it. If you do, I'll allow what you paid for your stuff and you can buy it from me.' "

After the usual warnings about breath holding, Wagner worked

Dan Wagner age 60, 1992.

his way down to the deep end of the pool, stood on one finger, and did a barrel roll. "I was no little fellow then, weighed about 230 pounds. After 5 minutes I came up, and said 'This is neat.' Jake looked at his wife and said 'He's hooked.'

Ice diving in Chicago from left to right; Don Oram, Bob Polley and Dan Wagner.

"It's been 38 years, so I guess he was right. I never took a course, but I so enjoyed what I was doing, that every week I would come out to the pool and...practice. Come spring, I was a swimming pool tiger." Wagner was hooked. He had cards printed that read, "Dan Wagner, Diver." He even went down to the local sheriff's office and told him, "If you ever need a diver for anything, call me." Eight feet was his depth record at the time.

Although Los Angeles County had started a scuba program by then, there was no organized instruction in the rest of the country. The way Wagner learned scuba was the way it was done in those days. He could hardly wait for June, when the water would be warm enough for a real dive.

One night in April the sheriff's office called: "We need a diver. There's been a car pushed into a quarry in Blue Island. We're not sure if there's people inside; we haven't been able to locate it."

Dan said he could be there in an hour, then called Jacobs, who had an air station and compressor at his farm outside of town. He agreed to accompany Dan. "When I got out there Jake is putting a big line of rope in the back of his station wagon. I asked what the rope was for. He says, 'That's to tie around your waist. I'm going to hold...the other end up on the bank. Give me a jerk and I'll pull you out.' I thought 'My God, what have I done?'

"This was April in Chicago, and there were no such animals as wet suits. All I had was...a pair of sweats...Around this quarry is (a) mob of people, there's all these flashing lights, (and) two or three little rowboats. There's newspaper reporters out there, asking 'Is this the diver?' What have I got myself into?"

Jacobs gave him a waterproof flashlight. From the rowboat, Dan dropped overboard and started sinking. "Now everything in the world is going through my mind. In those days we heard about bottomless pits, monsters in quarries. And it's dark. The great big waterproof flashlight worked just about two minutes. I'm wondering when am I going to hit the bottom? I'm blowing and my ears finally clear. It seemed like an eternity before I got to the bottom. I had no idea how deep I was. Visibility was zilch. I'm feeling my way along, on a lot of adrenaline, didn't even feel cold. You know how (it is), trying to find something and scared to death of the next thing you touch?"

Visibility was zilch. I'm feeling my way along, on a lot of adrenaline, didn't even feel cold. You know how (it is), trying to find something and scared to death of the next thing you touch?

Finally beginning to feel the cold, Dan surfaced. The sheriff asked if he wanted to go out further. "Yeah," he replied, and dropped down again. "I wasn't as scared then; if I had been sweeping I would have found it. They finally pulled me back up and now I'm shaking, my lips are blue. They asked, 'Would you like a cup of coffee before you try again?' Yeah.

"So I'm holding this cup of coffee and I hear this voice, 'Let me through, goddamn it, let me through.'...A very familiar voice, it was my father. There I was, supposedly an adult, married, 24 years old, but my father had heard (about it). He says 'What in the name of hell are you doing down there?' I'm shaking like hell and I say, 'Dad, I'm looking for the stolen car.' He says 'Get the hell out of there, you're blue.' I says 'I've got to find the car, there may be people in it.' He says, 'They aren't going to be any deader tomorrow.'

"Everybody had to agree with my father. I was blue, shaking like I was freezing to death, which I was. It convinced the sheriff that I should quit for the night."

Before returning to the quarry the next day, Dan made a run to the local dive shop and bought a rubber dry suit, which was all they had then. The salesman at the shop was Dick Bonin, who later made his mark as the founder of Scubapro.

Back in the quarry, he finally found the car. There were no bodies, just cement blocks in the trunk for weight, no engine, and the steering wheel had been tied. Dan Wagner was now an experienced open water diver.

The story made the papers and Wagner enjoyed his 15 minutes of fame. Then it was back to reality as a tool and die maker at the Ford plant in south Chicago, and helping Jacobs in the Harvey Y pool. Eventually he began teaching his own classes, with Jake's blessing and that of the YMCA director. It was a 32 hour course, significantly expanded over those taught by his predecessor. Like other Chicago area instructors, he was giving out his own certification card, using home-study materials for students developed by E.R. Cross, and distributed locally by Bonin's company, Divemaster.

Dan Wagner (r) and Don Oram on Chicago lakefront, June 1959.

In 1956 the Ford plant had a major layoff. Dan's union contract provided a guaranteed annual wage, so he took the money and became a full-time diving instructor. Classes expanded to five YMCAs, plus afternoon sessions for businessmen at the Sheraton. Setting up his garage as a dive shop, he bought a compressor which was mounted on wheels and towed out to the quarries on weekends. The name of the shop was Dan's Diving Den, his motto: "Have Compressor, Will Travel." At the time, there were only three other dive shops in greater Chicago.

Open water diving in the area wasn't very exciting. The water in Lake Michigan was cold all year round, and 5-foot visibility was a good day. A lot of the local diving went on in strip mines and quarries, where people would look for lost objects and run compass courses.

Wagner recalls, "If you were willing to work on the Braille system, you could find anchors, rods and reels. Chicago is noted for its smelt fishing, and people lost all kinds of things along that whole lakefront area." One day he demonstrated to a reporter how to make money diving. On a single tank, he said he could find enough money's worth of gear to buy his equipment. Dan let the writer choose any spot along the lakefront where people fish, so he wouldn't think he had been set up. "I was sticking my neck out. (But) I went down and found all kinds of goodies. Two perfectly good rods and reels (this was fresh water, it isn't going to mess them up)...anchors, somebody's wallet, (with) 40 dollars in it. I come up with over a hundred bucks worth of odds and ends. Back then you could buy a tank and regulator for that. He wrote a nice story about it."

In the winter, hardy midwestern divers go under the ice. In 1958, Wagner and George Kronberger claimed a depth record of 140 feet under the ice in Lake Geneva, Wisconsin. In the 38 degree water, he claimed to be comfortable in his 3/16" wet suit.

Scuba diving in Illinois was beginning to get organized. The Illinois Council of Skin and Scuba Divers was formed in 1955. Wagner thought up the name, and later was elected Board of Directors for 6 years, and twice was named Diver of the Year. He also was instrumental in forming the Sheriff's Department Underwater Recovery Team, and headed it up for several years. "Part of the reason we wanted to help was macho, ..part of it was that there was nothing else to do underwater in Illinois. We (also wanted to get away from) that motorcycle... image, which was the image of diving at that time." Through trial and error they devised the first underwater search patterns, which are still in today's manuals. "Our goal was that someday the police and fire departments would have their own teams, and instead of going out to find bodies, they would be able to save lives."

Part of the reason we wanted to help was macho, ...part of it was that there was nothing else to do underwater in Illinois. We (also wanted to get away from) that motorcycle... image, which was the image of diving at that time.

By the late 1950s a dozen Chicago YMCAs had scuba programs. Wagner was part of a committee that set up the first teaching standards. This eventually led to the first national certification of instructors, held in Chicago in 1959. Wagner attended that course but failed the written test. He was allowed to retest and passed.

By this time he was involved in photography. "I had never been a land photographer (but) people kept asking me 'What do you see down there?' I decided ...to get a camera and a housing to show them." At first he bought a still camera to shoot slides. Then a friend, working for Bell and Howell, was allowed to buy one movie camera a year at cost. M &E sold a universal housing that fit the Bell and Howell 200 EE, a 16mm camera with electric eye exposure control. It had to be wound by hand, but accepted a cassette holding 50 feet of film. Dan took it to a quarry west of Chicago and shot two rolls with a friend, Jimmy Lee.

Jimmy was a singer at the Chez Paree, Chicago's most renowned night club. One of the regular customers was Jim Thomas, who had a sports and outdoor T.V. show, syndicated throughout the midwest, and was doing a story on a hunting and fishing resort in Saskatchewan, near the Arctic circle. Thomas wanted some underwater pictures. Jimmy informed him that his buddy was an underwater photographer.

"So my third roll of film was shot for money, up at the fringe of the Arctic circle. They gave us a guide, Solomon Cook, a Cree Indian. The guides were totally amazed, they had never seen divers before. They called us 'Something that Goes Below.' (I was) 'Big

Beaver.' We just told Solomon to follow the bubbles. Whenever we came up,... there was Solomon with the boat. We got some good color pictures of walleyes underwater, caught on a rod and reel.

"I progressed from being an individual diver, to teaching, to shoot-

Dan Wagner directing recovery team divers.

ing a lot of (film and) video without ever having gone to a tech school for photography. I've won a lot of awards. Now when I shoot...it helps turn on thousands of people instead of one or two."

In 1960 Dan developed a tumor in his inner ear. It was benign and not connected with diving, but destroyed his sense of balance and eventually required surgery. Unable to work for several months, Dan lost everything he had and went bankrupt. He went back to work in a tool and die shop, but began to tire of Chicago's long cold winters. Florida, where he had made a few previous dive trips, offered an attractive alternative, and in 1963 Dan moved down there.

Once again he was working as a tool and die maker, but his goal was to get back into scuba instruction. The local YMCA had no pool, but there was a fishing tackle store in town that also sold dive gear. Dan offered to teach classes and bring in new customers, but the owner wasn't interested. "He said 'You can teach people all they need to know in 15 minutes.' I said 'Fine, but don't forget the name, because I'm going to teach.' I went to another fishing tackle place in Melbourne and asked if they would be interested in a dive operation. I told them I've got a bunch of equipment up north, I'll bring it down here and set up an air station. I'll just sell the air and teach, you guys sell equipment." They bought the idea and Wagner was back into diving.

He also began hanging around with a treasure hunter named Mel Fisher, who was looking for Spanish wrecks. In those days, nobody took Fisher seriously. But Wagner began shooting movies of his voyages, which later became part of the definitive film of the successful search for the *Atocha*. Today, Wagner's video is the one that Fisher shows in his Key West treasure museum.

The best diving was located offshore, but in the 60s Florida had no full-service dive boats. There were some bare boat charters, but most didn't even have a compressor. Wagner decided there had to be something better for divers. In 1975, he and a pair of partners bought an old 83-foot boat, which they christened the *Sirenia*. "In all my life and all the work I've done, I never worked so hard and so long for so little. On its fourteenth trip the captain put it on the reef in the northern Bahamas. Because of the age of the boat we couldn't get insurance and I lost everything I had.

"I flew back with the last $1000 we had in the bank, (which) we used to charter the plane that took the passengers back. I said, 'I don't know how I'm going to get the money or how I'm going to do it, but I'm going to build a brand new boat (that) will have all that a boat is supposed to have, and it will run dive charters.'"

The *Sirenia* sank on May 22, 1976. Two years later, the first US Coast Guard approved vessel with a SOLAS (Safety of Life at Sea) certificate ran its first trip. It was called the *Impossible Dream*. For six and a half years, Wagner ran trips from Florida to the Bahamas. The boat developed an international reputation as the class act in its area. During that time he also discovered underwater video, and shifted his creative talents to that field. But misfortune struck again. A new second captain ran the boat into the Northwest Channel light in the Bahamas, doing over a half million dollars worth of damage. "So that put me out of the boat business for a while. Then you've got to fight the insurance company, so you've lost it all three times."

Today the Wagner family is once again running a charter boat. "It took two years and my wife, Inez,... a very strong willed, determined woman, very dedicated to boats. I said, 'We'll get another boat under one condition. You and Scott (her son) run the boat. I'll promote (it) but I want to shoot pictures, that's what I enjoy most.'" Determined that there would be no second captain to run into a light, Inez got her 100-ton ocean operators license. She said, "We don't need a second captain, I am he."

The new boat is called *Dream Too*. "There's nothing that Scott can't fix on that boat. They do fabulous. I've been free to shoot pictures.

"By being in the right place at the right time, I've been able to shoot treasure recovery with Real Eight, and was fortunate to be there (the day after) the *Atocha* was found. I put that into a documentary that is still shown today by Mel Fisher because he thinks it's better than **National Geographic's**...I'm not **National Geo**, but I know what (Mel) went through, and told the story that way. Since then I've developed ten videos as documentaries. One on a juvenile delinquent program that turns hard core delinquents...into useful citizens, and they use scuba diving to do it. The thrill that they get from diving replaces the thrill they got being chased by the police. The filming is helping a lot more than running a boat would do, that's why I do it.."

Dan Wagner teaching David Hartman to dive, July 1979.

According to Spencer Slate, current president of the Florida Dive Operators Association, Dan's greatest contribution to diving is through his films. "He's got the best material ever done on Mel Fisher, footage no one else has, and also has shot some wonderful films to promote diving in Florida." One of them is **"Dive Florida"**, the official FADO film illustrating the highlights of the state's diving.

"I'll soon be 61," Dan reveals, "and I can still outflipper the best goddamn 25 year old that ever put on a set of fins. Last year I went out with Slate (on) a whale release. (It was the) first time in history that shortfin pilot whales had ever been saved and released back to the wild...I went off like a bat out of hell shooting (pictures of) this whale, (which) I later sold..to the TV stations. A 30 year old was (also shooting),...he was all unhappy. Slate pointed out, 'When the whale took off, you left that guy just like you had a motor on your ass.' That made me feel good. There's another reason he couldn't sell his footage. It had my butt in it."

Even today, the biggest problem in diving, and the reason this sport has not grown like it deserves, is this macho (thing)... not being willing to work together because that guy over there is going to get ahead a little more than (you) will.

Wagner has one complaint about the diving scene today. "When I was doing recovery work, people got mad because my name appeared in the paper. When a reporter walks up and wants to know what's going on, are you going to tell them to walk up to that old lady over there and ask her? Everybody was so afraid I would get my name out there instead of his name, it was a cutthroat thing. Even today, the biggest problem in diving, and the reason this sport has not grown like it deserves, is this macho (thing)...not being willing to work together because that guy over there is going to get ahead a little more than (you) will. Learn from these big peo-

ple. You work together, grow together, and everybody shares together. I don't understand why diving can't learn that.

"Dan Wagner is responsible for killing a lot of fish, grabbing a lot
of lobster...(tearing) some coral, but... if I had known what I should have
done, I wouldn't have done it
that way. We have a responsibility to tell people the story,
to show them there are still a
lot of things that are fun in this
sport and to show them how to
enjoy them. To give back some
of what we've taken."

Dan Wagner is a survivor.
After nearly four decades,
despite setbacks that would

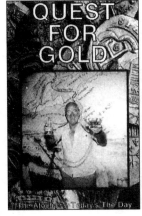

have caused most people to quit, his enthusiasm for diving is greater
than ever. He has conveyed this through his films, his charter boats,
and to students through his teaching. This writer is proud to have
been one of those students, 35 years ago in Chicago. Thanks, Dan.

The videos I have completed for home video viewing are
designed to educate and entertain. In doing that they will properly promote our underwater environment and friends. The **Reef Fish
I.D.** videos are the first to go with a **Reef Fish I.D.** book and contain
over 300 Caribbean reef fish. The music videos are open captioned
identifying over 50 different underwater friends in each video.

RALPH ERICKSON

John Cronin was angry. The midwestern sales manager for US Divers had driven from his Chicago home all the way to Western Illinois University, to help staff an instructor course. It was a tedious drive on a two-lane road, following tractors going 20 miles per hour. On arrival, he was informed the course had been canceled. This was the final straw. Cronin called his friend, Ralph Erickson, and set up a meeting at a restaurant in suburban Morton Grove.

ERICKSON RECALLS, "JOHN COMES IN, he's standing there all red in the face and says, 'It's time, it's time.' I asked, 'Time for what, John.' 'It's time to start an organization.' "

The first thing they discussed was a name. Cronin said, "Ralph, I don't give a damn what name we have as long as the word 'professional' is in there."

Erickson: "Right away my ears went up. I'm a professional teacher, now we're talking. And I said, 'How about, Professional Association of Dive Instructors?' John said 'PADI.' I said, ... 'You had that name figured out all along.' I don't know if he did or not ...I always accuse him ...because he's Irish, he wanted it to be called PADI. He'll say that if I selected it, it would have been Swedish, like VIKING or something."

I always accuse him... because he's Irish, he wanted it to be called PADI. He'll say that if I selected it, it would have been Swedish, like VIKING or something.

So out of their frustration over dealings with the prevailing national instructional organization, Cronin and Erickson founded the agency that today dominates diving instruction throughout the world. Current estimates credit PADI with over 60% of certifications worldwide.

Continuing their planning, they discussed a logo. Cronin wanted a globe similar to the **National Geographic** logo, with longitude and latitude. "I suggested we make a circle with Professional Association of Diving Instructors and we'll put the world inside with the

Ralph Erickson, Racine Quarry, 1978.

dive flag...Do you remember US Divers used to have Cousteau divers with torches on their catalog?...We want a torch, but we'll use the kind that the pathfinders use in the paratroops." Erickson had been a paratrooper in World War II. He designed the logo with

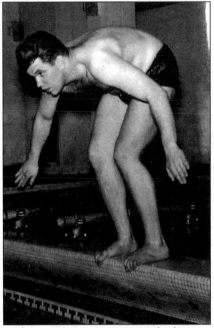

Erickson, swim instructor at Portage Park, Chicago Park District, 1946.

mechanical drawing tools and press-on letters. The diver was drawn by an artist friend, who opted for an instructor card in lieu of a fee.

Erickson had difficulty fitting in all the letters. This was before copying machines, so every time he added something new, all the circles and lines had to be redrawn by hand. It took two weeks, but finally all the letters fit. "The latitude and longitude lines came from the Navy navigation book, and that was the first PADI logo. Two years later we got a call from an instructor who said, 'You spelled professional wrong.' I had left out the letter E...That was the only way I could get it to fit, and we had been using it for 2 years. So then we got the thing done professionally."

Ralph Erickson's contributions to PADI didn't end with the name and the logo. The concepts of a progression of courses with emphasis on open water dives — the cornerstone of diving instruction today — originated with him. This was consistent with his background as a swimmer, teacher, and coach. Although diving didn't come to the forefront of his life until later, Ralph's early experiences set the stage for what was to follow:

1937. Owen Churchill brought his newly invented swim fins to Chicago's Lane Tech High School. Coach John Newman invited one of his swimmers to try them out. Erickson thought they were magnificent.

1939. At age 16, he was a lifeguard for Chicago Park District. Someone brought a homemade diving helmet: a water heater cut in half, with a manual pump to supply air. They tried it out at 15 to 20 feet in Diversey Harbor. Water temperature was 60°, visibility about 5 feet. That made little difference, because there was no window in the helmet anyway. They had to hold it above their heads to see, then bring it down to get a breath.

Erickson was a fine swimmer, placing third in the 100 freestyle in the state meet (behind a world record holder and an Olympian), and received a scholarship to the University of Southern California. A freshman when war broke out, he enlisted in the Army and became a paratrooper with the 82nd Airborne Division. His first combat jump was in Holland, he later fought in the Battle of the Bulge, and was wounded on the Rhine four days before the war in Europe ended. That arm injury, combined with his father's lingering illness, ended Erickson's swimming career. In 1946 he enrolled at Northwestern University, and began coaching swimming at Chicago's Portage Park.

> I could stand on my head... do somersaults... lay on my back, I could do anything I'd want, which is the one thing that I really love about diving. The other stuff is incidental ...Sure, I like to look at pretty things, but that's the essence of diving...

The Chicago Park District bought its first Aqualungs in the early 50s, and lifeguard captains would get together on their days off to use them in Lake Michigan. Sometimes they would hold the anchor of a powerboat, being dragged across the bottom looking for wrecks. They were close, but because of the poor visibility, never found one. "Some of the guys had spear guns...I didn't particularly care about shooting fish, I was just going down to enjoy the weightlessness. I could stand on my head...do somersaults...lay on my back, I could do anything I'd want, which is the one thing that I really love about diving. The other stuff is incidental ...Sure, I like to look at pretty things, but that's the essence of diving...I don't think anybody who dives a lot would disagree..."

Occasionally they would dive The Crib, an offshore structure that housed the intake for Chicago's water supply. "We'd go down to the bottom and through the opening...look around the rooms up there, look down the hole going down to 200 feet, and the tunnel that goes inshore to a pumping station. ...We couldn't go into that; the water was too cold because we didn't have any suits.

"Around 1959 I got a dry suit: the kind that you pull the pants all the way up to your armpits, then you fold it back down below your knees, then you put the shirt on and that goes all the way down below your knees, then you roll it up and that's your seal. I had an extra large but it wasn't big enough, so I could never wear anything underneath. It was a little bit better protection than nothing, so I was always cold when we went down deep. We went up to Racine Quarry (Wisconsin), I'd get down to about 40-45 feet and watch the others go down to 60 feet because they had clothes on underneath. I finally got a wetsuit and was in my glory; I could go anyplace I wanted."

By the mid 50s, Erickson was teaching and coaching at Elmwood Park High School in the western suburbs. He was also teaching scuba privately, although he wasn't certified, even as a basic diver. In those days in Chicago, there were no certification courses. "I rented pools and taught in a lot of high schools, and in almost all the country clubs on the north shore. I taught Mrs. Wilson and Mrs. Armour and Mrs. Swift (of the meatpacking families) at the most exclusive country club in the Chicagoland area.

Erickson, teaching an early scuba class.

"I gave my own cards under Erickson Underwater Diving School. Everyone had to make one dive with me up in Racine Quarry . They paid $18 for the pool session and $10 for the dive.

"I got hold of Bev Morgan's book for US Divers. Most fantastic book I ever had...that's where I learned the most. I told Bev ...'I learned to dive from your book.' He said, 'I wish I had a quarter for everyone who said that.' "

Erickson wrote an instructional book of his own in 1961. Entitled **"Under Pressure,"** it was co-authored by Al O'Neill, a partner in Demone manufacturing company, which produced an early single-hose regulator. Like Morgan's book, this was intended as a sales tool for the regulators. Unfortunately, Demone went out of business before many of the books were sold.

In 1961 Erickson went through the first NAUI instructor course at the Shamrock Hotel in Houston, Texas. "There were 65 of us and my NAUI instructor number is 35...I don't think it taught me anything about teaching diving. It was to see whether or not you could swim real well, or you could run real well, or if you could use your scuba gear...But we had a lot of lectures by a lot of great people: Captain Bond, Al Behnke, Andy Rechnitzer, Al Tillman. And Neal Hess, he started NAUI."

It was after this experience that Erickson wrote his book. He also became involved in the Illinois Divers' Association, publishing their newsletter, **"The Snorkeler"** This kept him up on local dive activities and gossip. "I had a hell of an intelligence system in Chicago. Everybody ...would call and ...tell me everything that was going on...I had information which nobody else had...

"I was the only certified instructor in the Chicago area outside the YMCAs and they were doing it for nothing. The dive stores had their own instructors who were not certified, but giving out their own cards. And they were charging $18. I wanted to raise the level. NAUI wouldn't let us have an Instructor Training Course in the midwest. They were all either on the west coast or the east coast. This went on for four or five years."

The first midwestern NAUI course was the aborted attempt at Western Illinois, that provided the impetus for the formation of PADI. In the beginning PADI was a two-man operation. Cronin took the program that Ralph had written out and promoted it among dive shop owners on his midwestern sales routes. Any working instructor at a dive shop could automatically qualify to become a PADI instructor. So every dive shop owner became an instructor. After six months, they ran their first Instructor Training Course. Cronin had been an instructor for Aqualung Diving School in New York in the 1950s. He taught the equipment sections, Erickson did the rest.

> I got hold of Bev Morgan's book for U.S. Divers. Most fantastic book I ever had... that's where learned the most. I told Bev... 'I learned to dive from your book.' He said, 'I wish I had a quarter for everyone who said that.'

The original PADI basic program consisted of six pool sessions and one mandatory open water dive. At the time, some people were still getting certified with only pool dives. That was soon upgraded to two open water dives. Then an incident occurred that made Erickson raise the ante to five.

It was the early 70s, and he was at Racine Quarry checking out a group of students from Loyola University. A high school student came out of the water in distress, wearing cutoff jeans, weights, and obsolete gear. He had lost his buddy. Erickson searched, and found the partner's body at 60 feet. The boy had panicked and ripped off all his gear in a vain attempt to reach the surface. "So, I went home and thought about it...From that moment on there's going to be five open water dives in order to get certified. I'm not doing it any more unless there's five. And we're going to charge $100 for it. I was getting $20 for the two dives."

PADI's concept of learning progressions had begun earlier. At the time, most organizations offered only a basic and an instructor course. The one exception was NASDS, which had Senior Diver. Erickson decided on steps called Master Diver, Assistant Instructor, and Instructor. Cronin ran this idea by Frank Scalli, US Divers' eastern sales manager. "Frank said we can't really use Master Diver because the Navy has it. I said, 'You're right, we'll just switch this around and call it Divemaster.' and this changed the whole thing. The word divemaster had been around but nobody had ever used it, and I had to set up criteria for it. We were wrong.. We should have made it Master Diver and inserted Divemaster afterward. I had specialties laid out at the time, but I didn't call them specialties. I had wreck diver, night diver, search and recovery. I had the names, but didn't call them specialties. Nick Icorn coined that term and ...Dennis Graver took it a little bit further.

Frank said we can't really use Master Diver because the Navy has it. John showed me and I said, 'You're right, we'll just switch this around and call it Divemaster.

"In swimming you have your progressions, Boy Scouts have them, skating has them. Almost every organization had a ladder and that was a natural thing; it didn't take much brains to do it....Except, in the diving world...it didn't take off until about 1980 when the advanced program started to go. It took that long for the damn thing to be integrated into the ideas and minds of the diving instructors."

The story of how PADI specialties began illustrates Erickson's inventiveness and pragmatism. "This guy called me up (he made $350,000 a year) and said, 'I don't know if you remember me, but I took your course three years ago at Glenbrook High School and never made the check out dives. Can I take them now?' I said, 'Sure...but I require five dives now.'...I told him it would take one dive a day, so it would take 2 1/2 weekends. He said 'What's it going to cost me?' I said, '100 bucks,' and held my breath...He said, 'Okay.'

"So the we made the five dives and I said, 'Here's your card, you're certified.' He asked, 'What's next?' I said 'Advanced Diver.' (By that time PADI had been in existence for quite a while, but we didn't have a program for advanced diver.) He said 'When can I start?' I said 'Tomorrow...at the beach up in Evanston, when you get off work.' He said 'I'll meet you there at 5:00. What's it going to cost me?' 'A hundred bucks.' We met there and had to walk about 50 yards to the water's edge. Now I had to come up with something for advanced diver, didn't I? So I invented it on the spot. I said, 'We're going to do natural navigation. We have these ripples in the sand, they're parallel to shore. You're going to go out against those and you're going to use an armspan. You're going to go 10 of them out and you're going to follow the ripples and go along the ripples to the right, the same thing, and come back towards shore and come back until you come here.

"While he's doing that, I'm thinking 'What do I do next?' He came up and said 'What do I do next?' 'A circle.' He did the circle, then the same question: 'What do I do next?' 'A triangle.' 'What do I do next?' 'A series of U's.' Which is the greatest thing I ever did - a U pattern, because everybody needs that for search and recovery...On the second dive we did compass navigation and on the third we made a night dive. The fourth dive was a deep one in the 90-foot trench at Racine Quarry, and the fifth was a wreck dive. He asked 'What's next?' We had eliminated Senior Diver (because NASDS had senior diver) and went right to Divemaster - which was the wrong thing to do. But that's what we did. He took the Divemaster course and said, 'What's next?' I said, 'Instructor.' So he went through an ITC and became an instructor."

Oak Street Beach Lifegaurd crew – Chicago Park District, 1942.

The Chicago Park District Northside lifeguard crew, break the one-mile world's record for the whale boat, 1941. Foreground left, Tommy Bastable and Ralph Erickson right.

PADI's house organ, the **Undersea Journal**, appeared as soon as the organization was launched. Erickson wrote the entire first issue, putting phony names on the articles. "One was my mother's maiden name, and I got a call from a guy out in Canada who said 'My name is that name and I might be a relative.' I threw that thing in the wastepaper basket as fast as I could."

By this time, Erickson was coaching at Loyola University, and he paid the athletic department secretary to type the first issue. Ralph pasted it up, using press-on letters for headlines. Printing was a problem on their limited budget, so they went to an orphanage that had a printing press. Cronin negotiated the price of 1,500 copies for a bottle of whiskey. Erickson asked, "John, how did you know he was going to take a bottle of whiskey?'

Cronin replied, 'He's Irish, has a red nose and he's about 55-60 years old. I know he drinks." Once the **Undersea Journal** was launched, articles began coming in from instructors. And subsequent printing was paid for in cash.

In swimming you have your progressions, Boy Scouts have them, skating has them. Almost every organization had a ladder and that was a natural thing; it didn't take much brains to do it...

In the late 60s, PADI ran their first public event, a film festival at Lane Tech High School. Jacques Cousteau made an appearance, and they filled the 2,500-seat auditorium. Experts gave seminars on topics like photography, wreck diving, and safety. "And then John went out to California and we didn't do that anymore...Harry Shanks took it up at the YMCA and made it Our World Underwater."

Cronin was transferred to California in 1969 to become US Divers' national sales director. Before long, he was president of the company. By 1970 PADI was still essentially a two-man operation. Cronin asked if Ralph would mind if he moved the headquarters to California. He replied, "No, that's the only way it is going to grow."

A combination of promotion, innovation, and business sense put PADI on top, and once they got there they never looked back. Nick Icorn was the first full-time training director, followed by Dennis Graver. Icorn's major contribution was meaningful emergency ascent training, while Graver developed the modular scuba course. An integral part of the modular course was based on the unit study questions used in Erickson's text for his scuba classes at Loyola University.

Even though headquarters had moved to California and the staff expanded exponentially, Erickson continued to wield a key influence in the organization. Meanwhile he was pursuing his other career as a swimming and water polo coach.

Loyola had hired him because he could coach both sports, but he immediately realized that the chances of succeeding in swimming, with virtually no scholarships, were impossible. So he turned his major efforts to water polo. "We were beating everybody in the midwest, and then we got into the east coast and beat them. Then we'd go out to California get beat badly. In 1972 we got invited to the NCAA in Albuquerque, New Mexico and (the athletic director) said 'The first time you get beat, you come home...' So we played San Jose State and got beat 22-1 and we came home. We didn't get to play Yale. They got 7th place and we got 8th as a result."

Once the NCAA began funding travel to the National meet, Loyola was invited every year but 1981. They always finished between fifth and eighth, beating virtually all but the California teams, which continue to dominate the sport. Erickson retired from Loyola in 1987, but is still active in diving. Recently remarried, he runs a scuba instructor college with his wife, Karen, in Austin, Texas. "I made her an instructor in Cozumel seven years ago, she came back and took a staff course. I asked her to come up to Chicago to run a training center I had. She does everything I do, we are best friends.

photo by Bud Bertog

"All my friends are divers; if they don't dive I teach them how...Everybody I'm involved with is in diving.

At the 1992 DEMA show, Erickson received that organization's highest honor, the Reaching Out Award, for long-term contributions to the sport. "Cronin changed my life by saying 'professional' and 'the world.' If it weren't for that,....all I cared about was the lower third of Lake Michigan."

Erickson at Loyola Univerisity,1976 as waterpolo coach.

LEE SOMERS

Growing up on a farm in the flatlands of Illinois is hardly conducive to becoming a diving pioneer. Yet Lee Somers found a way to get underwater and make an impression in the worlds of Florida cave diving and university research. A college dropout and self-confessed diving bum, Lee eventually earned a Ph.D. and organized the nationally recognized program at the University of Michigan. He was the first president of the American Academy of Underwater Sciences, and is godfather of the Michigan Mafia, a group of young turks who have changed the way we look at diving.

BRETT GILLIAM COINED THE TERM MICHIGAN MAFIA. It describes a group of instructors who came out of Lee Somers' intensive summer training courses at the University of Michigan. They include Paul Heinmiller, Bruce Wienke, Karl Huggins, Dan Orr and Phil Sharkey. All of them are running scientific diving programs at universities, or are on the cutting edge of today's decompression theory. Somers states, "One thing came out of that group: nobody ever told them what to do. It's a collection of people who are very independent minded, who truly love diving. Although all of us are affiliated with NAUI we don't go around beating the bush for them; it's diving...Diving came first, not beating the drum for an agency."

Diving has come first for Lee Somers all his life. It began in Champaign-Urbana, Illinois where his father was a tenant farmer, and there never was much money in the family. His mother made him join the Boy Scouts to learn swimming. Eventually he became a lifeguard and counselor at the scout camp in the area. One of Lee's fondest memories is of the day his mother brought him a pair of Owen Churchill fins for his birthday. The camp was in central Illinois strip mine country, and Lee did his first free diving in those flooded holes in the ground. "I didn't want anything in the world but those damn fins, and she saved up to buy them for me. In the early 50s I (had seen) **Silent World.** Two people made an impression on me in those days: Jacques Cousteau, and Richard Widmark in the movie **Frogman.**"

Lee Somers suiting up for a commercial dive in Tampa Bay, early 1960s.

At 16, he got a job lifeguarding in the town pool, a concrete oval about the size of a football field and 18 feet deep. Part of his duty was cleaning the bottom, using an old Jack Browne full face mask, and air supplied from the surface by an electric compressor. "An older gentleman at the pool had an Aqualung and let me use it for fun. He had to send it to Chicago on a Greyhound bus to be filled. I just couldn't pass up this fantastic piece of new equipment. I had no instruction, not even about not holding my breath. There must have been a great natural selection process and I survived it.

> I had no instruction, not even about not holding my breath. There must have been a great natural selection process and I survived it.

"I put together every cent I had and bought my own Aqualung...Ordered it through a sports shop in Champaign: a tank with inch thick harness attached by metal bands, a single stage Mistral or DA regulator...It wasn't a big deal moving from the pool to the strip mines. I had been to the same depths breath-hold diving, 30 to 35 feet...I ordered a wet suit in pieces and glued it together in my living room. (There was) more water inside the suit than out.".

What did Lee get from being underwater in a strip mine? "It seemed like there was nothing else I wanted to do, it was like a magnet. On a good day, visibility was about ten feet. At scout camp there was a lot of pond weed, sort of attractive in its own way. It wasn't science or macho, just the feeling of being underwater."

Somers went to one semester of college and decided it wasn't for him. So he took off for Florida, where it was warm, and where he could dive. He took on a variety of jobs from mowing parks to operating a swimming pool and went diving whenever possible, with any buddies that happened to be around. Lee's first Florida scuba dive was in Crystal River, but there were no manatees. "I didn't even realize they were supposed to be there. But there was a little cavern, where I went back as far as I could, and liked it. That was the beginning of my cave diving."

Among Lee's jobs during that period was marine construction, tending divers on Mark V and Jack Browne outfits. He got to dive the units in Tampa Bay and offshore in the Gulf of Mexico, but was put off by the shallow water and bad visibility. It was no better than the strip mines in Illinois. "Those were the years I was like a little kid who had to taste everything." He gravitated to caves because they were easy to get to, with no boat fee. Divers would buddy up with people they met at the site, and learned by discussing past experiences. Recalling one of his favorite caves, Lee says, "It was 165 to the bottom, 110 at the top of a debris cone. We entered into an area of poor visibility, yellowish brownish like tannic acid, then dropped though that into clear salt water. At the bottom the decomposition product was hydrogen sulfide, so you came out smelling like rotten eggs. It was fun until we found out you shouldn't spend much time down there. There were about six deaths in that sinkhole and many of us suspect that it was probably hydrogen sulfide.

"With no instruction we learned to calculate air supplies, safety factors, (and) decompression stops." There were no organized groups yet, but cave divers made it their business to read the diving literature of the time: the Navy manual, the manual supplied with the Aqualung, and E. R. Cross' **Underwater Safety**.

> People ask, 'What did diving in that swimming pool do for you?' I learned complete absolute relaxation, being at one with the water and with the apparatus. It was hours and hours of repetitive experience.

Somers recalls one of his favorite dive sites of the early days. "We would go to one little spring...with a good, swift current. We would tie a line, drop into the cave, and ride the line until it whipped us out to the end, then pull ourselves back. At 60 feet underwater, it was just like a carnival ride. Once I got out to the maximum extent of the line, started looking around, and got into an alcove where the current wasn't as strong. When I turned around, the other two guys had gone and the line was nowhere in sight. I had a light, but was a couple of hundred feet back in (not a lot by today's standard), had no pressure gauge, no buddies, and no line. Fortunately I just stayed close to the wall and worked my way out. The light went out about 75 feet from the entrance. I wasn't even upset with my buddies, but today I'd have killed them.

"The good divers of those days didn't just say, 'I'm a diver,' and jump off into 300 feet of water. You understood your environment. Everything was done in increments. People ask, 'What did diving in that swimming pool do for you?' I learned complete absolute relaxation, being at one with the water and with the apparatus. It was hours and hours of repetitive experience.

Lee's regular buddy of the time was Don Leadbeater, another pioneer cave diver. "In the early 60s..Don found a pond in a swamp area near Weeki Watchee Springs, with an opening that went straight down into a cave. We called it Leadbeater's Sink; today the name is Eagle's Nest. It is probably one of the most famous cave diving locations in Florida. I went with Don and another diver, so I count myself as the third person in there. We went to a depth of about 230 feet. You swim through a 60 foot shaft that opens into a large room.

When shining our lights down there, it was just like dropping through the ceiling of a big auditorium. As far as we could see, it was just beautiful."

During the summers, Lee would return to Illinois. It was there he

finally received his first certification, as an instructor with the Illinois Council of Skin and Scuba Divers in 1960. A year later he was part of the first YMCA instructor course run in Chicago, the second in the nation. "The people who certified me had just certified themselves

Lee Somers and Martin Nemeroff, M.D. (Hyperbaric Medical Specialist) at the University of Michigan.

that morning." They included the gurus of local diving: Dan Wagner, Skeet La Chance, Vern Pedersen, Joe Strykowski, and Ray Hoglund.

"During the years between colleges I would describe myself as a diving bum." Florida had been fun, but now it was time to go back to school. He enrolled in the University of Illinois, and in three years graduated with a degree in physical education. Lee earned part of his expenses by selling dive equipment out of his home, and teaching classes on campus and at the local YMCA. Skeet La Chance had set him up as a dealer. "I didn't make a lot of money, but learned about the diving industry."

He earned a trip to California for the national spearfishing championships, as a member of the Illinois team. Tryouts were held in Lamont Quarry, but nobody hit a fish. So they moved the operation to Lake Geneva, Wisconsin, where candidates were tested on their breath-hold diving ability. "One dive earned my trip back there. They had us diving down to these people in scuba on the bottom, and swim around for them. They kept moving progressively deeper, to 70-75 feet. I swam down and slapped one of them in the head. Next thing I knew I was on an airplane to California, with my weight belt strapped around my waist.

"During my first experiences in California I never had a tank on. What a wonderful group of people. Folks like Jim Christensen and Del Wren welcomed us with open arms. I remember somehow my shoes got locked in the back of Gustav Dalla Valle's car and we had to chase him down in a restaurant to get them back. Jim helped me load six-packs of Coors into my airplane bag because it wasn't available on our side of the Mississippi. One of the reasons I'm in diving is that we're a family. We have our disputes, but when I go anyplace in the world, I have family there."

Back at the University of Illinois, Somers entered a master's program in geology. Then he received a call from his former advisor, Jack Hough, who had moved to the University of Michigan. They needed somebody to start a diving program. "Jack said I should work on my Ph.D. I said, 'I don't want a Ph.D.' He said, 'You'll need it and you're going to get it.'" Lee finished in 1969, and was hired at Michigan to teach physical education, oceanography, and work with Sea Grant, one of the first such programs in the nation. He has been there ever since.

> One of the reasons I'm in diving is that we're a family. We have our disputes, but when I go anyplace in the world, I have family there.

During summers, Lee worked as a commercial diver any place he could find an assignment. He and Bob Anderson brought their experience with surface-supplied gear back to the university, where it was introduced to scientific divers. It was used in geological and biological studies throughout the Great Lakes. Ultimately they began doing saturation diving as well, in Hydrolab at Freeport and St. Croix.

"In the early 70s I went with Joe McInnis and was asked to participate on Arctic One. I crossed the border with a Zodiac boat and a station wagon packed solid with everything you could think of. We loaded it all on a Canadian Forces C-130 and headed for the high Arctic. This was the first of Joe's many ventures into the area. Four of us stayed two weeks in Resolute Bay, living in a tent part of the time and diving. It was science, it was adventure, testing whether a small expedition of this nature could be done."

Dissatisfied with the textbooks available for his classes, Somers wrote the first research diving manual, which was published by Sea Grant in 1972 and circulated throughout the country. Unlike Connie Limbaugh's Scripps manual which merely outlined rules and procedures, this was an instructional book in loose-leaf form, covering everything from diving theory to underwater transects . The reason for the loose-leaf format was to make it easy to update. Two years later that became obsolete when NOAA published its diving manual. Somers was on the editorial committee which produced that book.

The American Academy of Underwater Sciences was originally formed in California to combat OSHA's attempts to regulate scientific diving under commercial rules (see Jim Stewart chapter pp. 118-

127). When the battle was won, its founders realized that a need still existed to disseminate information on techniques, share knowledge, and present a united front in future battles with regulatory bureaucracies. To do that effectively, they would have to go national.

And to attract members from other areas, the first president would have to be somebody outside California. They selected one of the founding members, Lee Somers. Today, AAUS is a leading worldwide organization for diving scientists.

After a dive, from left to right; Tom Mount, Jim Sibthrop (left rear), Lee Somers and Jim Nums (right rear), 1992.

Looking at the state of diving today, Somers voiced a few concerns. "People today go from beginner to instructor in (less) time than it took us to know what we were really doing at 30 feet underwater. In fact, I'm still learning how to be a diver.

"I don't classify most people coming into diving today as divers. They haven't paid their dues. Also, we experienced divers are losing our rights. We are treated the same as a person who just took a basic course. (You) go to a resort and ...you are talked down to, you are treated like this incompetent moron who is there to kill himself, destroy the reef, and destroy their business.

"We need to bring back the diver's rights. That's the reason for my involvement with tri-mix and nitrox. Every diver shouldn't be diving deep, or diving gases. All of us thoroughly believe that. It's a matter of extending our capabilities. All diving is accepting a certain level of risk. My range will be whatever I deem proper for the particular set of circumstances. That varies from day to day, environment to environment, and who I'm with. I've been at far greater risk with some people at 30 feet than with Tom Mount at 270."

Reminiscing on his life and career, Lee says, "I will be remembered for being a pain in the ass for a lot of people, and for the positive influence I might have had on thousands of students...Diving gave me a life, diving gave me a family. Today I have my heroes, from all different ranks: George Bond, Ed Lanphier, Vern Pedersen, Glen Egstrom, Jim Corry, Karl Huggins, Mike Hughes, Larry Cushman, Tom Mount, to name a few.

"One of the things that's really irritated me about the modern era:...there are the agencies, but they don't have any of the names...They've replaced names with organizations. And believe me, PADI didn't build diving. And NAUI didn't build diving. They've forgotten where diving came from. They've forgotten Bernie Empleton and Jim Stewart and Connie Limbaugh and Doug Fane. That is the saddest part of what I see today. In all instruction programs, there is no history...no times, no places, no faces."

Underwater Educators
Tom Mount

"I WAS DIVING ON THE WALL IN ANDROS and we had a girl that sounded to the bottom on us. We were at 300 feet already. I saw her and caught her at the 400 foot mark. I used to be a Water Safety Instructor Trainer and believed the only thing worse than a single drowning was a double drowning, (so) was very actively checking myself. I reached down and grabbed her by the tank valve, gave one power stroke, and my whole vision field just totally collapsed...went to red with black dots. To this day when I close my eyes and think about it I can see it. So I climbed up the wall. It's amazing, you use more discipline than you think you can, because Dick Williams dropped down to 310 and took her from me. After we got out of the water, I asked him 'Why didn't you help me?' 'You looked all right,' (he replied). Well, I was blind as a doorknob at that time. Somewhere above 300 I started getting little blocks of vision. I didn't get it all the way back, just a block at a time. That was one bout with oxygen toxicity."

Tom Mount calmly recalled this incident without any braggadocio, in the same matter-of-fact tone that most people would use to describe a Sunday drive. But Tom's diving career has always been about pushing the limits of the envelope, whether in caves or in deep, open water using mixed gases. He has been a scientific, military, and commercial diver, was one of the founders of the National Association for Cave Diving, and developed many of the techniques in use today. Mount's kind of diving will shock some people raised on strict training agency precepts, and he is the first to admit it's not for everybody. Today he is a photographer, instructor, consultant, and president of the International Association of Nitrox and Technical Divers.

When Tom Mount was about nine years old he read a book about a hard-hat diver and decided then that was what he wanted to do. "My dad was an air force pilot, so we bounced all over. I went to college two years, then joined the Navy in '58. A Richard Widmark movie on Navy frogmen turned me toward scuba, so I joined to get into UDT."

Instead of arming explosives, Mount was assigned to disarm them, as a member of EOD (exploding ordnance disposal). The work was done underwater, and Tom considered it a bit more dangerous than UDT. On active duty during the Cuban missile crisis and the Bay of Pigs era, Mount was involved in some operations he still refuses to talk about.

Tom Mount in the early 1960s with cave diving gear.

He doesn't mind talking about recreational and training dives in that era. "The first navigation dive, I thought I was gonna fail. It was obvious we were concerned about sharks. They wanted to downplay sharks, but to have some fun they talked about barracudas. My team leader had stolen my bathing suit, which I didn't know. He just happened to have one in white with gold braid...and the way to attract barracuda is to put something shiny in the water. In those days, there was barracuda all over the place in Key West. So on my first open water swim I hit the water, a 25 foot barracuda (3 foot to today's eyes) was circling underneath me, and I thought he was going to bite me right in the groin. It's pretty hard to navigate when you have both hands covering your groin, and your buddy's head is out of the water because he didn't want to look at it. So we missed by 100 yards on our first try. They laughed and let us do it again.

> **There was an immediate market for the sub machine guns. Not being familiar with the law, we got visited by the FBI, (who) informed us of (it), so we ceased that activity.**

"Everything I did in the Navy turned me on to diving more and more. I would have made a career of it except I didn't like the idea of somebody always having a throttle over my activities. From the time I got out I was conniving what I could do to stay in this."

After being discharged in 1962, Tom opened a dive shop in Titusville, Florida. It was a baseline business that would allow him to do other things as well. He earned a contract to install underwater communication cable up and down the Atlantic missile test range, based with Lockheed at Cape Canaveral.

There was also a salvage operation. Mount could have struck it rich except for two problems. "Our team of three partners, young and foolish, trusted each other explicitly. One skipped with the bank account, all the investors' money, and left us high and dry. The wreck we found was loaded with steel, brass radiators, Thompson submachine guns, and several cases of 45s still in cosmoline. There was an immediate market for the sub machine guns. Not being familiar with the law, we got visited by the FBI, (who) informed us of (it), so we ceased that activity.

"I was active in cave diving and deep diving from the day I got out; they have always been two of my greater loves in diving. Deep is defined as 200 plus. With the equipment we had, that was much deeper than we should have been.

"I read a book by Captain Bill Royal which should have scared me out of cave diving instead of getting me interested in it. He and Eugenie Clark wrote...about some near misses in a place called

Ponce de Leon Springs (Deland, Florida), which enticed me to go see what it was all about. After the first ten minutes of the dive I was hooked on it forever." Tom began teaching cave diving in 1962, although there was no such certification at the time. "We formed a club called the Aquamarine Cave Dwellers, a hardy group, with rules that wouldn't apply today. This was pre BCs, pre pressure gauges, the penalties were pretty severe. Everybody had to free dive to 100 feet to get in. To keep people out, they had to sign an agreement that if they died they had to donate their gear to the rest of the club, but it didn't really deter anybody. We had a lot more cave divers than we thought we would. Everybody in those days was a multi-faceted diver.

Today if I had a choice between a cave and the ocean, it would by far be the ocean, it is so full of life. But cave diving totally captured my soul for about ten years, it was all I lived for.

"In those days we would make a tank dive in the morning, then free dive seven hours afterwards. It was a whole different ballgame."

In 1967 Dave Desautels, Larry Briel, Dale Malloy, Jim Sweeney and Tom started an organization, which evolved the following year into the National Association for Cave Diving. "We did it through concern. People were dying in the caves and we were usually the ones called to pull them out. Legislators were threatening to close them; we decided we had to do something to protect what we loved.

"Today if I had a choice between a cave and the ocean, it would by far be the ocean, it is so full of life. But cave diving totally captured my soul for about ten years, it was all I lived for.

"On my first cave dive — Ponce de Leon — I made the same mistake as a lot of people in those days. I made what I thought was a pretty good safety reel, put a 1/4 inch line on this big spool, a broomstick through it, put a thimble on the end, and proceeded to take the line in. It worked great going in. Coming out, with no buoyancy control, the line got in several line traps. It took me about four times as long to get out as it took to get in.."

In the early 60s Tom hooked up with Frank Martz, his cave diving buddy for many years. "Every week we did deep stuff like Eagle's Nest, in the 200 foot plus range. I did a lot of stuff in the Bahamas with him later on, which is where he got killed."

Mount was the first to emphasize proper buoyancy compensation and proper trim for cave divers. He introduced kicking above the midline of the body, and ran seminars on those skills. "But parallel thoughts always happen, so every time you think you did something first, you find someone else moved on it before you did.

"Frank Martz is probably the real pioneer. He invented the first really good light system, the Martz Lights. Most lights used in cave diving today are based on his principles: rechargeable, aircraft landing light bulbs. Just before he died, he developed halogen lighting systems He invented the first compact, jam-free safety reel. Between my emphasis on technique and his on equipment I think we made some major contributions.

> I have a hard time understanding diver burnout because I don't see how anybody can walk away from the feeling of just being underwater... It's like a very deep state of meditation... in a completely peaceful world.

"Our first BCs were a bit more economical than today's. We used to stop at the dump on the way to the dive site and pick up a Clorox bottle. Kept it underneath our hips to keep our feet up. If you were going really deep you used two Clorox bottles. The guy who invented that technique was Hal Watts.

"Frank got a regular gate valve, put it on a high pressure hose, and made the first inflatable BCs we know of. He presented it to Dick Bonin at Scubapro and Dick thought it was pretty hot. So pretty soon everybody else started coming out with it.

"In technical diving today, everybody has gone to back inflation. With double tanks it's the only way to fly. I love At-pacs. They can say what they want to about how you float; if you're unconscious, you're dead.

"I instituted one of the first air rules (not the one we use today). Most rules accepted today are not like the ones in recreational diving where a bureaucrat sits behind a desk and says, 'This sounds good, let's do it.' Rules in technical diving evolve because someone got killed or had a near scare.

"We were working a cave called Madison Blue Springs...put some line in it, got an offshoot that someone later named the Mount offshoot. We were doing what we call visual gaps, leaving 75 feet past the line to go into a new part of the cave. We were a very competitive community. You don't want anybody to see where your line starts because you don't want someone else to add to it till you get through working it. About 75 feet back, running the lines in there, we were cutting our air close. I put the reel down and couldn't find the tile because it was buried down in the clay. It totally zeroed the visibility out on us. We made a wrong turn, corrected it, and managed to get back to the permanent line. We always carried pony bottles in those days...left them at a restriction we called the half hitch. About 50 feet before the half hitch I turned to my Partner, Dick

Williams, an M.D., and gave him the out of air sign. He says he was already out. So we breath-held through the restriction, got our pony bottles, and got out. We had such severe CO_2 headaches, we lay on the bank about an hour after we were done decompressing. Before we got dressed I said, 'From now on I'm taking my air, dividing it by half, and adding 200 pounds to it.' The half plus 200 pounds was the predominant cave rule for about five years, then evolved to the third rule (a third in, a third out, and a third in reserve).

"We got involved in some of the deeper cave diving stuff, and had the crap scared out of us a couple of times. Frank and I were down about 260 feet, diving around a madman named Pete, who used to cut lines when he got tangled. We didn't know he came into the cave after us, got tangled, and cut the line. That's bad. What was really bad, he turned, snagged the line on his fins, and took the line right out the cave. And he silted it out. So Frank and I got back up to 250, there was zero visibility, no line. We had to use wall referencing and memory and finally got out. By the time we were through decompression, we were finally cooled off. Besides you couldn't really say much to Pete. He and some of the guys he dived with used to have guts contests. For amusement they used to shoot apples off their heads. With guns. If that wasn't enough, they sometimes put apples between their legs. So you really didn't want to challenge the guy.

"Remember the old SOS computer? When he got cold and tired of watching it, he would just come up. He had the distinction of being airlifted out of this place four times."

Before the start of NACD, cave diving had a fantastically bad record. "I took seven years layoff from it, because for a while every time I went to go cave diving they asked me to do a body recovery. I would hide in the woods and still they'd find me. Finally Scheck Exley matured as a cave diver and he started doing them, which made me very happy. It's a quieter scene now, they have recovery units. You don't get called in the middle of the night any more."

In 1969 Tom sold the dive shop to become the diving officer at the University of Miami. "A very exciting time. I had the best of both worlds, spending about 125 days a year at sea. We had money, funding, all that which you don't have in research diving any more. I got involved in saturation diving, we were doing dives on Hydrolab about every other month for two years. I supervised the Flare project (Florida Aquanaut Research Expedition), a mobile habitat thing. I was involved in Tektite II (another habitat project). I also started the first university use of mixed gases to my knowledge. We took divers as deep as 340 to 350, on the quiet because it was something you didn't talk about in those days. We had people going to 240 on air, finding more and more marine life people thought didn't exist. The biologists wanted to go deeper, so we started offering helium courses... Had about 50 scientists trained in it.

Sat diving is probably not the best thing to do to your body, but the more I did it, the more I wanted to do.

"When I left the university in 1976, they dropped the program. (There was) not a single accident of any type, no cases of DCS. We did surface decompression, a lot of exotic commercial type diving operations. We had a tightly supervised program, patterned after Jimmy Stewart's program at Scripps...a 100 hour basic course, one mile swims, 50 meters underwater to qualify, breathing from bare tanks — things that people shudder over today. Because we had stress management training we had virtually zero accidents."

At the university, Mount became heavily involved in saturation diving. "Sat diving is probably not the best thing to do to your body, but the more I did it, the more I wanted to do. The only time I ever got burned out was when Sylvia Earle and I did the first co-ed sat dive in Hydrolab. She froze me to death. That's the hardest working person I've ever been in the water with. It was January, we spent seven hours a day in the water. About three hours before decompression we sent all our gear up, including my wet suit. Sylvia talked me into doing one last dive with her. By the time we got through decompression, it was the coldest I have ever been in my entire life."

Summing up the university years, Tom states, "I had six weeks vacation a year, but never took any because they put me every place I wanted to be." Why did he leave? "I knew if I stayed, that was where I would be the rest of my life and there is a time to move." In addition, he wanted to finish his own college degree.

Since then, Mount has directed the YMCA scuba program in Key West, was a manufacturer's representative, and has done consulting work. He has become seriously involved in photography, and co-authored a book on underwater modeling with his wife, Patti. "I'm trying to see the world, but almost every place I've been, I want to go back to."

As president of the International Association of Nitrox Divers, Mount has some definite opinions on technical and deep diving.

"You've got to admit it exists, and recognize that people have to be trained in it. Everybody's doing it, everybody has always been doing it; they finally recognize it after thirty years.

"Several things have got to be addressed. I don't think it's something everybody needs to do, ought to do, or be enticed to do. People call me, say, 'I've got my divemaster card, I want to get into tri-mix.' I tell them, 'Make another 200 to 300 dives, till you are bored with what you are seeing now, before you venture into something else.' It's more demanding, more equipment dependent, you need more discipline, got to observe gas rules. The biggest killer in deep diving today is that people don't manage their gas.

> People call me, say, 'I've got my divemaster card, I want to get into tri-mix.' I tell them, 'Make another 200 to 300 dives, till you are bored with what you are seeing now, before you venture into something else.'

"The second biggest killer is...a parallel with what happened in the early 60s in cave diving. In the early 60s we started hitting between 260 and 300 feet and didn't have any accidents. In the late 60s we were getting accidents on the same profiles. Compared to the *Andrea Doria,* for a long time there were very few accidents. Today there are some. The parallel you see: in the early days of cave diving the bottom times were very short. As the bottom times extended we started having problems with people getting hurt. That segment of wreck diving is just starting to evolve, where cave diving was 20 years ago. The longer your central nervous system clock runs at that depth...there's no guarantee you're going to convulse, but the probability is there.

"Also today it is more easily accessible, so we are getting some marginally qualified people down there. But you are beginning to see some controls coming in. They don't want legislation, and are beginning to form organizations."

Tom has the following advice for today's divers: "Get good training, don't push yourself too fast. Just really enjoy everything you do. I still have every bit as much fun on a 30 foot reef dive. If I had a choice of diving a 250 foot wreck or sitting in the Red Sea in 50 feet of water, I'll tell you where I'd be: the Red Sea. Really enjoy what you have and stop to look at things. Most divers miss what they are really doing; they see the big grouper but not the community on the reef.

"Second, be respectful of the environment. When I started diving, there was a place called Dapple Shoals in Florida. You hit the water and at about 40 feet you started seeing jewfish. By the time you got down to 90 feet there were 400 pounders there. Now you are hard pressed to find one jewfish. And it was my generation that destroyed them. The species that we protect do come back. "

Tom sums up the allure of the underwater world this way: "I don't think any diver can explain why he is attracted to diving, it's just the feeling of being underwater. I love diving and am as enthused about it today as the day I first put on a tank. I still log dives, and even averaging well over 300 a year, I've lost none of my enthusiasm. I prefer to do it with a camera in my hand but it's just being there. I have a hard time understanding diver burnout because I don't see how anybody can walk away from the feeling of just being underwater...It's like a very deep state of meditation...in a completely peaceful world. I hope I can do it until the day before they put me under the ground."

INDEX OF NAMES